Lecture Notes in Computer Science   7840

Commenced Publication in 1973
Founding and Former Series Editors:
Gerhard Goos, Juris Hartmanis, and Jan van Leeuwen

James Noble   Ralph Johnson
Uwe Zdun   Eugene Wallingford (Eds.)

Transactions on Pattern Languages of Programming III

 Springer

Editors-in-Chief

James Noble
Victoria University of Wellington, School of Engineering and Computer Science
P.O. Box 600, Wellington 6140, New Zealand
E-mail: kjx@ecs.vuw.ac.nz

Ralph Johnson
Siebel Center for Computer Science
201 North Goodwin Avenue, Urbana, IL 61801, USA
E-mail: rjohnson@illinois.edu

Managing Editors

Uwe Zdun
University of Vienna, Faculty of Computer Science
Währingerstraße 29, 1090 Vienna, Austria
E-mail: uwe.zdun@univie.ac.at

Eugene Wallingford
University of Northern Iowa, Department of Computer Science
Cedar Falls, IA 50613, USA
E-mail: wallingf@cs.uni.edu

ISSN 0302-9743 (LNCS)   e-ISSN 1611-3349 (LNCS)
ISSN 1869-6015 (TPLOP)
ISBN 978-3-642-38675-6   e-ISBN 978-3-642-38676-3
DOI 10.1007/978-3-642-38676-3
Springer Heidelberg Dordrecht London New York

Library of Congress Control Number: 2013939834

CR Subject Classification (1998): D.2.11, D.2, D.3, D.1, K.6

Typesetting: Camera-ready by author, data conversion by Scientific Publishing Services, Chennai, India

Printed on acid-free paper

Springer is part of Springer Science+Business Media (www.springer.com)

Preface

It is our pleasure to present the third volume of Springer's LNCS *Transactions on Pattern Languages of Programming*. TPLOP aims to publish the best and most substantial work in design patterns, recognizing outstanding patterns and pattern languages, and making them available to the patterns community — and indeed, to the wider community of programmers and software developers.

This volume — like all the volumes in TPLOP — contains revised and reviewed articles that were first presented at one of the Pattern Languages of Programming (PLoP) conferences. Every paper submitted to a PLoP conference is shepherded by an experienced pattern writer who provides several rounds of detailed feedback to the authors. If the paper is considered ready, after the shepherding is complete the paper will be accepted to the conference itself, where a group of pattern authors will read the paper in depth, provide detailed feedback to the authors, and discuss the paper in a structured writers workshop. After the conference, authors are expected to make another round of improvements to the paper, taking into account the findings of the workshop. Only then may the paper be eligible for consideration by TPLOP: Many papers have several rounds of shepherding and reviewing before they are ready. Every paper considered by TPLOP receives at least three reviews ab initio, from experts in the paper's domain as well as pattern experts. Each article in this volume has been through this process before being accepted for publication in these Transactions.

This third volume contains five papers. The first paper, from longtime patterns contributor Andreas Rüping, is in the classic PLoP conference style: eight patterns that describe how data can be transformed as part of data migration. The patterns are clear, concise, and immediately practically applicable. The following three papers are substantial collections of interrelated patterns, or pattern languages. Christian Köppe's pattern language describes how to teach design patterns, drawing heavily upon Christopher Alexander's *A Pattern Language* for form and presentation. Eduardo Guerra, Jerffeson de Souza, and Clovis Fernandes present eight patterns for building reflexive frameworks, in substantial detail, based on analyses of 14 successful systems. Andreas Ratzka organizes 18 patters for multimodal interaction design. These larger articles, containing many patterns, describing their interdependencies, and based on considerable analysis, typically draw together several shorter papers presented at different PLoP conferences. TPLOP has a particular role in recognizing and presenting these more substantial works.

The last paper, from Neil B. Harrison and Paris Avgeriou, reflects the maturity of the patterns movement in another way: Rather than presenting new patterns, this paper describes a technique for conducing architectural reviews of software systems based upon patterns. The paper then goes on to present the results of an exploratory research study of applying pattern-based reviews to nine small software systems.

Once again, we believe the papers in this volume collect and represent some of the best work that has been carried out in design patterns and pattern languages of programming over the last few years. We thank the conference shepherds, the workshop groups, and the TPLOP reviewers who have ensured we continue to maintain this standard. Finally, we thank the authors for sharing the fruits of their insights and experience.

March 2013

James Noble
Ralph Johnson
Uwe Zdun
Eugene Wallingford

Organization

Table of Contents

Transform! Patterns for Data Migration........................... 1
    Andreas Rüping

A Pattern Language for Teaching Design Patterns................... 24
    Christian Köppe

Pattern Language for the Internal Structure of Metadata-Based
Frameworks 55
    Eduardo Guerra, Jerffeson de Souza, and Clovis Fernandes

User Interface Patterns for Multimodal Interaction 111
    Andreas Ratzka

Using Pattern-Based Architecture Reviews to Detect Quality Attribute
Issues – An Exploratory Study 168
    Neil B. Harrison and Paris Avgeriou

Author Index... 195

Transform!
Patterns for Data Migration

Andreas Rüping

Sodenkamp 21 Å, D-22337 Hamburg, Germany
andreas.rueping@rueping.info
www.rueping.info

Abstract. When an existing application is replaced by a new one, its data has to be transferred from the old world to the new. This process, known as data migration, faces several important requirements. Data migration must be accurate, otherwise valuable data would be lost. It must be able to handle legacy data of poor quality. It must be efficient and reliable, so as not to jeopardise the launch of the new application. This paper presents a collection of patterns for handling a data migration effort. The patterns focus on the design of the migration code as well as on process issues.

Introduction

There are many reasons that may prompt an organisation to replace an existing application, usually referred to as the legacy system, by a new one. Perhaps the legacy system has become difficult to maintain and should therefore be replaced. Perhaps the legacy system isn't even that old, but business demands still require some new functionality that turns out difficult to integrate. Perhaps technological advances make it possible to develop a new system that is more convenient and offers better usability.

Whatever reason there is for the development of a new system, that system cannot go operational with an empty database. Some existing data has to be made available to the new application before it can be launched. In many cases the amount of data will be rather large; for typical business applications it may include product data, customer data, and the like. Since this data is valuable to the organisation that owns it, care must be taken to transfer it to the new application accurately.

This is where data migration enters the scene. The data models of the old world and the new will probably not be the same; in fact the two could be fundamentally different. The objective of data migration is to extract data from the existing system, to re-format and re-structure it, and to upload it into the new system ([11], [2], [7], [8], [9], [10]).[1]

---

[1] Data migration is different from database migration. Database migration refers to the replacement of one database system by another, which may make some changes to database tables necessary for technical reasons. Database migration is outside the scope of this paper However, data migration includes the transfer of data from one data model to another. This is what this paper is about.

J. Noble et al. (Eds.): TPLOP III, LNCS 7840, pp. 1–23, 2013.

Migration projects typically set up a migration platform in between the legacy system and the target system. The migration platform is where all migration-related processing takes place, as Figure 1 illustrates. Similar diagrams can be found in the literature ([9], [8]).

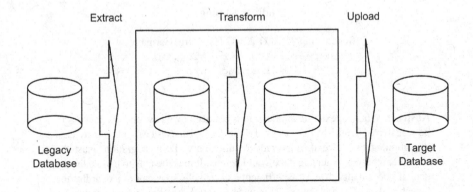

Fig. 1. Overall migration process

The technical basis can vary a lot:

- The migration platform often contains a copy of the legacy database (as indicated in the diagram), so that the live database remains undisturbed from any migration efforts. An alternative strategy is to extract the legacy data into flat files.
- The migration platform may also contain a copy of the target database.
- Various technologies can be used for the actual transformation, including Java programs, PL/SQL scripts, XML processing and more.

While database vendors make tools available that cover most of the extraction and uploading functionality, the actual transformation usually requires custom software. The transformation depends heavily on the data models used, and so differs from one migration effort to the next.

Migration projects involve quite a few risks. According to the literature ([11], [9], [10], [5], [6]), the most common risks include the following:

- The legacy data might be complex and difficult to understand.
- The legacy data might be of poor quality.
- The amount of data can be rather large.
- The target data model might still be subject to change.

As a consequence, care must be taken for a migration project to be successful. A failed data migration could easily delay the launch of the new application.

The patterns in this paper address these requirements. They demonstrate techniques and strategies that help meet the typical requirements of a data migration project. The patterns are targeted at software developers, architects and technical project leads alike.

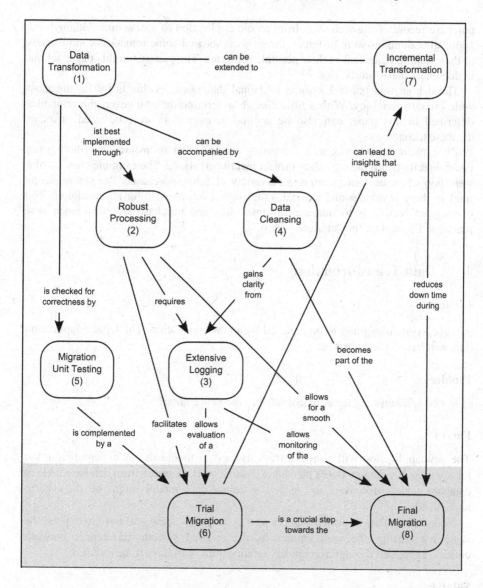

Fig. 2. Overview of the patterns

Figure 2 gives an overview of the patterns and briefly sketches the relationships between them. Six patterns address the design of the migration code, while two patterns (those in the grey-shaded area) focus more on the data migration process.

I have mined these patterns from three migration projects in which I was involved as developer and consultant. The first was the data migration made necessary by the introduction of a new life insurance system. The second was the migration of the editorial content for an online catalogue for household goods from one content management system to another. The third was the migration of customer data and purchase records for a web shop from an old application to a new one. Although the application domains were different, the projects showed some remarkable similarities in their requirements and in their possible solutions. The patterns in this paper set out to document these similarities.

Throughout this paper I assume relational databases, as this is by far the most widespread technology. With a little change in terminology, however, the principles described in this paper can also be applied to migration projects based on other database technology.

I'll explain the patterns with a running example that is inspired by (though not taken directly from) the web shop project mentioned above. The example consists of a web shop where customers can make a variety of online purchases. The system keeps track of these purchases and maintains the contact information for all customers. The overall perspective is to migrate customer data and purchase records onto a new platform. I'll explain the details as we go.

1   Data Transformation

Context

A legacy system is going to be replaced by a new application. The legacy application data will have to be migrated.

Problem

How can you make legacy data available to the new system?

Forces

The new application will almost always use a data model that is different from the legacy system's data model. You cannot assume a 1:1 mapping from database table to database table. Moreover, the legacy system's data model might be difficult to understand.

Nonetheless, data imported into the new system's database will have to express the same relationships between entities as the original system. References between entities, expressed through foreign key relationships, will have to be retained.

Solution

Implement a data transformation that establishes a mapping from the legacy data model to the target data model and that retains referential integrity.

The data transformation will be embedded into the overall migration process, which in most migration projects consists of three major steps [8]: first, all relevant data is exported from the legacy system's database; next, the data transformation is performed; finally, the transformation results are imported into the new application database.

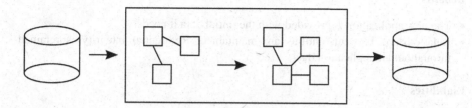

Fig. 3. DATA TRANSFORMATION

The actual transformation consists of the following steps:

- The transformation iterates over database tables, reading one entity after the other, while taking all its related entities into account as well.
- In each iteration, related entities are transferred into an object structure that matches the new application's data model. Because related entities are processed together, references between entities can be established and referential integrity is maintained.
- Some data models are too complex to allow the transformation to work this way, especially when cyclical references occur. In such a case, the transformation process needs to be extended, for instance by splitting up the transformation and storing intermediate results in temporary files.

A data transformation can be implemented in different ways. One option is to operate directly on database records, for instance with a PL/SQL script. Because running migration scripts on the live legacy database is almost always a bad idea, the original legacy data has to be exported into a database within the migration platform where the actual transformation can then be performed.

An alternative is to export data from the legacy database into a file-based representation, also within the migration platform. In this case the legacy data can be processed by Java programs, XML processors and the like.

In any case, the resulting objects represent the new system's data model. The transformation process stores them in a format that an import mechanism of the target database understands.

Example

In our web shop data migration, all relevant data records are exported from the legacy database into flat files, one for each database table. These files are read by a Java component that implements the transformation by iterating over all customers. For each customer, it takes the customer's purchases into account as well, as these maintain a foreign key relationship to the customer.

The transformation process creates a customer object for every legacy customer entity and a new purchase object for each legacy purchase entity. In addition, the transformation process creates address objects for all a customer's addresses, which in the legacy system were stored within the customer entity.

After a fixed number of customers, say 10.000, have been processed, the customer, address and purchase objects created so far are stored in the file system from where they can later be imported into the new database.

Benefits

- The new application is provided with the initial data it needs.
- Relationships between entities are maintained. Referential integrity is retained throughout all application data.

Liabilities

- Implementing the data transformation requires a good deal of domain knowledge [11]. It's next to impossible to map an old data model onto a new one without understanding the domain logic behind all this data. It's therefore crucial to involve domain experts into the migration effort. It's a good idea to use their knowledge for powerful MIGRATION UNIT TESTING (5).
- Establishing a correct data transformation can still be difficult, especially if the legacy system's data model is flawed or the two data models differ a lot. You may have to apply DATA CLEANSING (4) in order to solve possible conflicts. You should use EXTENSIVE LOGGING (3) whenever the data transformation encounters any problems.
- Depending on the overall amount of data and the transformation complexity, a data migration can require a long execution time. In practice, several hours or even several days are possible.
- The transformation process can have significant memory requirements, especially if large groups of data have to be processed together due to complex relationships between entities.
- If the overall amount of data turns out to be too large to be processed in one go, you may opt to migrate the data in batches. A common strategy is to Migrate Along Domain Partitions [12], which means to apply vertical decomposition to the overall application and to migrate one subsystem after the other.

2   Robust Processing

Context

You have set up the fundamental DATA TRANSFORMATION (1) logic necessary to migrate data from a legacy system to a new application. It's now time to think about non-functional requirements.

Problem

How can you prevent the migration process from unexpected failure?

Forces

Legacy data is sometimes of poor quality. It can be malformed, incomplete or inconsistent. Certain inconsistencies can in principle be avoided by the introduction of database constraints. However, legacy databases often lack the necessary constraints.

Despite all this, the transformation process must not yield output that, when imported into the new system, leads to database errors such as unique constraint violations or violations of referential integrity. (For the new database the relevant constraints will hopefully be defined.)

Moreover, the migration process should not abort due to flawed legacy data. While it's true that a crashed TRIAL MIGRATION (6) tells you that a specific entity is problematic, you don't get any feedback regarding the effectiveness of the migration code in its entirety. For a serious TRIAL MIGRATION (6) this is unacceptable.

For the FINAL MIGRATION (8) robustness is even more important. The FINAL MIGRATION (8) is likely to be performed just days or even hours before the new application will be launched. If unexpected problems caused the migration process to abort, the launch would be seriously delayed.

Solution

Apply extensive exception handling to make sure that the transformation process is robust and is able to cope with all kinds of problematic input data.

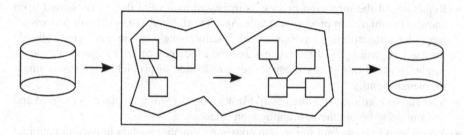

Fig. 4. ROBUST PROCESSING

The most common cases of problematic input data include the following:

- Missing references (violations of referential integrity in the legacy database).
- Duplicate data (unique constraint violations in the legacy database).
- Illegal null values (non-null constraint violations in the legacy database).
- Technical problems (illegal character sets or number formats, and the like).

Exception handling can take different forms depending on the technology you use to implement the DATA TRANSFORMATION (1). Exception handling mechanisms are available in many programming languages, including Java and PL/SQL.

Sometimes you won't be able to detect invalid data by evaluating entities in isolation, but only by evaluating entities in their relational context. In some cases, if you discard a specific entity, you will have to discard some related entities as well — entities that the DATA TRANSFORMATION (1) processes together.

In the aftermath of a migration run you will have to analyse what exceptions have occurred. In the case of a TRIAL MIGRATION (6) this will tell you where the migration code needs improvement. During the FINAL MIGRATION (8) (directly before the new application is launched) ideally no exceptions should occur. If they do, the problematic data will have to be handled manually in the target database.

Example

The web shop data migration applies exception handling to detect any illegal data formats. For example, names and addresses should consist of valid characters and prices should be non-negative numbers. If illegal values occur, an exception is caught and the flawed entity is discarded. The migration process won't crash.

The migration also discards purchases that refer to a non-existent customer, at least for the time being. In principle, such purchases shouldn't exist, but unfortunately there are some dangling references to customers.

As the migration code is gradually improved, some DATA CLEANSING (4) mechanisms are added so that exceptions are largely avoided; the few remaining problems are handled manually.

Benefits

- Reliability of the migration process is increased as invalid data is prevented from causing the migration process to crash. As a TRIAL MIGRATION (6) will process all input data, regardless of possible data quality issues, it can give you valuable feedback regarding the effectiveness and the efficiency of your migration code. A single TRIAL MIGRATION (6) can detect a multitude of problems, not just a single problematic entity.
- You can be confident that the FINAL MIGRATION (8) will take place as planned and without delay before the new application is launched.
- You can also be sure not to run into constraint violations when importing data into the target database.

Liabilities

- The migration process must never skip any invalid legacy data without further notice. Whenever problematic data occurs EXTENSIVE LOGGING (3) must document what entities have been discarded.
- If there is a chance that flawed legacy data can mended, you can plan to apply DATA CLEANSING (4), which reduces the amount of exceptions that will occur and will need to be handled.

3   Extensive Logging

Context

You have implemented the DATA TRANSFORMATION (1) logic required for your migration project. ROBUST PROCESSING (2) ensures that problematic input data is discarded if otherwise it would cause runtime exceptions.

Problem

How can you facilitate the analysis of problems that may occur during the transformation of possibly large amounts of data?

Forces

A data migration usually involves a huge amount of data — clearly too much data to monitor manually. Moreover, the migration process can last for several hours or days. You need to keep track of the current status while the migration is up and running.

Because ROBUST PROCESSING (2) is usually required, illegal data may have to be discarded during the DATA TRANSFORMATION (1) process. However, it's crucial to know what data had to be deleted and for what reasons.

Solution

Enhance your transformation process with extensive logging mechanisms.

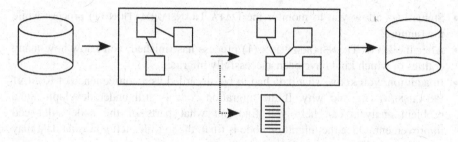

Fig. 5. EXTENSIVE LOGGING

Relevant logging includes the following:

- Count every entity that undergoes a DATA TRANSFORMATION (1), classified by type (legacy database table).
- Count every entity that is made available to the import into the new database, classified by type (new database table).
- Log every entity that is discarded in the process of ROBUST PROCESSING (2). Also log the reason why the entity was discarded, such as the exception that was thrown.
- If the migration code includes aspects of DATA CLEANSING (4), log every entity that is corrected or otherwise modified.

In addition, log status messages at certain intervals throughout the migration process. These status messages should explain how many entities of what type have been processed so far. They can also include the current memory usage or other parameters that may prove useful for system configuration.

The technical details of logging depend on the technology you use for the DATA TRANSFORMATION (1). A transformation implemented in PL/SQL will probably use a specific database table for logging. A Java-based transformation might use Log4J or any other filed-based logging mechanism. Either way it's important to make sure that logs won't be lost in case the system crashes.

Example

The web shop data migration logs the number of legacy customers and legacy purchases that are processed, as well as the number of customers, addresses and purchases that are created for the new database.

In addition, comprehensive log entries are written for each entity that has to be discarded (ill-formatted entities, but also purchases without customer). These log entries include as much information about the discarded elements as possible to make a straightforward problem analysis possible.

After a migration run the logs are analysed thoroughly. Special attention is given to the purchase records that has to be discarded due to non-existing customers. Domain experts look into the data and analyse what needs to be done.

Benefits

- Status logs allow you to monitor the DATA TRANSFORMATION (1) process while it's running.
- After the DATA TRANSFORMATION (1) process has finished, you know how many entities of which kind have been successfully migrated.
- In addition, you know what data had to be discarded as a consequence of ROBUST PROCESSING (2), and why. If the migration code is still under development, a problem analysis can help you find out what parts of the code still need improvement. Once the migration code is final, the log files tell you what data may require manual treatment.

Liabilities

- Log files can easily use up a significant amount of disk space.
- Logging can make the migration process slower.

4   Data Cleansing

Context

You have implemented the DATA TRANSFORMATION (1) logic for your data migration project with some ROBUST PROCESSING (2) that handles illegal data from the legacy system. Still, the legacy system might contain data that isn't exactly illegal, but isn't useful for the new application either.

Problem

How can you prevent the new application from being swamped with useless data right from the start?

Forces

A legacy system's data base often contains outdated or incomplete data; sometimes it's appalling how poor the data quality is ([11], [5]). Some problems with data quality are of technical nature — problems that could in principle be avoided by the definition of database constraints, which, however, are sometimes lacking in legacy systems. Other problems are caused by data that is invalid in terms of the application domain.

For an existing application invalid data is rarely ever corrected. Many legacy systems work reasonably well despite a low data quality, so people sometimes feel the least expensive way to handle poor data quality is simply to ignore it.

However, you can no longer ignore data quality issues when introducing a new application. First, launching a new application based on flawed data would be unsatisfactory. Second, there are technical reasons why it may be impossible to migrate flawed legacy data. If, for instance, the target database makes better use of constraints than the legacy database did, object that violate referential integrity couldn't be imported successfully.

Handling flawed data is a process known as data cleansing [11]. Data cleansing can take place at different points in time within the overall migration process. One approach is to handle flawed data early on in the legacy database, which offers the advantage that the DATA TRANSFORMATION (1) need not be concerned with data cleansing issues ([9], [10]).

However, when legacy data is migrated, every single entity has to be checked for validity anyway to make ROBUST PROCESSING (2) possible. Handling flawed legacy data during the DATA TRANSFORMATION (1) is therefore a powerful option too. In addition, this option bears the advantage that the data cleansing can be applied to groups of related entities, as these entities are typically migrated together.

Solution

Enhance your transformation processes with data cleansing mechanisms.

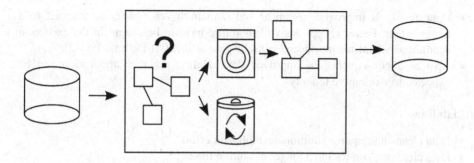

Fig. 6. DATA CLEANSING

Data cleansing can either mean to remove the invalid data or to try to correct it. Concrete solutions depend on the individual situation. Ultimately it's a business decision what data should be cleansed. Typical examples include the following:

- Data that violates constraints of the application domain.
- Data that is outdated and no longer relevant.

As data cleansing requires a good deal of application logic, it's usually a good strategy to encapsulate it into dedicated methods, which can then be invoked from the overall DATA TRANSFORMATION (1) process.

Apply EXTENSIVE LOGGING (3) to all cases of data cleansing, so that it's clear what changes to the application data have been made.

Example

In the past, the software team in charge of the web shop never got round to improving the quality of customer data. Now, however, the chance has come to do just that.

On the one hand, data cleansing addresses the problem with orphaned purchase records that point to non-existing customers. A function is added that tries to retrieve the missing customer data for purchases too recent to be simply ignored. The function consults a database table that stores transaction details — a table that so far wasn't considered.

On the other hand, data cleansing also aims to get rid of data that is no longer needed. Customers are removed if they haven't made a purchase within the last 7 years. In addition, the process looks up potential customer duplicates — distinct customers, though with the same name and address. Moreover, postal codes in customer addresses are validated and, if possible, corrected automatically.

Looking up customer duplicates makes the transformation process somewhat more complex. It's necessary to maintain the set of customers processed so far in order to detect duplicates. If a duplicate is detected, the two entities are merged into one.

Benefits

- Data quality is improved: technical and domain-driven constraints are met to a larger extent. Fewer exceptions will therefore have to be caught in the exception handling mechanisms introduced with the goal of ROBUST PROCESSING (2).
- Also as a consequence of improved data quality, the new application can be expected to work more reliably.

Liabilities

- Data cleansing requires addition development effort.
- Data cleansing can lead to a longer execution time.
- Data cleansing can become so complex that more than one pass can be required to perform the necessary corrections.

5   Migration Unit Testing

Context

You have implemented a DATA TRANSFORMATION (1) characterised by ROBUST PROCESSING (2) and DATA CLEANSING (4). You have added EXTENSIVE LOGGING (3) to monitor the transformation process. It's crucial for the success of your migration project that the transformation you have implemented is indeed correct.

Problem

How can you catch errors in your data transformation process?

Forces

Correctness is essential for any data migration effort. If the DATA TRANSFORMATION (1) was misconstrued, the new application would be initialised with flawed application data, which would give it a bad start.

However, the mapping from the old data model to the new one can be complex and difficult to understand. Detailed knowledge of both the old and the new system is required to define a correct mapping.

Solution

Write unit tests based on a representative test data in order to check the transformation process for correctness.

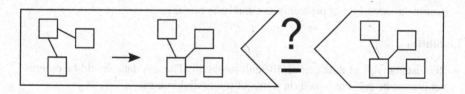

Fig. 7. MIGRATION UNIT TESTING

Ideally, the migration team will DEVELOP WITH PRODUCTION DATA [12], which suggests that the test data should be an excerpt of the legacy system's live database. The set of test data must be large enough to guarantee sufficient coverage, while on the other hand it should be compact enough to be still manageable.

- The unit tests should compare the outcome of the DATA TRANSFORMATION (1) with the expected results. Run the test suite automatically with each change you make to the migration software while it's still under development.
- In case the DATA TRANSFORMATION (1) applies DATA CLEANSING (4), an automated test can check that flawed data is properly mended.
- In addition, tests can verify that the EXTENSIVE LOGGING (3) works fine: the log files must contain the expected entries regarding invalid legacy data.

- Finally, you can import the results of the DATA TRANSFORMATION (1) into the new application and see if you can perform typical uses cases on the migrated data.

Much in the vein of test-driven development [1], it's essential to apply unit tests right from the start of your migration effort. This way, you get early feedback regarding the accuracy of your migration software.

Example

Representative test data consists of a set of several customers along with their purchase records. The customers should differ especially with respect to the number of their purchases, although other attributes (such as address information, preferred payment method, etc.) should vary too. A unit test can check that customers and purchases are migrated correctly, that their relationships are established, that the correct address entities are created, etc.

The test data also includes candidates for discarding, such as inactive customers, orphaned purchases, and the like. Testing can verify that the invalid data does not cause the transformation process to abort, that the invalid legacy entities are indeed discarded, and that the necessary log file entries are written.

Benefits

- Unit testing ensures that the transformation process works as it should. You get a good impression of how smoothly the new application will work on migrated data.
- If there are logical problems with the transformation — problems that probably result from a lack of understanding of the application domain — at least you'll become aware of these problems as quickly as possible.

Liabilities

- Representative test data can be difficult to obtain. The test data should be compact, yet it must be self-contained (in terms of referential integrity).
- Even if tests based on representative data run smoothly and show that the DATA TRANSFORMATION (1) works as it should, there is no guarantee that the overall migration will work reliably. A TRIAL MIGRATION (6) can shed more light on the overall process.

6   Trial Migration

Context

You have successfully applied MIGRATION UNIT TESTING (5) to the DATA TRANSFORMATION (1) mechanisms you have implemented. The overall process migration should be characterised by ROBUST PROCESSING (2).

Problem

How can you avoid problems with the processing of mass data during the execution of your data migration process?

Forces

MIGRATION UNIT TESTING (5) gives you a good idea regarding the accuracy of your DATA TRANSFORMATION (1).

However, unit tests cannot prove that your migration software meets its robustness requirements. You simply cannot anticipate all possible risks. Even if you plan to discard illegal legacy data, there might be instances of illegal data you didn't foresee.

You cannot foresee the exact system requirements for your migration process either. What if the process fails due to lack of memory, or because there was no disk space left when trying to store a file? Keep in mind that in practical cases a DATA TRANSFORMATION (1) can easily require several gigabytes of memory and that EXTENSIVE LOGGING (3) can lead to log files that amount to hundreds of gigabytes. You have to ensure ROBUST PROCESSING (2) despite these risks.

Moreover, you cannot start to plan the FINAL MIGRATION (8) unless you know how long it will take to complete. MIGRATION UNIT TESTING (5) cannot answer this question, only a realistic test using a complete set of legacy data can.

Solution

Run a series of trial migrations that each process a complete set of legacy data. Perform measurements on the process and the results and improve the data transformation logic until the results are satisfactory.

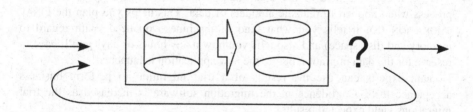

Fig. 8. TRIAL MIGRATION

The simplest way to obtain a complete set of legacy data is to create a dump of the legacy system's live database. A trial migration comprises the following tasks:

- Migrate the complete database dump.
- Test whether the overall migration process completes without aborting.
- Measure the time span the trial migration requires.
- Measure the amount of disk space required. This includes files generated by EXTENSIVE LOGGING (3), but also temporary files the DATA TRANSFORMATION (1) may require.

- Compare the number of legacy entities processed with the number of new entities that are created. Test whether these numbers are plausible.

Any trial migration benefits from EXTENSIVE LOGGING (3). You can evaluate log files or log tables to obtain the numbers of entities that were processed or discarded. A simple script can usually check the log files for plausibility and MEASURE MIGRATION QUALITY [12].

It's important to understand that a single trial migration isn't enough. Instead, the idea is to establish a process model that involves repeated trial migration runs ([9], [10]). If you manage to run trial migrations on a regular basis, you'll be aware of any effects that changes to the migration code or to the target data model may have. Once the trial migrations run consistently smoothly, you're ready for the FINAL MIGRATION (8).

Example

The trial migration uses a dump of the web shop's live data base, so it should cover all kinds of data that the real migration will have to face. Reliable conclusions regarding robustness become possible. In addition, the test shows how long the migration process will take and what size the log files will be.

A small shell script performs a few plausibility checks. For instance, the number of migrated customers and discarded customers are extracted from the log files. They must add up to the number of customers exported from the legacy database.

Benefits

- Reliability is increased as trial migrations verify that your overall migration process is robust and fail-safe.
- You get a concrete idea of the time and space requirements of your migration process when applied to realistic amounts of data. This helps you plan the FINAL MIGRATION (8): it tells you what kind of machines you need (with regard to memory and disk space) and also tells you how many hours or days you'll have to reserve for the data migration before the new application is launched.
- Domain experts can use the results of a trial migration to perform business acceptance tests. Confidence in the migration software is increased as the trial migrations yield expected results.

Liabilities

- In some organisations, getting hold of a dump of the live database can prove difficult. If the migration involves sensitive live data, it may have to be anonymized before it can be used for testing purposes.
- If a trial migration reveals that the overall DATA TRANSFORMATION (1) requires more time than expected, you may have to think about strategies to reduce application down time during the FINAL MIGRATION (8). A powerful strategy is to apply INCREMENTAL TRANSFORMATION (7).

7   Incremental Transformation

Context

A TRIAL MIGRATION (6) has revealed how long the migration of the complete legacy data might take.

Problem

How can you avoid unacceptable down times of your application while the data migration takes place?

Forces

A straightforward migration strategy is to migrate all data in one go. In this scenario, you have to shut down the legacy application before the data migration starts, since otherwise changes could be made to the legacy data that would not be reflected by the results of the migration process.

Depending on the amount of legacy data and the complexity of the DATA TRANSFORMATION (1), the overall migration process can take quite some time. Experience shows that, for large applications, data migration can require several hours or even several days. During this time neither the legacy system nor the new application will be available.

This may or may not be acceptable. A short down time is in many cases ok, but taking a business-critical application off-line for several days is almost always impossible.

Solution

If necessary, enhance the data transformation mechanism with the ability to process data records only if they haven't been processed before or have changed in the meantime. Such a transformation mechanism makes it possible to migrate the legacy data in batches and to keep the legacy system operational while the bulk of data is being processed.

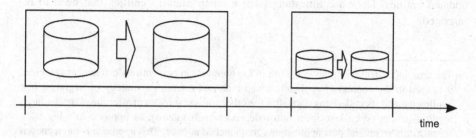

Fig. 9. INCREMENTAL TRANSFORMATION

Technically, the idea is to introduce a slightly more sophisticated DATA TRANSFORMATION (1):

- As with a standard DATA TRANSFORMATION (1), there is a mapping from the old data model onto the new one.
- Entities are processed only if they have been created or updated since the last data migration. A timestamp on the database can be used to make that decision.
- When data is imported into the target database, it isn't automatically created anew. If an entity already exists, it is updated instead.
- Entities aren't deleted in the legacy database after the initial migration, but are only marked for deletion. The version that was migrated before will be deleted in the target database during the next migration run.

This incremental approach[2] allows you to keep the legacy application operational while a large amount of data is migrated in a first migration run, which is likely to take some time. The second migration run will be much faster as it has to process only data that has been updated in the meantime. If necessary, there can be a third increment that will require even smaller time spans, and so on. Shutting down the legacy system will be necessary only while the last increment is being processed.

Because an incremental transformation is more complex than a simple DATA TRANSFORMATION (1), you should only opt for this strategy if there is a real benefit to it. There is hardly a justification for implementing an incremental transformation unless a TRIAL MIGRATION (6) has shown that migrating all legacy data in one go would take longer than you can afford to take the application off-line.

Example

A TRIAL MIGRATION (6) of the web shop's database has taken almost two days and it's definitely impossible to take the shop off-line for so long. There is a chance that the run time can reduced by making the code more efficient, but this alone won't solve the problem. The decision is made to apply incremental migration so that much of the migration process can take place a few weeks before the new application is launched.

The existing transformation code is enhanced so that it only processes new or updated entities. Database timestamps are used to identify entities that need to be migrated.

---

[2] The term incremental migration is used in the literature in two entirely different ways. First, it is used in the context of application migration and refers to a strategy of migrating one application and its underlying data after the other (or one subsystem after the other if a large application can be broken down into independent subsystems), as opposed to a big bang scenario where several new applications are launched at once. This approach is often chosen as a means of risk reduction [3], but can also be the consequence of an incremental software development method [5]. The second meaning of incremental migration refers to techniques of migrating only data that hasn't been migrated before, usually with the aim of reducing down times in mind. The latter is what that this pattern is about.

The next TRIAL MIGRATION (6) shows that there is reason for optimism. The first migration run still takes two days, but an incremental migration performed a week later completes successfully after only a few hours. This is a time span that is acceptable as an application down time during the FINAL MIGRATION (8).

Benefits

- Down times are clearly reduced. The time span between the shutdown of the legacy application and the launch of the new application, during which no application data can be written, can be kept relatively short.
- Some projects have reported that risk is also reduced provided you do a series of incremental migration runs. First, much of the data is migrated some time before the launch of the new application and, second, the closer you get to that date, the more familiar you are with migrating live data as you're doing one increment after the other [4].

Liabilities

- Implementing an incremental transformation is more complex than implementing a standard DATA TRANSFORMATION (1). For instance, the last modification date needs to be known for each entity, which may or may not be easy to figure out. Also, handling deleted elements may turn out difficult to implement. As said before, an incremental transformation should be implemented only if the benefits in terms of reduced down times justify the additional effort.
- Testing an incremental migration is equally more complex. It certainly requires several TRIAL MIGRATION (6) runs, consisting of two or more increments each. Whenever you make changes to the logic underlying the incremental transformation, you have to re-test the whole process, starting with the bulk migration and continuing with the smaller increments.

8   Final Migration

Context

You're approaching the launch of the new application. A series of TRIAL MIGRATION (6) runs has shown that the migration code is ready to go live. You may or may not have decided to apply INCREMENTAL TRANSFORMATION (7) in order to reduce system down time.

Problem

How can you avoid trouble when the new application is launched?

Forces

You have tested the data migration throughout a series of TRIAL MIGRATION (6) runs, but still you can't be one hundred percent sure that there aren't going to be problems. The risk of running into trouble may be very, very small, but if problems occur the consequences could be serious. The launch of the new application is at stake: if the legacy data cannot be migrated successfully, the new application isn't going to be launched.

It's not just possible problems that you need to be thinking of. At some point the legacy system will have to be shut down and from that point on the application will not be available until the new system is launched. From the latest TRIAL MIGRATION (6) you know how long the down time is going to be. It's wise to think about whether that down time should be on a specific date, a specific day of the week, a specific weekend, during the day or the night time, and the like.

Solution

Set up a checklist that includes all things that need to be done in the context of the final data migration, by whom, and at what point in time.

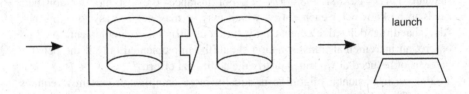

Fig. 10. FINAL MIGRATION

Some preparations are necessary to come up with such a checklist:

- You have to choose a migration date that is least problematic with regard to the expected system down time. You'll probably need to reach an agreement with many stakeholders to make that decision.
- In case you apply INCREMENTAL TRANSFORMATION (7), the final data migration will consist of several increments. Only the last increment will be take place immediately before the new application is launched. You'll have to set up a timeline from migrating the first bulk of data to the last small increment.
- You have to decide what hardware you're going to use. Ideally you'll use exactly the same hardware for the final migration that you've already used for the latest TRIAL MIGRATION (6). If this isn't possible, make sure to use equivalent hardware that is configured identically. In any case, keep a list of the commands necessary to execute the final migration tasks.

- Implement a fall-back strategy in case the data migration fails (or anything else goes astray). If nothing else works, you must at least be able to revert to using the legacy system.
- The final migration will produce EXTENSIVE LOGGING (3) just as the latest TRIAL MIGRATION (6) did. Keep a list of the log files or database tables that you may have to inspect during the final migration for monitoring purposes.
- Plan to do a few final tests in the live environment-to-be before the new application goes live. There cannot be extensive testing because the new application will have to be launched soon, but there is probably time for a few simple tests that completely rely on migrated data.

Last but not least, make sure the necessary team members are available when the final migration takes place.

Example

In order to avoid significant down times, the bulk of legacy data for the web shop is migrated a couple of weeks before the launch of the new application.

The decision is made to launch the new application on a Monday night, as this is when the web shop creates the smallest revenue. On that Monday night, only the last increment of legacy data is migrated. Since the migration includes only entities that were changed recently, the legacy database export, the transformation and the target database import together take only a few hours to complete.

A few final tests in the new live environment show that all necessary data has been migrated completely. The new application can be launched.

Benefits

- The benefit of being well-prepared is very likely a smooth ride through the final data migration process.

Liabilities

- There is no way to deny that the preparation takes quite some effort.

Conclusions

Data migration doesn't happen automatically. In a certain sense, a data migration effort constitutes a project in its own right. After its completion the migration software is expected to be executed only once, but nonetheless, or perhaps because of this, the requirements especially on correctness, robustness and efficiency are quite high.

In my experience the effort necessary to perform a successful data migration is often underestimated. If you are, or will be, involved in a data migration project, the patterns in this paper should give you a reasonable idea of what needs to be done and how, and should also give you a realistic feel for the underlying complexity.

Acknowledgements. I'd like to thank Filipe Correia who, as the EuroPLoP 2010 shepherd for this paper, offered valuable feedback on both its form and content. His detailed suggestions clearly helped me improve the paper.

Thanks are also due to the participants of the EuroPLoP 2010 workshop in which this paper was discussed. The workshop spawned many good ideas and helped me fine-tune the paper. Special thanks go out to James Noble, Jim Siddle and Tim Wellhausen for feedback at an amazing level of detail; James Noble also provided the winning suggestion for the title of this paper.

I'd also like to thank Christopher Schulz for the in-depth discussion on data migration we had in February 2012. This discussion provided a lot more insight and lead to a number of improvements.

Last but not least, thanks are due to the anonymous TPLoP reviewers for their comments and suggestions that helped me to round off this paper.

There isn't much literature available on data migration. The contributions listed below discuss related topics.

The paper by Martin Wagner and Tim Wellhausen [12] also contains patterns on data migration. Their paper and mine were parallel efforts, written independently though at the same time. There are a few overlaps. In general, their paper places emphasis on process and management issues, while the focus of this paper is mostly on technical aspects. Ultimately, the two papers complement each other.

References

1. Beck, K.: Test-Driven Development — By Example. Addison-Wesley (2002)
2. Bisbal, J., Lawless, D., Wu, B., Grimson, J.: Legacy Information Systems: Issues and Directions. IEEE Software 16(5) (September / October 1999)
3. Cimitile, A., De Carlini, U., De Lucia, A.: Incremental Migration Strategies: Data Flow Analysis for Wrapping. In: 5th Working Conference on Reverse Engineering. IEEE, Honolulu (1998)
4. The Economist.com data migration to Drupal (October 2010), http://drupal.org/node/915102
5. Fowler, M.: Incremental Migration (July 2008), http://martinfowler.com/bliki/IncrementalMigration.html
6. Keller, W.: The Bridge to the New Town — A Legacy System Migration Pattern. In: Devos, M., Rüping, A. (eds.) Proceedings of the 5th European Conference on Pattern Languages of Programs, EuroPLoP 2000. Universitätsverlag, Konstanz (2001)
7. Haller, K.: Data Migration Project Management and Standard Software: Experiences in Avaloq Implementation Projects. In: Dinter, B., Winter, R., Chamoni, P., Gronau, N., Turowski, K. (eds.) Synergien Durch Integration Und Informationslogistik, DW 2008, St. Gallen, Switzerland. LNI, vol. 138. Gesellschaft für Informatik (2008)
8. Haller, K.: Towards the Industrialization of Data Migration: Concepts and Patterns for Standard Software Implementation Projects. In: van Eck, P., Gordijn, J., Wieringa, R. (eds.) CAiSE 2009. LNCS, vol. 5565, pp. 63–78. Springer, Heidelberg (2009)

9. Matthes, F., Schulz, C.: Towards an integrated data migration process model - State of the art and literature overview. Technische Universität München, Fakultät für Informatik, Technical Report (2011), http://wwwmatthes.in.tum.de/file/attachments/wikis/sebis-article-archive/ms11-towards-an-integrated-data-migration/tb_DataMigration.pdf
10. Matthes, F., Schulz, C., Haller, K.: Testing & quality assurance in data migration projects. In: 27th IEEE International Conference on Software Maintenance, ICSM. IEEE, Williamsburg (2011)
11. Morris, J.: Practical Data Migration. British Computer Society (2006)
12. Wagner, M., Wellhausen, T.: Patterns for Data Migration Projects. In: Weiss, M., Avgeriou, P. (eds.) Proceedings of the 15th European Conference on Pattern Languages of Programs, EuroPLoP 2010. ACM Digital Library (2011)

A Pattern Language
for Teaching Design Patterns*

Christian Köppe

HU University of Applied Sciences Utrecht
Institute for Information & Communication Technology
Postbus 182, 3500 AD Utrecht, Netherlands
christian.koppe@hu.nl

Abstract. Pedagogical Patterns help in general with teaching. But the teaching of design patterns introduces a few specific problems like e.g. ensuring that the purpose of patterns is understood and that patterns are applied in the appropriate and correct way. This pattern language for teaching design patterns addresses these problems and offers solutions for teachers and trainers to solve them.

Keywords: Computer Science Education, Educational Patterns, Design Patterns.

1 Introduction

> I hear and I forget.
> I see and I remember.
> I do and I understand.
> Confucius

Teaching is a creational process, in the sense that it supports the creation of knowledge, skills, and passion in students. Successful creational processes are based on common patterns, as Christopher Alexander suggests in *The Timeless Way of Building* [1]. These patterns form a language, which can be used to address and solve the problems inherent in this creational process.

Patterns are well known in software engineering, mostly initiated by the publication of the book from the Gang of Four (GoF) [13]. Many books and papers have been written since, introducing a wide range of patterns and pattern languages and covering diverse fields as design, architecture, requirements, processes, and many others. Not much research on the successfulness of the application of these patterns exists, but practitioners often report that patterns are regularly mis- or overused or applied just like other software development techniques with insufficient results. Buschmann et al. state that "the very fact that there are many misconceptions, misinterpretations, and mistakes, however, suggests that something is often amiss in the popular perception and definitions of

---

* This article subsumes two earlier conference papers [20, 21].

J. Noble et al. (Eds.): TPLOP III, LNCS 7840, pp. 24–54, 2013.

the pattern concept" and that "such misunderstandings inevitably lead to inappropriate application and realization of the patterns themselves" [8]. One part of this problem lies in the inappropriate teaching of the patterns [3, 10, 15–17, 22]. To help in solving this problem we describe a pattern language for teaching design patterns. This language is an addition to the existing literature on teaching design patterns.

All patterns in this language use the pedagogical pattern ACTIVE STUDENT [7] and can also be categorized as pedagogical or — better — educational patterns. To increase the learning effect, the patterns should be taught from different perspectives [7] by the teachers or trainers and the students should apply them and experience the full lifecycle of them [25]. Different techniques can be used to do this, putting the focus on different parts of the patterns or on different moments in the lifecycle as well as some pattern-specific problems.

This pattern language is aimed at teachers or trainers who want to improve the results of teaching (design) patterns to students or learners in general. Some of the patterns are based on experience from previously given courses on Design Patterns [18]. Others come from published case studies and experience reports about teaching design patterns [3, 10, 15–17, 22] and include discussions on when to introduce patterns in a curriculum.

Applying these patterns requires extra preparation time for the teachers or trainers, but students will gain a deeper understanding of design patterns and patterns in general which enables them to succesfully study further patterns themselves. In order to compensate the extra time needed for implementing the patterns of the proposed language one could introduce just a selection of the patterns and leave the others for students' self study.

This language is also useful for pattern learners and pattern authors. Learners can become aware of the obstacles when first introduced to patterns. Authors will find help in some of the patterns — e.g. CONTEXT, PROBLEM AND CONSEQUENCES FIRST or BEST FITTING PATTERN CHOICE — to also take the learnability and applicability of their patterns into account by covering all aspects required for a successful pattern application.

2   The Pattern Language

Teaching design patterns has a lot in common with general teaching. Students need to be actively engaged in order to improve the learning process. Feedback should be given in an appropriate way and different perspectives should be used to enrich the students' experience [7].

There are also some questions specific to this domain, which also can be seen as learning objectives for teaching design patterns. The patterns in this language related to the questions are given after each question and are shown in the language map in Figure 1, whereby HOLISTIC PATTERN UNDERSTANDING serves as entry pattern of the language:

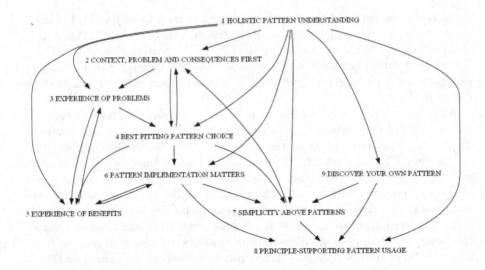

Fig. 1. Language Map - the arrows show relations between the patterns

1. How can we make sure that the concept of design patterns[1] — their purpose and their different aspects — is understood by the students and that the patterns are applied in the appropriate and correct way by them, taking the specific situation into account? (patterns 2 - 6)
2. How can we encourage students to keep looking at the whole design while applying patterns? (patterns 7 and 8)
3. How to show students that design patterns indeed offer good solutions to their problems? (pattern 9)

All patterns in this language are just parts of the whole language and should not be used in isolation. Even if the application of separate patterns would add some value related to the learning objectives, the combination of the patterns will lead to a much deeper understanding in total: the whole is greater than the sum of its parts.

These patterns use a version of the Alexandrian pattern format, as described in [2]. The first part of each pattern contains a sketch, a quote and a short description of the context, followed by three diamonds. The sketch and quote are intended for representing the core of the pattern in a recognizable way. However, the ideas behind the sketches are summarized at the end of the paper. In the second part, the problem (in bold), the background, and the forces are described, followed by another three diamonds. The third part offers the solution (again in bold), the qualification of the pattern, the consequences of the pattern application — which are part of the resulting context — and a discussion of possible implementations. In the final part of each pattern in italics, we present some known applications.

---

[1] This work focuses on the design patterns as described in [13], but is partly also applicable for other patterns.

The design patterns presented in the book from the Gang of Four use a format which differs from formats used in other pattern languages or pattern catalogues [13]. However, the basic parts of patterns are also included in the GoF format. The intent and motivation parts for example describe the context, the problem and some forces and consequences — although to a lesser extent than most other pattern descriptions, as the patterns from [13] are low level and apply only to the relatively small domain of OO-languages. We decided to use the more general terms as introduced by Alexander et al. in [2] for this language, namely *context*, *problem*, *forces*, *solution*, and *consequences/resulting context*. Using these terms broadens the applicability of the patterns of this language, as all these terms and their related pattern parts can be found in nearly all pattern formats. The described patterns are therefore applicable independent of the description format of the design patterns to be taught.

Although initially the patterns of this language were intended for application of teaching software design patterns only, it showed that some of the patterns are on a higher level/qualification. These patterns actually form true invariants in the context of teaching patterns of any domain. These patterns are marked — using the notation as introduced by Alexander — with two asterisks. The patterns which are only applicable in the context of teaching (software) design patterns, but form invariants in this domain, are marked with one asterisk. The patterns which are only applicable in specific circumstances and therefore do not represent an invariant, are not marked with an asterisk. A reasoning about the given qualification of each pattern is included in the description of the pattern directly after the solution statement.

Pattern 1: HOLISTIC PATTERN UNDERSTANDING**

Also known as: Understand Design Patterns.

If you want to make beautiful music, you must play the black and the white
notes together.
Richard M. Nixon

During the first semesters of their study, students have obtained good knowledge of the basic concepts and techniques of their study. For a computer science student this is knowledge of programming and (object-oriented) principles as well as a good understanding of non-functional requirements like modifiability, reusability, or more general maintainability. You now want to introduce (design) patterns and make sure that the students understand and apply them as intended.

Patterns are conceptually different from other design techniques or methods, and not taking this into account when teaching them often results in students applying patterns in an inappropriate way.

When beginning with patterns, students tend to apply them blindly without thinking of the overall consequences. It seems to students that some intelligent people invented the design patterns and that using them automatically leads to a good design.

Abstraction. The concept of a pattern is often not well understood by the students, as patterns are at a higher abstraction level than e.g. programming language constructs or the graphical UML notations. This higher abstraction level makes it harder to understand what a pattern is and how to apply it. But if the overall concept of a pattern — and specifically that of a design pattern — is not understood, then there is a high probability that patterns are not applied properly.

Incompleteness. Students have to learn a lot of diverging concepts and techniques. These are often loosely coupled and not highly coherent and it is sometimes sufficient to have a good understanding of an appropriate subset of them in order to pass examinations or assessments. This is different with design patterns, as applying them incompletely — in the sense of not taking care of all aspects — increases the chance of incorrect application.

Goals. Design patterns are often used to realize non-functional requirements of a software system. Understanding the impact design patterns can have on the overall design of such a system is necessary in order to see if the goals are reached and the requirements are indeed implemented. This requires a thorough understanding of the consequences of pattern application.

Therefore: assure that students understand *all* aspects of patterns, their lifecycle, and how their use relates to the overall context by addressing these aspects, the lifecycle and the relations explicitly when teaching patterns.

This pattern is marked as true invariant, because independent of the domain it is important to understand the whole idea of patterns. Also with patterns of domains other than software design people tend to focus mainly on the solution part. This pattern can be implemented by choosing the appropriate patterns of this language, dependent of the domain and the context the patterns are taught in.

First of all, the students need to know *all* parts of a pattern. Quite often the knowledge of patterns focuses mainly on the solution. CONTEXT, PROBLEM AND CONSEQUENCES FIRST helps in avoiding this problem. As the students do not have a lot of experience with the problems addressed by the patterns and therefore do not see the benefits the patterns offer, expose them to the EXPERIENCE OF PROBLEMS — by showing them what happens when not addressing the problem properly — themselves. Make sure they make the BEST FITTING PATTERN CHOICE for resolving their problems and give them the EXPERIENCE OF BENEFITS of a correctly applied pattern. A concrete PATTERN IMPLEMENTATION MATTERS, as without implementing a pattern themselves the whole concept of patterns will stay abstract for students.

The description of the resulting context forms an important part of a design pattern. The problem should be solved without introducing too much complexity, so the students should always put SIMPLICITY ABOVE PATTERNS. The main goal of design patterns is to help in making a good design by applying PRINCIPLE-SUPPORTING PATTERN USAGE.

Understanding design patterns should include the full lifecycle of these patterns — not only their application, but also their evolution [17, 25]. Patterns emerge through careful observation of good solutions and the extraction of the common parts of these solutions. Applying DISCOVER YOUR OWN PATTERN helps in understanding the pattern evolution.

After the students' understanding of design patterns, their parts and their lifecycle has improved, they can apply them more effectively. This will help in improving their designs, but also their design process, as the application of design patterns requires a careful consideration of all aspects of patterns.

The implementation of this pattern requires a time-intensive preparation and has to take the teaching environment into account. In settings which make use of GROUPS WORK [7], small classes and direct teacher-student interaction different approaches can be used including discussions and presentations. In a setting with large student groups and classical lectures and work assignments, the implementation of this pattern (and the other patterns of this language) should be included in the design of the assignments.

This pattern was used as new outline for the course "Patterns and Frameworks" at the Hogeschool Utrecht - University of Applied Sciences. The course was given earlier and some shortcomings were identified [18]. The new structure of the course based on this pattern addresses these shortcomings.
In the beginning the focus is put on the concepts of object orientation and UML. Then a short history of patterns was presented to the students, describing the way Alexander et al. collected their pattern language [2]. The first exercises made use

of the patterns CONTEXT, PROBLEM AND CONSEQUENCES FIRST, EXPERIENCE OF PROBLEMS, BEST FITTING PATTERN CHOICE, EXPERIENCE OF BENEFITS, *but also* DISCOVER YOUR OWN PATTERN *(see the application sections of these patterns for the concrete implementation). Different exercises also made use of* PATTERN IMPLEMENTATION MATTERS. *Later assignments in the course were of bigger scope, so the overall design of the students' solutions was also important. The patterns* SIMPLICITY ABOVE PATTERNS *and* PRINCIPLE-SUPPORTING PATTERN USAGE *were applied in this phase of the course.*

This pattern also forms the main approach used by Eduardo Guerra from the Instituto Tecnológico de Aeronautica in Brazil when introducing design patterns for the first time.

The goal of the book Head First Design Patterns [12] is to teach a good understanding of design patterns. This pattern is also applied in this book as most patterns of this language are applied there as well.

Uwe Zdun, professor for software architecture at the University of Vienna, uses this pattern for the design of the work assignments in different courses on teaching architectural patterns, as there are large groups of students in the classical lectures. The assignments cover the different aspects of the patterns.

Pattern 2: CONTEXT, PROBLEM AND CONSEQUENCES FIRST**

Also known as: First Things First, Focus Beyond The Solution.

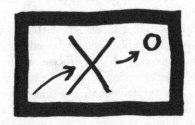

Success depends upon previous preparation, and without such preparation there is sure to be failure.

Aristotle

After an initial introduction to patterns, the students will be required to apply them as well. The application requires the choice of a pattern and the application of its solution. You now want to show students how to start applying patterns in a correct way.

❖ ❖ ❖

Students who start to learn patterns often go straight to the solution and apply it, hastily skipping the problem, context, forces, and consequences parts of the pattern.

Students often think that the obvious way to show that a pattern has been understood is by implementing its solution. This is reasonable considering that patterns are often presented with a strong focus on the structure of the *solution*.

Visual vs. Textual. The structure of the solution of a pattern is often re-presented with a diagram. Pictures and diagrams are easier to remember than text, so students focus on these while exploring patterns for themselves. Putting the focus mostly on the diagram without examination of the textual parts of the pattern description as well — which contain also the addressed problem(s), the forces of the pattern and the consequences — leads to a high chance that they are applying a solution without solving a real problem.

Focus. Many websites[2] which provide information on design patterns give a diagram of the structure of the solution as the first non-text element in a pattern description, which attracts the attention and therefore the focus of the reader as well. So it is not surprising that students tend to look at the solution first and then tend to try to implement this solution without further examination of what their problem consists of. But even experienced software developers often see the diagram as representation of a pattern — people think the diagram *is* the pattern [8].

Example-based Learning. If the students want to implement a pattern they look for example implementations of it. These example implementations often fall short if it comes to the description of the context and problem this specific implementation addresses, but also what the consequences are after applying the pattern. This encourages the student's perception that design patterns are just implementation techniques.

Therefore: Focus first on the context and the problem (including the forces) addressed by the pattern and the consequences of applying the pattern. Assure that the students understand the need for a good solution before applying the solution.

We consider this pattern a true invariant, as independent of the domain a specific pattern should only be applied after all relevant information has been gathered and analysed.

It has to become the "natural way" for students to follow the order implied in patterns. They have to focus first on the context, the problem, and the forces

---

[2] E.g. http://en.wikipedia.org/wiki/Design_pattern_(computer_science) or http://www.oodesign.com/

of a pattern, even if the solution is the first thing which is visually attracting their attention. This implicitly includes that the needed information is available to the students. If examples are used for learning, teach the students to first answer the question of why a pattern is used in this example, and only then to look at how it is applied or implemented. An awareness of the consequences of not respecting this order can be created by exposing them to the EXPERIENCE OF PROBLEMS.

To improve the consequences of CONTEXT, PROBLEM AND CONSEQUENCES FIRST, students should actively discuss the problem and context. Gestwicki and Sun state that "a discussion of the domain-specific problem leads to the justification of the design pattern" [15]. Different Active Learning patterns can be used to realize this [7]. However, teachers should be able to facilitate such a discussion. They are responsible for keeping the focus of the discussion on the important parts and preventing the discussion from drifting in unwanted directions. This requires teachers to have a good knowledge of the design patterns — especially of the addressed problems, the forces, and the consequences as well as possible variations. The set-up for such a discussion should also take social aspects into account: it is important to create and maintain an open and constructive atmosphere and aggressive or attacking behaviour should not be tolerated.

Gestwicki and Sun also emphasize in [15] that the first and most important part of applying a pattern is a good understanding of the context and the problem. The focus should therefore be put on these parts while learning design patterns as well as for the application of design patterns to solve real problems. Wallingford also describes an approach where the first step is to analyse the problem at hand and the context before actually applying the pattern [24]. Be aware that there are often different levels of problems, ranging from abstract problems like "I need to decouple these two system parts" to concrete problems like "I need to be able to add a new implementation of this algorithm easily". A discussion of the problem part should respect and reflect these levels.

In one exercise during the course on Patterns & Frameworks at the Hogeschool Utrecht students were required to study the FACADE *pattern from the GoF-book [13] and were then asked to summarize this pattern. Most students started to describe the solution, but when asked which problems the pattern addresses the answers became more vague and divergent. So the students got a second exercise (which was the implementation of* CONTEXT, PROBLEM AND CONSEQUENCES FIRST*). They were given 3 short problem descriptions and had to decide for which of these they would apply the* FACADE *pattern. They were encouraged to use the GoF-book and online sources to substantiate their decision. The students had to work first in groups of two and then in bigger groups of four (an application of* STUDENT DESIGN SPRINT *[7] in order to improve the communication between the students). Finally, one student of each group was randomly chosen to present the groups argumentation for which problem description the* FACADE *pattern can be applied (and why!) and for which not (and why not!), hereby making use of the pedagogical pattern* SHOTGUN SEMINAR *[7]. These argumentations were then subject to discussion of the whole class. This lead to a better awareness* of the problem and contexts which were addressed, but also the consequences of applying the pattern. In a follow-up exercise the students then had to implement the pattern. This way all parts of the pattern were covered, and they were covered in the correct order.

Kevlin Henney, an independent consultant and co-author of Pattern-Oriented Software Architecture Volume 5 (POSA5) [8], makes use of this pattern by giving a lot of examples involving consideration of context, forces and a clear understanding of the problem when teaching design patterns.

The authors of Head First Design Patterns [12] emphasize the analysis of the problem, the context, the forces and the consequences of applying a pattern prior to the real application as basis for a grounded decision for or against a pattern application.

The assignments given to students in courses on software architecture at the University of Vienna often include the need for determining the applicability of specific architectural patterns before their application. This includes a discussion of the context, problem and consequences sections of the patterns to be applied.

Pattern 3: EXPERIENCE OF PROBLEMS

Also known as: Feel The Pain

The aim of the wise is not to secure pleasure, but to avoid pain.

Aristotle

Students often have (naturally) a limited experience in the domain of their study. This experience is mainly based on some school projects, but these school projects are of limited scope themselves due to time constraints and other environmental factors like the size of classes or the teaching model.

❖ ❖ ❖

Students often apply patterns without understanding why the problem really is a problem. They are not aware of the consequences if this problem is not addressed properly.

The required functionality of a software system can be implemented in countless ways. Only a few of these ways equally respect and balance the non-functional requirements of the system too, while the others often lead to a BIG BALL OF MUD [11]. Many problems related to non-functional requirements emerge long after they have been caused.

Shortened Software Lifecycle. As students' projects are often of limited scope, these non-functional requirements — even if gathered and described in the beginning of the project — are not obviously necessary and of value to students, as the phase where these requirements become important is mostly out of the scope of the project. The need for — and advantage of — the consideration of these requirements during design becomes hence not obvious to the students.

Sparse Experience. The problems which are addressed by the different design patterns are often ones that students have never experienced by themselves [25]. The consequences of high coupling, low cohesion, low modifiability etc. are not obvious to them, so they often just implement the required functionality without thinking about possible consequences for the non-functional requirements.

Therefore: Let the students experience the problems addressed by a pattern first hand before they implement the pattern. Help them to understand what consequences it has if these problems are not addressed appropriately.

This pattern is specific for teaching design patterns to students without prior (excessive) design experience. It also can be inappropriate to let pattern users experience the problems addressed by the patterns, e.g. when teaching pedagogical patterns one should not enforce the problems addressed by pedagogical patterns. We therefore do not consider this as sufficiently high-level to be marked with one asterisk.

Experiencing a problem yourself improves the awareness of this particular problem, but also the awareness of why a problem should have been understood properly before solving it. This might require the adaptation of some existing exercises in a way that also the phases of the software lifecycle are covered so that the problems can actually be experienced. In software engineering projects most often this will be the integration or maintenance phase. So possible applications of this pattern could be the task of implementing a new requirement which has huge impact on the current design, or the integration of a new component in a software system.

Astrachan et al. used this technique as well [3]. They based it on the idea that "good design comes from experience, and experience comes from bad design" (attributed to Fred Brooks and Henry Petroski according to [3]).

An important aspect is that the students should not have the experience of complete failing up to the point of loss of motivation. Struggling with the problem and having difficulties to solve it are necessary part of the solution, but should not have a negative effect on the students' self-confidence. This requires a sensible application of this pattern: the period where the students actually "feel the pain" should be long enough to make the point, but not longer.

Immediately after feeling the pain of an unsolved problem, the students should look for the BEST FITTING PATTERN CHOICE and, when found, should see and have the EXPERIENCE OF BENEFITS which the solving of the problem gives them. Astrachan et al. describe this as the *before and after model* [3].

The application of this pattern is often not necessary in commercial contexts, where trainings in design patterns are given to somewhat experienced software developers or designers. These people often have a good understanding of the problems, as they have experienced them themselves and these problems were often the reason for following the course on design patterns.

We implemented this pattern in a workshop using Class-Responsibilities-Collaboration (CRC) cards as introduced by Beck and Cunningham [6]. Prior to the introduction of the Observer pattern [13] the students were asked to think of classes and a mechanism which automatically represents changes different values on different display types (which is actually one of the most often found examples of a possible Observer-application). They were required to use the CRC cards for the design process. After finishing their designs, they had to replay a simple change of one value including the automatic refresh of all representations. Then they had to add another representation and to discuss what they had to change in their design and how difficult this was. This way the students recognized that even a small addition of another display can require a relative large amount of changes.

This pattern can also be found in an exercise Cinnéide and Tynan gave their students [10]. The students had to implement an extension for two different solutions which were given to them. One of these solutions made use of design patterns while the other solution was using an ad-hoc implementation without a good design. The students struggled with the ad-hoc solution, trying to figure out the complex control flow and where to put what code in order to implement the extension. They therefore experienced the maintenance problems generated with this bad design and were able to compare this experience with the one made while extending the well-designed solution, which used design patterns. So this exercise implemented both EXPERIENCE OF PROBLEMS *and* EXPERIENCE OF BENEFITS.

Eduardo Guerra also uses this pattern in his lecture on "Understanding Design Patterns" (in combination with DISCOVER YOUR OWN PATTERN *and* EXPERIENCE OF BENEFITS). *He starts there to work towards a complex UI-menu structure, initially without making use of the later introduced* STRATEGY *Pattern. During this design process many problems are detected and identified, which shows the students that the straightforward approach presented by Guerra obviously leads to design problems.*

In the book Head First Design Patterns [12] much attention is spent on the problems the design patterns are addressing. All these problems are discussed in detail and also related to the principles possibly violated by applying a simple solution to them.

This pattern is also implemented in the assignments given by Uwe Zdun in his course on software architecture at the University of Vienna.

Pattern 4: BEST FITTING PATTERN CHOICE**

Also known as: Perfect Fit.

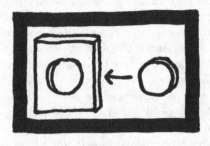

> Fine art is that in which the hand, the head, and the heart of man go together.
>
> John Ruskin

Teaching patterns usually involves a larger set of somehow related patterns. Books are often used in such courses which contain patterns covering different aspects of a certain domain. After being exposed to the patterns, the sheer amount of them — and in some cases their similarities — make it difficult for students to immediately choose and apply these patterns in the intended way.

Students often choose inappropriate patterns without exploring if the problem they have is the same as the problem addressed by the pattern. And even if this fits, the context or forces may be different or the consequences are worse than the original problem. If pattern names are part of the vocabulary of a domain, choosing an inappropriate pattern also leads to miscommunication.

One of the underlying problems is that students have difficulties with determining which pattern to use for a specific problem [22], even if the problem is described properly.

Solution-focussed. Some design patterns describe similar solution structures for solving different problems, like the ADAPTER, PROXY, and FACADE patterns. The differences between these patterns are mainly in their intentions. If not all parts of the pattern are examined, then it might seem that different solutions could be applied to solve the problem at hand. Technically all these solutions could be working, but often the role-names of pattern participants — as suggested in the the GoF-book [13] — are used as parts of the class- or method-names of the concrete pattern implementation. Using the solution of the wrong pattern would therefore communicate the wrong intention.

Vague Problem Description. Some design patterns offer different solutions to similar problems, like the INTERPRETER and COMMAND pattern. If the design problem is — or can — only be vaguely identified, then it's hard to determine which pattern to use, because it can seem that the problem/context-part of more than one pattern matches the problem. It also will be harder to understand the consequences completely.

Big Problem Space. Often there is more than one design problem which needs to be addressed. Choosing a pattern based on just one of these problems could have a negative effect on the other problems.

Example-based Learning. If examples are used which come from books or websites, then these examples often do not state a (sufficient) reasoning of why the applied pattern has been chosen to solve the example problem. This can be because there is not really a problem at hand, which is often the case with e.g. websites which focus on the *implementation* of patterns and not the correct *application*. Students tend to look for examples where patterns were applied in a context similar to their own. But if this example application is based on the wrong decisions or a misunderstood problem, then also the students will apply the possibly wrong pattern.

First Shot Solution. While looking for an applicable pattern, students tend to stop after finding the first possible *solution* to implement. So they are using "first possible solution" as stop condition for their search, which is faster than determining *all* possible patterns, studying their descriptions and making a well-grounded choice of one these patterns. Even if this is technically working, it could communicate a wrong intention.

Therefore: Ensure that the students have analysed the design problem, context, forces, and consequences sufficiently, and that all match with the pattern they choose. It is also important that the resulting context and the fitting to other applied patterns and the overall design has been taken into account.

This pattern is a true invariant. Independent of the domain, problems can look similar in different contexts or different solutions exist for the same problem with different consequences. The correct application of patterns always requires a careful consideration of the possible alternatives and grounded choice for one of them.

A metaphor will demonstrate this pattern: A good doctor will not immediately subscribe aspirine when one has headache, but will look at all — or the most — possibly relevant symptoms in order to determine the real cause of the headache and the appropriate treatment of it. She will also take possible adverse reactions and interactions with other medicines into account.

Applying the solution of this pattern requires that the students have all needed information available and examine the CONTEXT, PROBLEM AND CONSEQUENCES FIRST. A sensible analysis of the existing problems and the applicable patterns increases the chance of applying the correct pattern. The application of patterns often requires trade-offs [25]. The results of such a sensible analysis form the basis for making these trade-offs.

The design patterns described by the GoF in [13] are grouped in three categories: behavioral, structural, and creational patterns. These categories can help with scoping the problem spaces of the specific patterns. So determining the category where a problem actually belongs to could help to decrease the number of pattern candidates which have to be examined. Knowing that there are not that many pattern candidates left can help in the decision to examine them all vs. choosing the first possible solution found.

The problem space should be kept small when applying this pattern in the beginning of a course on design patterns. It is necessary that students first grasp the idea of patterns and do apply them in small scale examples [22].

However, applying BEST FITTING PATTERN CHOICE also includes a discussion of traditional, naïve, and non-patterns-based approaches for solving the problem at hand [15]. This ensures that if a pattern does not offer the best solution or comes for the price of a much higher complexity in the resulting context, then it is better to put SIMPLICITY ABOVE PATTERNS and use one of the traditional or naïve approaches.

One application of this pattern was included in an exercise during the course on Patterns & Frameworks at the Hogeschool Utrecht which was done after introducing the students to the design patterns ADAPTER, PROXY, and FACADE. They were then given following problem statement and asked to choose one of the previously taught patterns for solving it: "A client needs only to access the last results and the table of a football administration system". All three patterns were chosen by some students, and we encouraged a discussion about why the different patterns were chosen. It was made clear that probably all of them could be used to implement the required functionality, but that only the FACADE pattern matches with the real problem and also communicates that. This way the students were made aware of the fact that it is not sufficient to just apply a solution of one pattern, but to make sure that pattern and problem match and therefore the implementation also communicates the intent of the pattern application.

In other discussions the students were constantly asked why they did not use another pattern. The teacher here asked on purpose for incorrect patterns in order to initiate a discussion and create an awareness of making sure that indeed there is a BEST FITTING PATTERN CHOICE.

The authors of Head First Design Patterns [12] mention that before applying a pattern the user should study other patterns first which look like they could be applicable too. Based on the matching of the different parts — they name intent and applicability, which include the problem, context and also consequences of a pattern — with the situation at hand a fitting pattern can be selected.

Bauer and Baumgartner cite BEST FITTING PATTERN CHOICE *(under the synonym PERFECT FIT) in their forthcoming book on E-Portfolio Patterns [4]. They encourage students to make use of it when applying the patterns from the book for the creation of their E-Portfolio. This is an example from the domain of education.*

In the assignments given in the course on software architecture at the University of Vienna the students are required to give the rationale behind their choice of applied patterns. This included a discussion of the problem, context, and consequences of the applied pattern, but also a rationale of why other patterns were not applicable.

Pattern 5: EXPERIENCE OF BENEFITS*

Also known as: Rewarding Sweets.

> Let's face it, a nice creamy chocolate cake does a lot for a lot of people; it
> does for me.
>   Audrey Hepburn

Giving the students the EXPERIENCE OF PROBLEMS helps in intrinsically motivating them to do something about these problems. Naturally, these problems often can be solved in many different ways and students often tend to apply the most straight-forward approach to solving them which often is not the best possible one. Their motivation to apply a pattern for solving the problem is initially often only extrinsically motivated by the teacher.

❖ ❖ ❖

It is hard for students to see the advantages generated by correctly applied pattern solutions if they are only told to them. This has negative impact on the intrinsic motivation of the students to use patterns outside of the educational setting.

After students had the EXPERIENCE OF PROBLEMS, they start to understand why a solution is needed to solve a problem. But purely applying a pattern is only part of the story.

Shortened Software Lifecycle. The correct appliance of patterns creates a resulting context, which offers in some cases advantages (e.g. better modifiability). Even if the students apply a pattern correct to reach this, they often miss the part that they really get advantage out of this, as the student projects often stop right before getting to this phase of the lifecycle.

Curricula. It seems that computer science and software engineering curricula still focus mainly on the activities prior the deployment and maintenance phases in the lifecycle of software systems.

Belief. Purely hearing from the teacher that a solution is a good solution because it offers some advantages which actually can't be experienced by the students themselves, requires a high belief of the students in what the teacher says. Some students experienced that some teachers don't have reasonable arguments for why some things are good and have to be done in the way the teacher wants to. Their belief is therefore dependent on their previous experiences with specific teachers.

Motivation. If students do not believe in the advantages of applying patterns, then they probably get their motivation purely out of the grading or teacher's feedback they receive. If this is the only thing of value for them it is likely that they do not apply patterns again or that they still apply them in an incorrect way. This extrinsic motivation is therefore not very helpful in teaching design patterns.

Therefore: Give the students rewarding sweets — something of value or satisfaction for the students — by letting them experience the benefits one gets after or during the correct application of a pattern first hand.

In the domain of software design the benefits of applying patterns can — and should — be demonstrated to students. But in other domains this is not always possible, as the real implementation of a pattern solution might be out-scoping the teaching context (e.g. when trying to show the benefit of Alexander's TOWNS pattern). Therefore this pattern is considered as an invariant in the context of software design patterns.

This pattern is closely related to EXPERIENCE OF PROBLEMS, but both patterns cover different aspects. While EXPERIENCE OF PROBLEMS shows what happens when the problem is not addressed, EXPERIENCE OF BENEFITS reveals what happens when the problem is appropriately addressed and solved, using the pattern selected as BEST FITTING PATTERN CHOICE. While the main focus should be put on the benefits, the liabilities also need to be addressed.

EXPERIENCE OF BENEFITS can be realized using an existing implementation of a pattern solution. This implementation can then be used as basis for a follow-up assignment, where the focus is led on making use of the benefits of the correct pattern application. This way the students can experience the advantage themselves. However, the implementation can be of different origins: as PATTERN IMPLEMENTATION MATTERS, the students may already have implemented a pattern in the correct way themselves. But also a solution can be given to the students by the teacher which includes a correct implementation of a pattern.

In some cases it might be sufficient to only discuss the benefits. For example, Gestwicki and Sun introduced the STATE design pattern by comparing it with earlier designs made by the students and discussing the shortcomings of these designs and the possible benefits from the application of the STATE pattern [15].

The implementation described by Cinnéide and Tynan focusses more on the advantages a pattern can offer during its implementation [10]. They used a problem-based approach in order to let the students "appreciate the flexibility provided by the pattern". The students had to implement a solution without using a specific pattern and then implement it again using this pattern, showing them that using the pattern was the more easy way.

Warren states that students should experience the full lifecycle of a pattern so that they really appreciate the benefits [25]. Using this pattern reduces the need for projects which cover the full software lifecycle, as it simulates the phases which can not be included in student projects due to time constraints. This increases the awareness of the consequences of applying patterns and also offers a way for introducing activities to the curriculum which are related to phases in the later part of the software development lifecycle.

In one exercise the students were asked to implement a small cook-administration system. All cooks made use of one of a few preparation strategies, and the students were asked to use the STRATEGY pattern to realize this. In a follow-up assignment they were asked to add another strategy and assign it to one of the cooks. Furthermore they had to describe how difficult it was to realize this and how long it took them. Their answers showed that they experienced it as an easy task which was implemented in a few minutes. So they had a noticeable benefit after the application of the STRATEGY pattern.

*Cinnéide and Tynan used this pattern [10]. The students were offered two solutions, one implemented in an ad-hoc way and one using the OBSERVER design pattern. They were required to add a new view for both solutions. This way they were able to **experience** the simplicity offered by the solution which used the OBSERVER pattern instead of just reading about it, which increases the under-*

standing of the advantages of applying patterns. As stated earlier, this implementation combines EXPERIENCE OF PROBLEMS *and* EXPERIENCE OF BENEFITS *in one exercise.*

Pattern 6: PATTERN IMPLEMENTATION MATTERS*

Also known as: Implementation Matters.

> Knowing is not enough; we must apply. Willing is not enough; we must do.
> Johann Wolfgang von Goethe

The concept of patterns is often abstract to students when first introduced to it. Especially the solution of a pattern is described on a high abstraction level, which makes it hard for students to see how this solution could or should be implemented in a concrete context.

The students have difficulties with implementing the solutions of patterns if they only read or hear about them. It is hard for them to add the information necessary for the pattern implementation, which has been abstracted away during the definition of the pattern.

Similar to programming techniques, it is not sufficient to just know about the solution a specific design pattern describes in order to use it in the intended way. E.g. the concept of recursion should be implemented and played with in order to get a real understanding of it. The process of unfolding to specific needs is generally an essential part of using abstractions like patterns.

Abstract vs. Concrete. Design pattern solutions are usually given in an abstract way. The participants are described and the structure is shown in a class diagram. However, all these stay on an abstract level for the student. Even if a sample implementation is given for a specific problem, the students still might have problems on how to apply the pattern for *their own* concrete problem. It is not an easy task applying an abstract solution to a concrete problem.

Implementation Complexity. Some patterns are easy to implement, while others are much more complex. This difference is not easily comprehensible for students.

Code Generation. Some development tools offer support for the application of design patterns[3]. These tools generate most of the code which makes up the important parts of a pattern implementation. The students do often not study this generated code and take for granted that this code reflects the best possible implementation of the pattern solution independent of the rest of their implementation. So if they have to implement a pattern on their own — without using the generating facilities of such an IDE — or if they have to recognize patterns in source code, they are likely to fail.

Therefore: let the students implement some pattern solutions themselves.

With software design patterns it is always possible to implement them, and this helps students to understand the transformation from abstract pattern solution to concrete implementation better. However, this is not always easily possible in other domains. E.g. the patterns of Alexander can mostly not be implemented in the context of a course on architecture, and educational patterns at curriculum level might also be too big to be implemented during a course on didactics. This pattern is therefore considered as an invariant in the domain of teaching software design patterns.

As Ralph Johnson says in [16]: "...people can't learn patterns without trying them out.". It is hard for non-experienced programmers to realize the power of patterns without a concrete application of them [3].

The solution is supported by the pedagogical pattern PREFER WRITING [7], which encourages the use of written exercises and includes also the writing of source code.

Having students implementing design patterns on their own helps in getting a better understanding of the solution in general. If a concrete pattern implementation is given to the students, there will be a higher chance that they recognize the participants of the pattern and the roles they play. So even if they use code generation, having implemented a pattern on their own helps them in using it the correct way and to understand the generated code.

This pattern is just a part of the whole language and should not be used in isolation. PATTERN IMPLEMENTATION MATTERS can be used in combination with

---

[3] Design pattern generation support can be found e.g. in the Netbeans IDE or in the Eclipse IDE (using PatternBox, http://www.patternbox.com).

EXPERIENCE OF BENEFITS, but does not have to. After using PATTERN IMPLE-
MENTATION MATTERS it is advisable to also ensure a PRINCIPLE-SUPPORTING
PATTERN USAGE and that the students put SIMPLICITY ABOVE PATTERNS.

The applicability of this pattern depends on the domain of the patterns. If
the implementation is not realistic in the scope of the educational setting due to
time or space constraints, then alternatives as e.g. working with a prototype or
modelling the solution could be considered.

*Probably all courses on design patterns include the implementation of at least
a few of them. In our course the students had, among others, to implement
e.g. the* STRATEGY *pattern. This exercise was then also used to give them the*
EXPERIENCE OF BENEFITS. *Another exercise included the implementation of the*
FACADE *pattern. Many more examples can be found in the references section.*

In Head First Design Patterns [12] many implementation exercises are included.

*The assignments for the course on software architecture at the University of
Vienna all require the implementation of different architectural patterns.*

Pattern 7: SIMPLICITY ABOVE PATTERNS**

Also known as: Keep it Simple.

> Any intelligent fool can make things bigger and more complex... It takes a
> touch of genius - and a lot of courage to move in the opposite direction.
>
> Albert Einstein

When patterns are taught to students, then it usually is also expected that the
students apply them in some assignments or exercises. The implementation of
patterns nearly always increases the overall complexity in some way, either by
adding additional elements to a design or different activities to a certain process.

❖ ❖ ❖

While learning patterns students want to show that they understand the patterns by implementing as many of them as possible. Most often this adds unnecessary complexity without adding value.

The application of a design pattern often adds complexity to the design of a software system in terms of extra classes, methods or relations between objects and classes. But if applied in a correct way, design patterns can add value through improving the quality of a systems' design in respect of non-functional requirements. However, a software designer has to make sensible decisions on when to use a design pattern and how to implement it. These decisions include trade-offs between the added complexity and the improved quality.

Exhaustive Use. Students often seem to skip this trade-off and decide to use a pattern even if it is not necessary. This is probably related to their experiences in other courses, where they are required to show that they understood all concepts and techniques taught to them by applying them. When being taught Enterprise JavaBeans (EJB), they probably have to implement all sorts of EJB's. When introduced to specific UML diagrams, they probably are requested to make use of all of them. Exposing students to an increasing number of patterns seems to correlate with the amount of pattern implementations.

Decreased Necessity. With design patterns it is a different story. A typical larger assignment in a course which also teaches design patterns often does require the use of *some* of the learned design patterns, but most probably *not all* of them.

Complex vs. Straightforward. In some cases a problem or requirement could also be implemented — or designed — using a straightforward solution. Most pattern beginners tend to choose for still applying the pattern, thereby adding unnecessary complexity.

Therefore: Motivate the students to always give a rationale for all design patterns they have used. Make sure that they only apply a design pattern when they have not only examined the design problem at hand, but also the consequences of applying the pattern. The application of the pattern should add value to the overall design.

This pattern is considered as true invariant for the teaching of patterns of all domains, as the tendency of applying patterns excessively after being introduced to them can be found in nearly all domains.

To ensure that the students always have a rationale let them study the CONTEXT, PROBLEM AND CONSEQUENCES FIRST. A good understanding of the problem, the context, and possible consequences form the basis for the trade-offs which are part of the decision on when to use a pattern and when not. It has to be ensured that students understand that *not* applying the solution of a pattern if this is not appropriate is a good practice and higher valued than the simple application of the patterns.

While discussing the trade-offs, experience shows that the students put less emphasis on general principles of a good system design (like low coupling, high cohesion, etc.), so you have to emphasize that the students apply a PRINCIPLE-SUPPORTING PATTERN USAGE. Generally, make sure that they understand that the goal is not to apply as many design patterns as possible, but to create a good design that implements the requirements and that design patterns can — and should — help to do this.

Additional to an oral discussion of the trade-offs it could also be asked from the students to give a written explanation of the rationale as part of an exercise or assignment, if time and other conditions allow this. This also would include the application of PREFER WRITING [7].

We were delivering an earlier version of the course "Patterns and Frameworks", which was not yet based on this pattern language. During the final presentations of the project, one of the students gave as a rationale why he used a specific design pattern that 'they had to use a pattern and that he chose that one'. When asked if he really had a design problem and if he understands the consequences of applying this pattern, he had no answers. After starting to work with this pattern language, the students were required to present their solutions to the whole class and give a rationale for each pattern they were using. The other students were encouraged to ask questions about the design decisions made and also to state if they have possible alternative solutions. This way it became natural to the students to provide a rationale for all their decisions and trade-offs, which lead to decreased complexity of their designs.

In the book Head First Design Patterns the authors state that it is more important to keep the design as simple as possible and not to blindly apply design patterns [12]. They explicitly state that the most simple and straightforward solution should always be considered too, and that sometimes this is sufficient. They also explicitly suggest to remove a pattern from the design if this improves the simplicity of it.

Pattern 8: PRINCIPLE-SUPPORTING PATTERN USAGE*

Also known as: Principles Are Leading.

> Rules are not necessarily sacred, principles are.
> Franklin D. Roosevelt

In many domains principles are defined which guide practitioners in this domain and help them to realize *good* solutions. These principles are often taught before or during the introduction of patterns, but the relation between these principles and the patterns are not always obvious to the students.

❖ ❖ ❖

While learning design patterns students often focus on the implementation of the patterns in isolation, which regularly results in a bad overall design.

Good design of an object-oriented system is based on basic principles like high cohesion, loose coupling, etc. They should be taken into account while designing, and design patterns are just a tool to do so. As Warren states, the focus should be put on *doing* design by making effective use of design patterns [25].

Small Scale vs. Large Scale. Design patterns are often taught first using small examples. The design principles do not play a prominent role in these examples. However, when the examples become larger also the principles become more important. But the students often apply the patterns as in their small examples, which increases the chance of violating basic design principles.

Golden Design Bullet. Students tend to think that the pure application of patterns does automatically lead to a good design.

Therefore: Assure that the students understand that basic design-principles are more important than the patterns themselves and should therefore always be followed first. Emphasize that design patterns *can support* the implementation of these principles if applied correctly, but do not automatically so.

Not for all domains principles have been identified which form guidelines for creation in these domains. In software design these principles are well known and described, and because patterns are mainly intended to follow these principles, this pattern is considered as invariant in the domain of software design patterns.

This pattern is inspired by the framework process pattern IT'S STILL OO TO ME [9], which is applicable for the development of frameworks, but also for the usage of design patterns. Rasala states that one of the problems in teaching design is the "lack of clarity about fundamental issues" [23]. This problem is addressed by this pattern as well through making the fundamental issues —

the principles which have to be followed — explicit and leading. The correct consideration of the principles should be emphasized continuously by the teacher or trainer when teaching design patterns. This ideally is also reflected when assessing the students' practical work: not the multiple application of different patterns should be rewarded, but the support of the applied patterns for the realization of the design principles in the overall design.

Gestwicki and Sun define three main learning objectives for teaching Design Patterns [15]. The first and most important one is: "The student understands object-oriented design and modeling". This requires the constant reminding of the students what a good object-oriented design is based on. Through making the OO-principles leading, this learning objective could be more easily achieved.

As stated by Vlissides, design patterns are not necessarily object-oriented [5]. So the design principles don't have to be necessarily object-oriented. But the more important part is that whatever paradigm is used, the patterns should be used to support the principles valid for this paradigm.

EXPERIENCE OF BENEFITS can be used for the implementation of this pattern. If shown to students, the EXPERIENCE OF BENEFITS is often of value because of their maintenance of the design principles.

In our course we included in the discussions with the students also the resulting context. The students were constantly reminded of the design principles and had to explain how the resulting context conforms to these principles.

Eduardo Guerra introduces patterns in his courses at the Instituto Tecnológico de Aeronautica as examples of how to realize different principles. This way it is ensured that the focus of the course is primarily on these principles and that the patterns only help in realizing them, which also makes the difference between principles and patterns more clear to the students.

In Head first Design Patterns the authors make a distinction between different levels of pattern thinking [12]. They describe the highest level as Zen Thinking, which consists of thinking in object principles and applying patterns only if this naturally follows the object thinking. They also repeatedly emphasize the design principles and explain how the patterns are used to follow them. One example is the principle of loose coupling and how the OBSERVER pattern can help in realizing this principle.

Pattern 9: DISCOVER YOUR OWN PATTERN**

Also known as: Pattern Discovery.

> Nothing is so well learned as that which is discovered.
>
> Socrates

The students have enough knowledge of the subject addressed by some of the more simple patterns and they probably already applied the pattern solution without knowing that this was a pattern implementation. You now want to show the students where patterns come from.

Students see patterns as something that intelligent people have written. They don't understand that these mostly are captured "best known practices" and that experienced people use them without thinking about them.

Usually not much focus is put on where patterns come from. They are taught to students (and explained in textbooks) as if they are a mechanism invented by some experts. This does not increase the understanding of what patterns in general are and can do.

Not Invented Here. Some students prefer to design software (in assignments or projects) their own way. They think that patterns are just techniques which are invented by other people, but that they can do better. The students do not know that they already are applying implicitly some patterns.

Complexity Fear. Patterns are at different complexity levels. The VISITOR pattern from the GoF-book is certainly more complex and harder to understand than the SINGLETON pattern [13]. Especially when beginning with patterns, this complexity can be overwhelming. The students are afraid of doing it wrong, so they often decide to not use patterns. This experienced complexity is related to their perception that they have to understand the abstract mechanism of pattern application and that this mechanism is separate from their own programming and design experiences. They do not see both as parts of the same process.

Therefore: Show students how patterns emerge by letting them discover an existing and well-known pattern by themselves.

We consider this pattern as true invariant, taking into account that it is only applicable for patterns which match with the experience of the students or pattern learners. It was for example used for introducing pedagogical patterns during a lecturer's workshop and also during a presentation at the Dutch Conference on Computer Science Education in 2011 [19].

The experience of discovering something by yourself can lead to a higher learning effect than if it is just explained. While discovering something, one uses already existing knowledge. The parts of the new knowledge can be connected to the existing knowledge, which is the implementation of the pedagogical pattern EXPAND THE KNOWN WORLD and makes use of Constructivist educational theories where knowledge is built upon existing knowledge [7].

So, if students would discover a pattern by themselves, they can more easy connect and add it to their existing knowledge. They also recognize that discovering patterns is based on the experience of the ones looking for the patterns. James Coplien states that "it is difficult for designers to appreciate patterns fully, unless they have written one" [5]. Warren also describes the experience that one sometimes subconsciously applies patterns while designing [25]. This can be used for letting students make the same experience.

Pattern discovery — or pattern mining — is usually based on many examples. The implementation of this pattern therefore requires the existence of a group of implementations or designs, all solving the same problem. Then the pattern discovery steps as suggested by Alexander in [1, p.254-260] can be used:

> "In order to discover patterns which are alive we must always start with observation".

One realisation could be to give students prior to the teaching of a specific design pattern an assignment which includes the problem addressed by this pattern in a well defined context. Let them implement it — without using the pattern! — and present their solution to the class.

> "Now try to discover some property which is common to all the ones which feel good, and missing from all the ones which don't feel good."

Discuss all solutions in the class. Let the students vote on which solution or which parts of solutions are the best.

> "Now try to identify the problem which exists in (...)[4] which lack this property. Knowledge of the problem then helps shed light on the invariant which solves the problem."

Make sure they give arguments for why they've chosen one of the solutions as the best one and how this could be applied to equivalent problems. Then introduce the pattern and compare it with the students' solution. If the example is well chosen and the discussion stays focused on the important parts, the students' solution should be nearly identical to the pattern and, if at all, only differ in minor parts. This way, the students discovered the pattern themselves.

Before providing some known uses of this pattern it is interesting to mention that by far the most examples make use of the STRATEGY design pattern for the application of this pattern.

---

[4] Alexander uses entrances as example. The actual realisation depends on the chosen example.

This pattern was used in the beginning of a course on 'Patterns and Frameworks'. The students got an exercise where they had to give the design of a solution (with a UML-classdiagram) which solved the problem of maintaining a few cooks with different preparations. It should be easy to give a cook another series of preparations steps. After a short period all groups had to present their solutions and the group was discussing them. Some created a class for every cook (like cookChristian, cookJeroen, etc.), others made one class cook with an attribute name. Some decided to add a list to every cook with all preparation steps, while other solutions included an abstract class preparation with concrete implementations of different preparation strategies. The group decided after a discussion that this last solution was the best one. After that we introduced the STRATEGY pattern [13], which only differed in some minor details from the solution which was chosen as the best solution. In some later exercises and assignments the author experienced that the students' usage of the STRATEGY pattern was nearly always reasonable.

Weiss used this pattern as basis for an undergraduate CS course [26]. Using a series of ongoing assignments, all improvements of a small application, he introduced different problems which had to be solved and implemented by the students. The solutions to these problems were subject to group discussions, and the best solutions were then applied by the students. These solutions were actually implementations of specific design patterns, which was communicated to the students after they implemented them. This showed the students that design patterns are indeed good solutions to well identified problems.

Eduardo Guerra lets his students write a pattern themselves based on their prior experience, which is also an implementation of DISCOVER YOUR OWN PATTERN. He also works in his lecture on "Understanding Design Patterns" together with the students towards the best possible solution for implementing a complex UI-menu. The agreed-on best solution then actually is the implementation of the STRATEGY pattern, which gives the students the impression that they discovered this pattern themselves.

Kevlin Henney, independent consultant and co-author of POSA5 [8], often tells people in a design and code lab in a commercial training context to focus on problem identification and problem solving. The participants of this training already have certain design knowledge, but only knowledge of a small set of design patterns. During the retrospective after finishing the lab exercise sometimes patterns become visible which the participants applied without knowing it. Linking the pattern to the presented solution is then easy to grasp for the participants, and also shows them where patterns come from. Even though this is not a conscious application of DISCOVER YOUR OWN PATTERN, it shows the applicability of the idea behind this pattern.

Also the book Head First Design Patterns begins with the application of existing object-oriented knowledge following some basic principles, which finally leads to the implementation of the STRATEGY pattern [12]. But this is just mentioned at the end of this book section.

Clarification of the Sketches

The main ideas of the sketches are based on the drawings of Takashi Iba which he made on the copy of his print-out of my paper and gave me after the writer's workshop at the PLoP 2011 conference. I drew them myself again and modified some based on my own ideas. The main theme are an X and an O, which mostly represent pattern parts in an abstract way (and with sometimes changing associations). The following list tries to clarify my thoughts for each sketch:

- HOLISTIC PATTERN UNDERSTANDING — Teaching patterns is more than just explaining a part of them (mostly the solution). It is therefore not sufficient to study only X or O, but you have to take all relevant parts into account.
- CONTEXT, PROBLEM AND CONSEQUENCES FIRST — Students tend to move on to the solution (the O) quickly without taking the other relevant parts (the usually larger X) into account. So the focus should be on first going to X, and then move on to O.
- EXPERIENCE OF PROBLEMS — The X represents the problem, and the broken heart is used as metaphor for pain.
- BEST FITTING PATTERN CHOICE — The materialized O only fits perfectly into the hole if the diameter, the deepness, the color, and all other relevant aspects of both parts have been taken into account.
- EXPERIENCE OF BENEFITS — After implementing a pattern correctly, considering all the X's and O's, then a sweet reward emerges. The chocolate stands as metaphor for the positive consequences — the benefits — of the pattern application.
- PATTERN IMPLEMENTATION MATTERS — Just presenting the plan of the solution O does not automatically lead to the correct implementation of this solution (in this case the cube with the O). The process of translating this abstract plan to a concrete implementation offers deeper insights in the way pattern solutions have to be implemented in general.
- SIMPLICITY ABOVE PATTERNS — There are many patterns out there, and applying them blindly often leads to complex situations, shown in the chaotic lower part of the sketch. The upper part is more easy to grasp, containing only the things really needed.
- PRINCIPLE-SUPPORTING PATTERN USAGE — Even though it might seem appropriate to apply all the pattern solutions to solve a problem — the O's on the right side — it might happen that some of these solution applications lead to violations of some of the basic principles. These solutions should be initially rejected (as happens with the second O).
- DISCOVER YOUR OWN PATTERN — The metaphor of a mountain and the (unexpected) appearance of a pattern, represented by the X and the O, are used here. Most people know this feeling that when walking through mountains (which is hard to experience in the Netherlands) after reaching the top of a hill, a complete new scenario comes into sight, like e.g. a wonderful sea or a village located in a valley.

Acknowledgements. I want to thank my shepherd Nuno Flores, who helped me to improve the patterns prior to the EuroPLoP 2011. I highly appreciate the feedback which I got from the EuroPLoP 2011 writer's workshop members: Christian Kohls, Andreas Rüping, Claudia Iacob, Peter Baumgartner, Reinhard Bauer, and Dirk Schnelle-Walka.

I also would like to thank my PLoP 2011 shepherd Hugo Ferreira. And again it was great pleasure and honor to receive feedback from the members of the PLoP 2011 pedagogy workshop: Christian Kohls, Takashi Iba, Willem Larsen, Zhen Jiang, Javier Gonzalez-Sanchez, Helen Chavez-Echeagaray, Chikara Ichikawa, Mami Sakamoto, Tomohito Yamazaki, Kana Matsumura, Rinko Arao, Aya Matsumoto, and James Noble.

The comments and questions of Paul Griffioen and Mike van Hilst helped in making this work more accessible, also for non-pattern community members. Special thanks go again to Takashi Iba for giving me the inspiration for the sketches and to Christian Kohls, Kevlin Henney, and Uwe Zdun for their feedback on later versions of this language.

References

1. Alexander, C.: The Timeless Way of Building, later prin. edn. Oxford University Press, New York (1979)
2. Alexander, C., Ishikawa, S., Silverstein, M.: A Pattern Language: Towns, Buildings, Construction, later prin. edn. Center for Environmental Structure Series. Oxford University Press (August 1977)
3. Astrachan, O., Mitchener, G., Berry, G., Cox, L.: Design patterns: an essential component of CS curricula. In: Proceedings of the Twenty-Ninth SIGCSE Technical Symposium on Computer Science Education, SIGCSE 1998, pp. 153–160. ACM, New York (1998)
4. Bauer, R., Baumgartner, P.: Schaufenster des Lernens - Eine Sammlung von Mustern für die Arbeit mit E-Portfolios. Waxmann Verlag, Münster (2012)
5. Beck, K., Crocker, R., Meszaros, G., Vlissides, J., Coplien, J.O., Dominick, L., Paulisch, F.: Industrial experience with design patterns. In: Proceedings of the 18th International Conference on Software Engineering, ICSE 1996, pp. 103–114. IEEE Computer Society, Washington, DC (1996)
6. Beck, K., Cunningham, W.: A laboratory for teaching object oriented thinking. ACM SIGPLAN Notices 24(10), 1–6 (1989)
7. Pedagogical Patterns Editorial Board. Pedagogical Patterns: Advice for Educators. Joseph Bergin Software Tools (2012)
8. Buschmann, F., Henney, K., Schmidt, D.C.: Pattern-oriented software architecture: On patterns and pattern languages, vol. 5. John Wiley & Sons Inc. (2007)
9. Carey, J., Carlson, B.: Framework process patterns: lessons learned developing application frameworks. Addison-Wesley Longman Publishing Co., Inc., Boston (2002)
10. Cinnéide, M.Ó., Tynan, R.: A problem-based approach to teaching design patterns. SIGCSE Bull. 36(4), 80–82 (2004)
11. Foote, B., Yoder, J.: Big Ball of Mud. In: Pattern Languages of Program Design, pp. 653–692. Addison-Wesley (1997)

12. Freeman, E., Robson, E., Bates, B., Sierra, K.: Head First Design Patterns. O'Reilly Media (2004)
13. Gamma, E., Helm, R., Johnson, R., Vlissides, J.: Design Patterns. Addison-Wesley, Boston (1995)
14. Gestwicki, P.: Teaching Design Patterns Through Computer Game Development. Journal on Educational Resources in Computing 8(1), 1–22 (2008)
15. Gestwicki, P., Sun, F.-S.: Teaching Design Patterns Through Computer Game Development. J. Educ. Resour. Comput. 8(1), 2:1–2:22 (2008)
16. Goldfedder, B., Rising, L.: A training experience with patterns. Commun. ACM 39(10), 60–64 (1996)
17. Hundley, J.: A review of using design patterns in CS1. In: Proceedings of the 46th Annual Southeast Regional Conference on XX, ACM-SE 46, pp. 30–33. ACM, New York (2008)
18. Köppe, C.: Observations on the Observer Pattern. In: Proceedings of the 17th Conference on Pattern Languages of Programs, PLoP 2010. ACM, New York (2010)
19. Köppe, C.: Een tijd-(en grenze) loze manier van onderwijs: Pedagogical Patterns. In: Proceedings of the NIOC 2011 Conference, Heerlen, Netherlands (2011)
20. Köppe, C.: A Pattern Language for Teaching Design Patterns (Part 1). In: Proceedings of the 16th European Conference on Pattern Languages of Programs, EuroPLoP 2011, ACM, Irsee (2011)
21. Köppe, C.: A Pattern Language for Teaching Design Patterns (Part 2). In: Proceedings of the 18th Conference on Pattern Languages of Programs, PLoP 2011, ACM, Portland (2011)
22. Pillay, N.: Teaching Design Patterns. In: Proceedings of the SACLA Conference, Pretoria, South Africa (2010)
23. Rasala, R.: Design issues in computer science education. SIGCSE Bull. 29(4), 4–7 (1997)
24. Wallingford, E.: Toward a first course based on object-oriented patterns. ACM SIGCSE Bulletin 28(1), 27–31 (1996)
25. Warren, I.: Teaching patterns and software design. In: Proceedings of the 7th Australasian Conference on Computing Education, ACE 2005, vol. 42, pp. 39–49. Australian Computer Society, Inc., Darlinghurst (2005)
26. Weiss, S.: Teaching design patterns by stealth. In: Proceedings of the 36th SIGCSE Technical Symposium on Computer Science Education, SIGCSE 2005, p. 492 (2005)

Pattern Language for the Internal Structure
of Metadata-Based Frameworks

Eduardo Guerra[1], Jerffeson de Souza[2], and Clovis Fernandes[1]

[1] Aeronautical Institute of Technology – ITA
Praça Marechal Eduardo Gomes, 50 - Vl Acácias - SJ Campos – SP, Brazil
guerraem@gmail.com, clovistf@uol.com.br
[2] State University of Ceará – UECE
Av. Paranjana, 1700 , Campus do Itaperi - Fortaleza – CE, Brazil
jeff@larces.uece.br

Abstract. Metadata-based frameworks are those that process their logic based
on the metadata of classes whose instances they are working with. Many recent
frameworks use this approach to get a higher reuse level and to be more suita-
bly adapted to the application needs. However, there is not yet a complete best
practices documentation or reference architecture for the development of metadata-based frameworks. This paper presents a pattern language that focuses on
recurring solutions used in the internal structure of metadata-based frameworks
addressing the main problems faced in this kind of development. Based on the
pattern language, a reference architecture which identifies a base structure and
the main hotspots for metadata-based frameworks is defined.

Keywords: Metadata, Design Patterns, Pattern Language, Annotation,
Attribute-oriented Programming, Framework, Reference Architecture.

1 Introduction

Many mature frameworks and APIs used in the industry nowadays are based on
metadata such as Hibernate [2], EJB 3 [34] and JUnit [40]. However, most of them
have flexibility problems that can make it difficult or prevent their use in some
applications. For instance, the metadata reading mechanism of some frameworks
cannot be extended, which makes it difficult to retrieve metadata from other sources
or formats. This lack of flexibility in the metadata reading may demand changes, such
as annotation refactorings [54]. Examples of other design concerns are the following:
(a) how to make metadata extensible?; (b) how can the framework logic be adapted
according to class metadata?; (c) and how can specific framework metadata be shared
among other frameworks or components?

This paper presents a pattern language for metadata-based frameworks. The aim of
this research is to identify best practices both in the understanding and in the development of this kind of framework. The recurring solutions for common problems are
documented in a pattern language. The next subsections of the introduction explore

J. Noble et al. (Eds.): TPLOP III, LNCS 7840, pp. 55–110, 2013.

important concepts about frameworks and metadata. Then, the goal, relevance, and intended audience of this work are presented and explained.

1.1   Frameworks

A framework is a set of classes that supports reuse at larger granularity. It defines an object-oriented abstract design for a particular kind of application which enables not only source code reuse, but also design reuse [32]. The framework abstract structure can be filled with classes from its own library or application-specific ones, providing flexibility for the developer to adapt its behavior to each application. Besides flexibility, a good framework also increases the team productivity and makes application maintenance easier [59, 10].

A framework must contain points, called hotspots, where applications can customize their behavior [46]. Points that cannot be changed are called frozen spots. These two points usually define the framework general architecture, which consists of its basic components and the relationships among them.

In the first frameworks, the application classes had to be compatible with the framework protocol, usually by extending an abstract class or implementing an interface. The framework structures have evolved and recent ones use introspection [7, 13] to access at runtime the application classes metadata, such as their superclasses, methods, and attributes. As a result, it allows application classes to be decoupled from the framework abstract classes and interfaces. The framework can, for instance, search the class structure for the right method to invoke. The use of this technique provides more flexibility for the application, since the framework reads the classes dynamically, allowing their structure to evolve more easily [12].

For some frameworks, however, the information found in the class definition is not enough, since they need a domain-specific or application-specific metadata to customize their behavior [51]. Thus, they use additional class metadata defined by the application developer to customize framework behavior. In this paper this kind of framework is called a *Metadata-based Framework*, which can be defined as one that processes their logic based on the metadata from the classes whose instances they are working with [20, 22].

1.2   Metadata

"Metadata" is an overloaded term in computer science and can be interpreted differently according to the context. In the context of object-oriented programming, metadata is information about the program structure itself such as classes, methods, and attributes. A class, for example, has intrinsic metadata like its name, its superclass, its interfaces, its methods, and its attributes. In metadata-based frameworks, the developer also must define some additional application-specific or domain-specific metadata.

Even in this context, metadata can be used for many purposes. There are several examples of this, such as source code generation [6], compile-time verification [8, 48], and class transformation [47]. The metadata-based frameworks consume metadata at runtime and use it for framework adaptation. This distinction is important because the same goal could be achieved using different strategies [16].

The metadata consumed by the framework can be defined in different ways. Naming Conventions [4] use patterns in the name of classes and methods that have a special meaning for the framework. For instance, Java Beans specification [28] defines the use of access method names beginning with 'get' and 'set', and JUnit 3 [40] interprets method names beginning with 'test' as test cases implementation. Ruby on Rails [49] is an example of a framework known by using naming conventions. The conventions can also consider other information besides naming, such as an attribute type or the method parameters. The practice known as marker interface uses an empty interface to add a piece of metadata in a class.

Conventions usage can save a lot of configuration work, but it can only represent a limited amount of information. For some scenarios the metadata needed are more complex and code conventions are not enough. An alternative can be setting the information programmatically in the framework, but it is not used in practice in the majority of the frameworks. Another option is metadata definition in external sources, like XML files and databases. The possibility to modify the metadata at deploy-time or even at runtime without recompiling the code is an advantage of this type of definition. However, the definition is more verbose because it has to reference and identify program elements. Furthermore, the distance that configuration keeps from the source code is not intuitive for some developers.

Another alternative that has become popular in the software community is the use of code annotations, which is supported by some programming languages like Java [33] and C# [41; 43]. When using this technique, the developer can add custom metadata elements directly into the class source code, keeping its definition less verbose and closer to the source code. The use of code annotations is also called attribute-oriented programing [51] and can be defined as a program-level marking technique that allows developers to mark programming elements, such as classes and methods, to indicate application-specific or domain-specific semantics [55]. This technique introduces a declarative approach inside an imperative programming language.

For languages that do not support a native custom metadata configuration, an alternative can be the usage of hot comments [26], which is a software comment with an interpretable well-formed expression. The JavaDoc comments are an example of the usage of hot comments. XDoclet [56], a very popular tool before Java annotations, used JavaDoc comments to add custom metadata in programming elements. This information was often used to generate XML metadata descriptors to be consumed by frameworks.

1.3   Goals and Intended Audience

The intended audience for this work are framework developers and software architects who need to create frameworks whose behavior is based on class metadata. The pattern language explores each solution individually, presenting its forces and corresponding consequences in its usage. It also clearly identifies the main framework hotspots and frozen spots for this kind of framework. This paper is intended to be used as a guide for the design of metadata-based frameworks internal structure.

Previously to this study, there was not a work that identified best practices in the development of this kind of framework. Despite there being patterns with a similar structure, their usage in the context of metadata-based frameworks has never been registered before. Some of the patterns may be used in other contexts than frameworks, however it is not on the scope of this paper to document this kind of applicability.

The usage and development of this kind of framework is increasing and this fact can be verified by the use of a metadata-based approach in Java EE 6 specifications [29, 38, 36]. In this context, this work has the important role to disseminate the best practices for this kind of software, making it easier for framework developers to address the most common problems that can arise in their design.

2   Pattern Language Description

This section presents the proposed **Pattern Language for Metadata-based Frameworks** whose goal is to identify both the major problems occurring in implementing metadata-based frameworks and the recurring solutions for them found in existing ones. To reach this aim, an extensive study was carried out including a deep analysis of the internal structure of many existing open source metadata-based frameworks. Other frameworks were developed by the authors' research group to experiment existing and alternative solutions in different contexts. Solutions and best practices for recursive problems in this context were initially identified and documented in patterns [22]. As this research matured, the relationship among the patterns were consolidated and structured   in this pattern language.

The pattern language is composed of new patterns and specializations of existing ones. The pattern specializations present how existing practices are applied to a problem in this specific context. Despite the pattern structure and dynamics being similar to other patterns, the pattern context, forces, and consequences are different and specific to metadata-based frameworks. Since some patterns propose general solutions, it is not always obvious for a developer where they should be applied in this kind of framework. The documentation of these pattern specializations is also important in the context of the whole pattern language, since it registers their relationships with other solutions.

It is out of the scope of this pattern language to describe how metadata-based frameworks can be attached to an application architecture. The simplest case is when the framework entry point class is instantiated and used by the application, but it can also be transparent for clients in an application class Proxy [17], embedded in a container like in the EJB specification [34, 36] or even weaved with an aspect [23]. How the framework is instantiated does not provoke any change to its internal structure. For simplicity, the pattern language will consider, without loss of generality, that the client directly invokes the framework's methods.

Since the pattern context is frameworks, the pattern sections Structure, Participants and Dynamics are focused on object-oriented implementations. The diagrams presented in these sections are for illustration and should not be interpreted as the only possible implementation of the related pattern. Some pattern solutions could possibly be implemented in a different programming paradigm; however this is not addressed in this work.

The patterns are not intended to be language-specific and the documented solutions do not depend at all on any specific language feature. Although additional metadata can be defined in XML documents or in databases, most of the known uses were found in languages with features allowing the addition of custom metadata directly on the program code elements, such as Java annotations and C# attributes.

2.1   Patterns Overview

This section's goal is to give an initial idea of the pattern language and how each pattern fits in its context. The following gives a small description of each pattern:

- Metadata Container - This pattern decouples the metadata reading from the framework's logic by creating a container to represent metadata at runtime. A metadata reader populates the instance of this class, which is then used by the framework.
- Metadata Repository - This pattern creates a repository to store metadata at runtime, avoiding unnecessary metadata readings. The repository manages the metadata reading and is accessed by the framework to retrieve the metadata container.
- Metadata Reader Strategy - This pattern creates an abstraction of the metadata reading algorithm allowing it to have different implementations. It allows the framework to read metadata from different kinds of sources.
- Metadata Reader Chain - This pattern enables the metadata from more than one source to be combined during the reading. It uses a metadata reader that invokes a chain of other ones to compose the metadata reading algorithm.
- Metadata Reader Adapter - This pattern uses the metadata repository of another framework to get the existing metadata and set information in the metadata container. It allows metadata sharing among frameworks.
- Metadata Reader Delegate - In this pattern, the metadata reader delegates the responsibility to interpret pieces of metadata defined in annotations or XML elements to other classes. It allows the metadata understood by the framework to be extended by the application.
- Metadata Processor - In this pattern, the metadata container is composed of classes that maintain logic to process pieces of metadata. By implementing these class abstractions, it is possible to extend the framework behavior.
- Metadata Processing Layers - In this pattern, the logic processing is composed of many different layers, each one with different responsibilities. It allows each layer to evolve independently and also the framework functionality to be extended by adding new layers.

2.2   Pattern Language Navigation

There are a lot of paths that can be followed in the patterns implementation on a metada-ta-based framework. The running example presented with the patterns shows a possible path, but it is not the only one. Fig. 1 presents a roadmap that can help in the pattern language adoption. It starts with the implementation of Metadata Container and after that there are many possible paths that can be followed based on the framework needs.

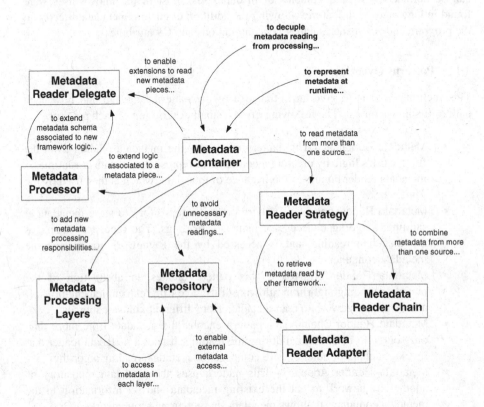

Fig. 1. Pattern Language Navigation

The pattern format used in the pattern language uses sections to organize its information. This kind of organization enables the reader to choose a subset of the sections which portrays a particular vision of the pattern language. The following paragraphs describe some possible paths in the pattern sections which can be followed to read this work.

For readers who prefer to have a more abstract view of solutions without concerning about implementation details, a possible path is to skip the Running Example section. The set of Running Example sections correspond to a pattern story which can be read separately from the patterns themselves. Another possibility for people who prefer to start thinking in more concrete problems is to read the entire running example first and then read more abstract information about the solutions in the patterns.

The solutions described by the patterns in the Structure, Participants, and Dynamics sections are focused on the object-oriented programming paradigm. Readers more interested in the abstract solution given by the pattern, perhaps for implementing it in a different program paradigm, can skip these sections and focus more on the Motivation, Problem, Forces, Solution, and Consequences sections.

2.3   Patterns Classification and Dependence

Fig. 2 illustrates the patterns classification and dependence. The dashed arrows represent that one pattern uses another pattern [44], meaning that for the implementation of a pattern, it is mandatory the implementation of the other. For instance, Metadata Reader Strategy uses Metadata Container. Other possible relationships between patterns are described in the Related Patterns section of each one.

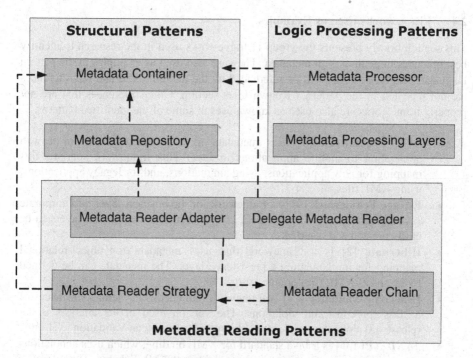

Fig. 2. Patterns Classification and Dependence

The patterns are classified in the following three mutually exclusive categories:

- **Structural Patterns** - These patterns document best practices about how to internally structure the classes of a metadata-based framework. They can be considered as the base of the pattern language, since many other patterns depend on their implementation. The structural patterns identify the main frozen spots that define the internal framework architecture. They are described in Section 3.

- **Metadata Reading Patterns** - These patterns document recurring solutions about the reading of metadata by the framework. They provide solutions to improve the flexibility in the reading process, allowing metadata sharing and metadata extension. The metadata reading patterns identify the main kinds of hotspots that can exist associated to the metadata reading process. They are described in Section 4.
- **Logic Processing Patterns** - These patterns document solutions in the design of the classes that process the main logic of the framework. They allow logic processing based on the class metadata to be extended and modified. The logic processing patterns identify the main kinds of hotspots that can exist associated to the framework metadata processing. They are described in Section 5.

2.4   Frameworks Used as Examples

This section briefly presents the group of frameworks used in the research to identify best practices in dealing with metadata. They are also used as examples in the pattern language. The frameworks will be referenced by the name in bold and the references are not repeated in the pattern's Known Uses section. Other references that are not properly frameworks are also used as known uses in some of the identified patterns.

- **ACE Framework** [5] uses metadata to map functionalities of a web application to mobile applications in Java. This framework supports this mapping for new applications, using annotations, and for legacy applications, using XML files.
- **Esfinge Framework** [9] is a framework for the business layer of a corporate Java EE application. It provides a layered structure that allows layers to be easily created and inserted.
- **Hibernate** [2] is a framework that uses metadata for object-relational mapping for implementing a persistence layer. The metadata can be defined by means of XML files or annotations.
- **Hibernate Validator** [24] is framework that checks in-memory instances of a class for constraint violations. The version used in the analysis is the release 4.0 alpha that implements the specification Bean Validation [37].
- **JAXB API** [35] is a Java standard for XML binding, which uses annotations on application classes to map them to the target XML Schema. The reference implementation is used in the analysis.
- **JBoss Application Server 5** [30] is an implementation of an application server that supports the EJB 3 specification [34].
- **JColtrane** [31] is a framework to parse XML files based on SAX [50] events. It uses annotations to define conditions for each method to be executed.
- **MentalLink** [21] is a framework that uses annotations for mapping between instances of an ontology and objects.

- **MetadataSharing** [52] is an implementation of metadata sharing among frameworks. A repository reads the metadata from many sources and then provides an API for the frameworks to retrieve the information that they need.
- **NUnit** [27] is a testing framework for .NET applications. It uses metadata defined in attributes to configure what each method means in the test execution, such as initialization, finalization, and test cases.
- **NHibernate** [39] is a framework for .NET applications for object-relational mapping using metadata. It is a similar to Hibernate, but for the .NET platform. Its NHibernate Validator component was also considered in the analysis.
- **Ohgma** [11] is a framework to implement Adaptive Object Models [61, 62, 57] in the .NET platform. It provides not only the core features to create a dynamic model, but also to persist and represent in user interface instances of this model.
- **SwingBean framework** [53] provides graphical components for creating forms and tables for a Swing desktop application in Java. These components use the metadata of an application domain class defined in an XML document to configure how the information should be retrieved or presented.
- **XapMap** [60], which stands for Cross Application Mapping, is a framework that maps entities of the same domain but implemented in different class structures. It provides a component that creates an instance of one structure based on an instance of another one. It also provides a proxy that encapsulates the access of an instance of one structure based on another one's API.

2.5   Running Example

The pattern language is illustrated in this work by means of a running example featuring the Comparison Component, a framework that compares instances of the same class and returns a list of differences among them. It will compare all the application class properties searching for differences. The metadata will be used to configure characteristics in the comparison algorithm for each class, such as properties to ignore, numeric tolerance, and objects to go deep into the comparison.

To understand completely this running example, it is advised for the reader to be familiar with Java language, specially to its metadata facility feature, usually referred to as code annotations. It is also important to understand the Java Reflection API, which is both used to dynamically invoke methods and to retrieve class metadata.

The comparison component provides three annotations to configure how the classes should be compared: @Ignore annotates properties that should not be included in the comparison; @Tolerance annotates numeric properties that should consider a specific numeric tolerance; @DeepComparison annotates compound properties that should be compared by using its own comparison component.

The framework entry point, represented by the class `ComparisonComponent`, has only one public method called `compare()`. This method receives two instances of the same class, considering that they are different versions of the same business entity. This method also returns an instance list of `Difference`, which is a class that has three properties representing the property name, the property value in the new instance, and the property value in the old instance. Listing 1 presents the initial implementation of Comparison Component without using any one of the proposed patterns. In each pattern, this implementation will be refactored to increase its flexibility and, in some cases, enabling the creation of new functionalities.

Listing 1. The initial source code for ComparisonComponent.

```
public class ComparisonComponent {
  public List<Difference> compare(Object oldObj, Object newObj)
        throws CompareException {
    List<Difference> difs = new ArrayList<Difference>();
    if (!newObj.getClass().isAssignableFrom(oldObj.getClass())) {
        throw new CompareException("Not compatible types");
    }
    Class clazz = newObj.getClass();
    for (Method method : clazz.getMethods()) {
        try {
            boolean isGetter = method.getName().startsWith("get");
            boolean noParameters = (method.getParameterTypes().length == 0);
            boolean notGetClass = !method.getName().equals("getClass");
            boolean noIgnore = !method.isAnnotationPresent(Ignore.class);
            if (isGetter && noParameters && notGetClass && noIgnore) {
                Object oldValue = method.invoke(oldObj);
                Object newValue = method.invoke(newObj);
                String propName = method.getName().
                            substring(3, 4).toLowerCase() +
                            method.getName().substring(4);
                if (method.isAnnotationPresent(Tolerance.class)) {
                    Tolerance tol = method.getAnnotation(Tolerance.class);
                    compareWithTolerance(difs, tol.value(),
                        newValue, oldValue, propName);
                } else if (method.isAnnotationPresent(DeepComparison.class)
                        && newValue != null && oldValue != null) {
                    List<Difference> difsProp = compare(newValue, oldValue);
                    for (Difference d : difsProp) {
                        d.setProperty(propName + "." + d.getProperty());
                        difs.add(d);
                    }
                } else {
                    compareRegular(difs, propName, newValue, oldValue);
                }
            }
        } catch (Exception e) {
            throw new CompareException("Error retrieving property", e);
        }
    }
    return difs;
  }
  private void compareWithTolerance(List<Difference> difs, double tolerance,
        Object newValue, Object oldValue, String prop) {
    double dif = Math.abs(((Double) newValue) - ((Double) oldValue));
    if (dif > tolerance) {
        difs.add(new Difference(prop, newValue, oldValue));
    }
  }
  private void compareRegular(List<Difference> difs, String prop,
        Object newValue, Object oldValue) {
    if (newValue == null) {
```

```
        if (oldValue != null) {
            difs.add(new Difference(prop, newValue, oldValue));
        }
    } else if (!newValue.equals(oldValue)) {
        difs.add(new Difference(prop, newValue, oldValue));
    }
  }
}
```

The implementation of the `compare()` method in Listing 1 first verifies if both instances are from the same class. After that, it retrieves all getter methods from the class and compares the values retrieved from both instances based on the metadata. The private methods `compareRegular()` and `compareWithTolerance()` are used by the `compare()` method respectively for the regular comparison and for the comparison using tolerance.

3 Structural Patterns

3.1 Metadata Container

Also Known as
Metadata Descriptor, Metadata Recipient

Context
Every metadata-based framework has to perform two distinct tasks: reading class metadata and executing its logic based on that information. The term *framework main logic* is used to indicate the functionality provided by the framework for the applications. If these two responsibilities are implemented mixed in the source code, the main logic execution will be coupled to that particular form of metadata definition and to the metadata reading process.

The drawback of this design choice is that it may impede the addition of new behavior both in metadata reading and in framework main logic. For instance, a change in how metadata are defined would impact entirely the framework process. Consequently, it can also impact the framework flexibility and maintainability.

Observing the `ComparisonComponent` implementation presented in Listing 1, the annotations are read at the same time that they are processed. For instance, the addition of a new annotation would demand a change that involves all the logic and not only the metadata reading. As another example, to read the same metadata from an XML file, it would be very difficult to reuse part of this source code.

Problem
How to decouple the metadata reading from the framework main logic?

Forces
- For a small metadata set, the source code complexity to read and process metadata in the same method is still manageable.

- The reading of metadata in all framework instantiations can make the framework stateless but it can become a performance bottleneck as well.
- The existence of an internal representation of the metadata can consume more runtime memory, which is a problem especially in embedded applications.
- The creation of an internal representation for metadata adds indirection in the source code which uses it.
- A representation of the metadata at runtime can be used to share this information among frameworks.
- Metadata reading mixed with framework main logic creates a dependence between the framework logic and how the metadata is defined.
- The creation of an internal representation for metadata adds indirection and can add unnecessary complexity for simple cases.

Solution

Metadata Container proposes creating a representation of metadata at runtime. This representation is used to exchange information between metadata reading process and framework main logic, as the main interface among them.

The metadata reading process should receive the target class and return a Metadata Container populated with all the information necessary for the framework execution. With the instance of the Metadata Container, the framework main logic can retrieve the desired metadata without relying on how it is defined.

Structure

In Metadata Container, the application class metadata is stored in an instance that represents it at runtime. Figure 3 illustrates the pattern structure. The MetadataContainer is the class that represents the metadata structure. It is also the main interface between the class responsible for reading metadata and the class that contains the framework main logic, respectively MetadataReader and FrameworkController.

The ApplicationClass represents the class for which the framework metadata is configured. This class is used by the MetadataReader in the metadata extraction and its instances are used by the FrameworkController in the execution of the main logic. The ApplicationClient represents the class which invokes the framework functionality in the application.

The FrameworkController can store the MetadataContainer instance internally as represented in the diagram. This is usually done when the class with the metadata is received by the FrameworkController in the constructor. Alternatively, the FrameworkController can be stateless and accepts invocations receiving the class with metadata as a parameter, consequently invoking the MetadataReader for each one.

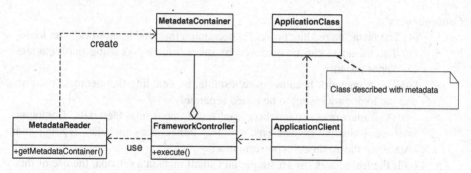

Fig. 3. Metadata Container structure

Participants

- MetadataReader - It is responsible for reading metadata wherever it is defined. It is used by FrameworkController to create an instance of MetadataContainer representing the ApplicationClass metadata.
- MetadataContainer - It is responsible for representing the ApplicationClass metadata at runtime. It is the main interface among MetadataReader and FrameworkController.
- FrameworkController - It is the framework class where the functionality is invoked by the application, also known as the framework *entry point*. It is responsible for executing the main logic and for being a controller for the other classes. It uses the data from MetadataContainer retrieved by means of MetadataReader to execute its logic.
- ApplicationClient - It represents the application class that invokes implicitly or explicitly the FrameworkController to execute the framework functionality.
- ApplicationClass - It represents the application class that has additional domain-specific or application-specific metadata, which is used by FrameworkController in its main logic.

Dynamics

When the application client accesses the entry point of the metadata-based framework, it invokes the MetadataReader that reads the metadata and returns an instance of the MetadataContainer populated with the class metadata. During the execution of the main logic, the FrameworkController accesses the required metadata using the MetadataContainer instance. The corresponding sequence diagram is shown in Figure 4.

As an alternative implementation of this pattern, the ApplicationClient can create the MetadataContainer instance explicitly. When using this approach, the client uses the MetadataReader to create the MetadataContainer and passes it to the FrameworkController in its constructor or as a method parameter.

Consequences
- (+) The metadata reading process is decoupled from the framework main logic.
- (+) The metadata can be retrieved by other frameworks using the Metadata Container instance.
- (+) The framework became more testable, by enabling the metadata reading and the logic processing to be tested separately.
- (+) A framework instantiation can reuse the same Metadata Container instance in distinct invocations, avoiding unnecessary metadata reading and improving the application performance.
- (-) If the framework uses a simple and small metadata schema, the use of this pattern can complicate unnecessarily its structure.
- (-) Both metadata reading and framework logic became coupled with the Metadata Container structure.

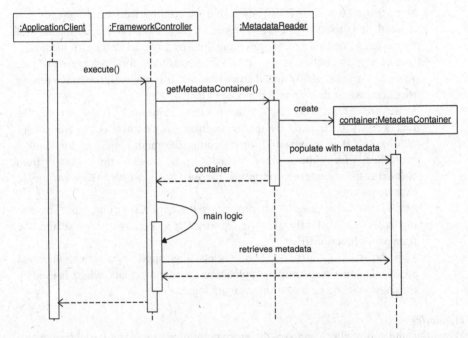

Fig. 4. Metadata Container sequence diagram

Known Uses

Hibernate uses, as a Metadata Container, an implementation of the interface ClassMetadata that can be retrieved from a SessionFactory instance. The SessionFactory is the class responsible for creating instances of Session, which is used by the application to interact with the framework. ClassMetadata contains all the information about a persistent class used by the framework.

Differently, in **SwingBean**, the class XMLDescriptorFactory provides a Facade [17] for the client to retrieve metadata, represented by the

`FieldDescriptor` interface. The client uses this instance to create graphical components, passing it as an argument to their constructor.

NUnit testing framework contains a class called `TestSuite` that contains all the information necessary for the execution of a test class, such as what methods should be executed before and after each test method. This class can be considered a Metadata Container which is created and consumed in each execution.

Running Example

To increase its flexibility, the Comparison Component, defined earlier in the Running Example, is refactored to decouple the metadata reading from the comparison logic. This step is necessary to allow both the implementation of metadata reading from other sources and the extension of the components logic.

In this example, the metadata container is represented by a class named `ComparisonDescriptor`, which is composed of a map of instances of `PropertyDescriptor`. The class `PropertyDescriptor` provides information about just one class property: property name, numeric tolerance, and whether it should be compared "deeply". In addition, the class `ComparisonDescriptor` has a map with the properties that should be included in the comparison. Each map entry contains the property name linked with the respective `PropertyDescriptor` instance.

The `ComparisonMetadataReader` class is represented in Listing 2. The `createContainer()` method receives a class as a parameter and returns the respective instance of `ComparisonDescriptor` created by using the annotations in the properties getter methods. When a property presents the annotation `@Ignore`, it is not included in the `ComparisonDescriptor` instance. The information provided by other annotations are obtained and stored in the descriptor.

Listing 2. Source code of ComparisonMetadataReader.

```
public class ComparisonMetadataReader {
    public ComparisonDescriptor createContainer(Class c) {
        ComparisonDescriptor descr = new ComparisonDescriptor();
        for (Method method : c.getMethods()) {
            boolean isGetter = method.getName().startsWith("get");
            boolean noParameters = (method.getParameterTypes().length == 0);
            boolean notGetClass = !method.getName().equals("getClass");
            boolean noIgnore = !method.isAnnotationPresent(Ignore.class);
            if (isGetter && noParameters && notGetClass && noIgnore) {
                PropertyDescriptor prop = new PropertyDescriptor();
                String getter = method.getName();
                String propName = getter.substring(3, 4).toLowerCase() +
                                  getter.substring(4);
                prop.setName(propName);
                prop.setDeepComparison(method.isAnnotationPresent(
                          DeepComparison.class));
                if (method.isAnnotationPresent(Tolerance.class)) {
                    Tolerance t = method.getAnnotation(Tolerance.class);
                    prop.setTolerance(t.value());
                }
                descr.addPropertyDescriptor(prop);
            }
        }
        return descr;
    }
}
```

The `ComparisonComponent` presented in Listing 1 is refactored to retrieve the `ComparisonDescriptor` from the `ComparisonMetadataReader`. It uses the Reflection API [13] to retrieve the properties values based on the information contained in the respective `PropertyDescriptor`. Then, it delegates the comparison to one of the methods `compareWithTolerance()`, `compareRegular()` or `compare()` method, in case of deep comparison.

Related Patterns
Metadata Container is the foundation of the proposed pattern language. Indeed in Figure 1, one can observe that all patterns depend directly or indirectly on it. The rationale behind this is that the decoupling between the logic and the metadata reading provides a structure that allows for each part to evolve independently.

This pattern can be considered related to Data Accessor [45], which encapsulates physical data access details in a single component, decoupling data access responsibilities. Accordingly, Metadata Container uses the same principle to decouple the metadata reading.

This same concept is also used in Property Loader [58], which loads and provides access to external configurable properties at runtime. In this pattern, the application uses the Property Loader to decouple its logic from the property reading. The greatest difference from Metadata Container is that the class which loads the properties and provides access to them is the same. In the proposed pattern, since metadata can have a complex structure, Metadata Container is used to store these values to be accessed by the framework.

3.2   Metadata Repository

Also Known as
Metadata Cache, Central Metadata Provider

Context
The functionalities of a framework are usually invoked more than once in the same application. For a metadata-based framework this fact means that the Metadata Container should be retrieved more than once. Specially when metadata is defined by external sources, the process of metadata reading can become a bottleneck for the application performance. The framework instances can keep the Metadata Container to other invocations; however, if other instances are created, the reading process would need to be repeated. It is also not desirable for the framework controller to accumulate the responsibility of managing the Metadata Container instances.

In this context, it is important to make the metadata available not only for distinct framework instantiations, but also among the framework components of the same instance. Having a central place to retrieve the Metadata Container, it would not be necessary to pass it as a parameter to other framework classes. This availability is also important to enable external classes to retrieve this information.

For instance, the previous `ComparisonComponent` implementations read the metadata in every invocation of the method `compare()`. In a scenario where many comparisons of the same class should be made, this can waste processing time.

Problem

How to make metadata available for repeated-use while avoiding unnecessary metadata readings?

Forces

- Having a single instance of the framework entry point can be easier in some architectures, but under other circumstances, it is not possible. For instance, when the framework entry point is a proxy, it should have an instance for each application class instance encapsulated.
- The framework controller should not be responsible for managing instances of Metadata Container.
- Having a central place to retrieve metadata can open the possibility for external classes to retrieve metadata.
- When metadata is cached, the additional runtime memory consumed is traded for a reduced processing time in metadata reading.
- Lazyly loading the metadata can allow a fast initialization, but it can slow the application execution when the metadata is retrieved for the first time.
- Pre-loading the metadata can accelerate the application execution, but it can also slow down the application initialization.
- If the framework allows for changing metadata at runtime, any implementation which caches the metadata read in memory should handle concurrency issues.

Solution

Metadata Repository proposes creating a central repository where metadata can be retrieved. This repository is responsible for managing the metadata reading process and internally storing the Metadata Container instances already obtained. Consequently, it can perform the metadata reading at the most appropriate time, such as in the application initialization or in the first time which that metadata is needed. His internal metadata storage avoid unnecessary metadata readings.

The Metadata Repository can also be used for all the framework components to easily access a class metadata. This can avoid passing the Metadata Container as a parameter to all of them. This repository can also enable an external access to the framework metadata, which can be used by the application or by other metadata-based frameworks.

Structure

In Metadata Repository, a single class instance is responsible for managing the metadata reading and internally storing the class metadata. In the first reading of the metadata, the `Repository` caches the information and makes it available to any other component that needs it. The Metadata Repository can be implemented as a Singleton [17], however other patterns such as Dependency Injection and Service Locator [14] can also be applied.

Figure 5 introduces a class diagram of the pattern. In this structure, `FrameworkController` does not directly access `MetadataReader`. In fact all of the metadata accesses occur via `Repository`, which has a common base of metadata, represented by instances of MetadataContainer, which is shared between all FrameworkController instances.

Participants
- MetadataReader - It is responsible for reading the metadata wherever it is defined. It is used by Repository to retrieve instances of MetadataContainer and store it internally.
- MetadataContainer - It is responsible for representing the metadata of an application class at runtime. It is stored internally by the Repository.
- FrameworkController - It is the framework entry point. It is responsible for executing the main logic and for being a controller for the other classes. It uses Repository to retrieve metadata represented in instances of MetadataContainer.
- Repository - It is responsible for managing the access to MetadataReader and internally storing the instances of MetadataContainer. It has a single instance and provides metadata to all instances of FrameworkController or to any other classes that might need it.

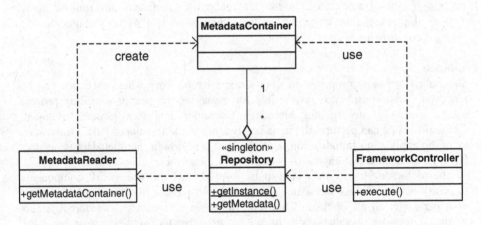

Fig. 5. Metadata Repository structure

Dynamics
The sequence diagram in Figure 6 illustrates the algorithm for accessing metadata using the Repository. Moreover, if the metadata is not read yet, Repository collaborates with MetadataReader to retrieve the metadata represented by an instance of MetadataContainer. Then, in further accesses, the metadata is already stored inside Repository and is returned without an additional reading.

Consequences
- (+) The unnecessary metadata reading can be avoided and therefore the application performance can be improved.

- (+) The application can choose to use the repository to load all metadata when the application starts or to load it only when the application needs them.
- (+) The metadata is available in a central point to be accessed by other software components, facilitating to share metadata.
- (+) Different framework classes can access the metadata directly from the repository, eliminating the need to pass MetadataContainer as a parameter among them.
- (-) For a framework whose instantiation uses a singleton class shared by all the application, the creation of a repository may be unnecessary.
- (-) For frameworks which need to process metadata only once, such as for testing or instance creation, repository is unnecessary.
- (-) For applications that can change the metadata at runtime, it is necessary to control the access in the MetadataContainer for concurrent modification.
- (-) The storage of metadata in the repository can increase the usage of runtime memory by the application in exchange of a saving in the metadata reading processing.

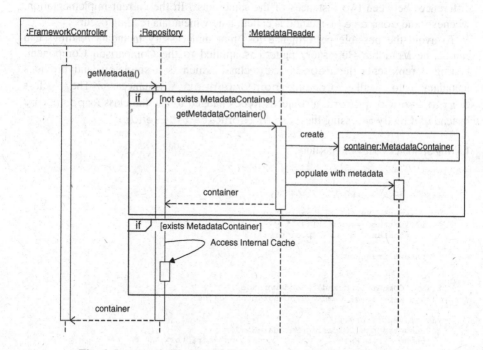

Fig. 6. Sequence of FrameworkController using Metadata Repository

Known Uses

The **Hibernate** framework provides the class SessionFactory, which is responsible for creating Session. Further, the Session class provides an API for the application to persist and retrieve entities from the database. The SessionFactory has an encapsulated repository and provides methods to retrieve metadata. As a consequence, each instance of `Session` created receives a reference to this `SessionFactory`, which is a central place to retrieve the metadata for all instances.

The **NHibernate** contains a class named `Mappings` which contains the metadata already obtained by the framework and can be considered a **Metadata Repository**. This class is invoked when the framework loads configurations and mappings. This data is then retrieved by other components during the framework execution.

XapMap provides a component that creates an instance of one schema based on an instance of the other schema and also provides a proxy that encapsulates the access of an instance of one schema based on the other schema API. Both components of the framework access the metadata through a singleton repository, which guarantees that the metadata will not be read again for the same class, even if it is accessed by different classes.

Running Example

The application that uses the Comparison Component creates an instance of `ComparisonComponent` and then calls the `compare()` method to get the differences between two instances of the same class. In the current implementation, whenever the `compare()` method is called, a new metadata reading occurs.

To avoid the possible performance loss that unnecessary metadata readings can cause, the **Metadata Repository** pattern is applied to the Comparison Component. Listing 3 represents the `Repository` class, which is a singleton, and provides metadata to all `ComparisonComponent` instances. The class `ComparisonComponent` also needs to be changed to use the class `Repository` instead of directly accessing the `ComparisonMetadataReader`.

Listing 3. Source code of Repository.

```
public class Repository {

    private static Repository instance;

    public static Repository getInstance(){
        if(instance == null){
            instance = new Repository();
        }
        return instance;
    }

    private ComparisonMetadataReader reader;
    private Map<Class, ComparisonDescriptor> cache;

    private Repository(){
        reader = new ComparisonMetadataReader();
        cache = new HashMap<Class, ComparisonDescriptor>();
    }
    public ComparisonDescriptor getMetadata(Class clazz){
        if(cache.containsKey(clazz)){
            return cache.get(clazz);
        }
        ComparisonDescriptor cd = reader.createContainer(clazz);
        cache.put(clazz, cd);
        return cd;
    }
}
```

Related Patterns

Metadata Repository is important to allow metadata sharing. Therefore the Metadata Reader Adapter uses the repository of another component to read and adapt the metadata format. The Metadata Processing Layers divides the logic of the metadata-based component in many processing layers and using Metadata Repository is recommended to provide a common place to access metadata without the need to pass the Metadata Container as a parameter among them.

Metadata Repository can be considered an adaptation of the pattern Repository [15], which is specific for the information retrieved from data-mapping layers. This pattern is also related to the patterns Cache Accessor and Demand Cache [45], which provide a structure for caching data retrieved from a data source. It is important to highlight that the Metadata Repository differs from those patterns because it is not used only for performance reasons, but also performs an import role for metadata sharing and facilitates the metadata access from different framework classes. Other patterns related to cache [45] can also be applied in a Metadata Repository implementation to improve its functionality.

4 Metadata Reading Patterns

4.1 Metadata Reader Strategy

Also Known as

Metadata Reader Switch, Exchangeable Metadata Reader

Context

The metadata reading is an important part of a metadata-based framework. The choice of how the metadata about the application classes should be defined is crucial to the framework usability. Since the framework can be used in different applications, they can have different needs for the metadata definition.

Different strategies for metadata definition have different consequences on the application that uses it. For instance, annotations are usually less verbose and closer to the source code, while XML files can easily be changed without the need to recompile the code. If the metadata should be defined for legacy code, the use of code annotations is not possible.

If the metadata definition provided by the framework does not fulfill the application requirements, its usage is usually discarded. When this incompatibility is identified late in the framework adoption, the framework is often misused. For those reasons it is important for the framework to support different sources and formats of metadata.

As an example, in `Repository` presented in Listing 3, the class `ComparisonMetadataReader` is directly instantiated. Additionally, the framework does not provide an abstraction for the metadata reading class. Consequently, it is not possible to change or extend how the metadata is obtained in a specific framework instantiation.

Problem

How to allow the framework to support metadata reading from different sources and formats?

Forces

- The application could already have the metadata needed by the framework in other sources.
- The use of external metadata definition can make it modifiable at deployment time.
- Code annotations bring the metadata definition closer to the source code, usually making it easier to maintain.
- The use of annotations is sometimes not possible in legacy classes, which demand usage of other metadata definition strategies.
- Different applications may have different needs for metadata definition in the same framework domain.
- The same application can have different needs for metadata definition for distinct class sets.

Solution

Metadata Reader Strategy proposes abstracting the metadata reading component to enable the exchange of its concrete implementation. By changing the implementation of metadata reader, it is possible to change the algorithm which is used to obtain the Metadata Container to be used by the framework. Distinct reading implementations can access metadata form different sources and formats.

The framework also needs to allow the application to configure the concrete Metadata Reader Strategy which should be used in a particular instantiation. That can be made by using factories, configuration files, or Dependency Injection [14]. The use of factories is specially advised when distinct metadata readers should be used for distinct sets of classes.

Structure

The Metadata Reader Strategy uses a similar structure of Strategy [17] but for metadata reading purposes, its structure is introduced in Figure 7. There, an interface is used to abstract the metadata reading, and different classes can implement it to read metadata from different sources. A Singleton [17] is used to retrieve the correct metadata reader instance, but other factory implementations can be adopted as well. Dependency Injection [14] is another alternative that can be used to set the correct reader in framework.

The interface AbstractMetadataReader abstracts the reading of metadata and is implemented by any ConcreteMetadataReader. The MetadataReaderClient represents the class that needs to read metadata. If the component uses the structure of Metadata Container the client will be FrameworkController. Otherwise, if it uses Metadata Repository structure the client will be Repository.

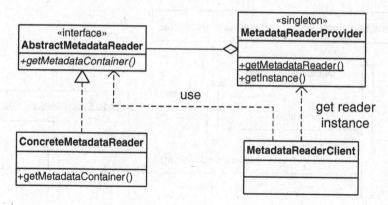

Fig. 7. The structure of Metadata Reader Strategy

Participants

- AbstractMetadataReader - It represents an abstraction of a metadata reader. It must be implemented by any ConcreteMetadataReader.
- ConcreteMetadataReader - It is responsible for reading metadata from one specific source and implements the AbstractMetadataReader interface.
- MetadataReaderClient - It is the class that needs to directly retrieve metadata from a reader, which can be a Repository or a FrameworkController depending on the component structure. It is coupled only with AbstractMetadataReader and not with one specific implementation.
- MetadataReaderProvider - It is responsible for providing the correct ConcreteMetadataReader instance that the MetadataReaderClient should use for each application class.

Dynamics

The client uses MetadataReaderProvider to retrieve the correct instance of a ConcreteMetadataReader. This class can have some logic that returns different readers to read metadata from different classes. It is especially useful if different sets of classes in the application require different readers.

As an alternative implementation, the MetadataReaderProvider is not necessary if the client set the ConcreteMetadataReader instance as a parameter or using dependency injection. The need for the MetadataReaderProvider can also be eliminated by the use of **Dependence Injection** [14] on the MetadataReaderClient. Figure 8 shows a sequence diagram that represents how the MetadataReaderClient retrieves the MetadataContainer by using this solution.

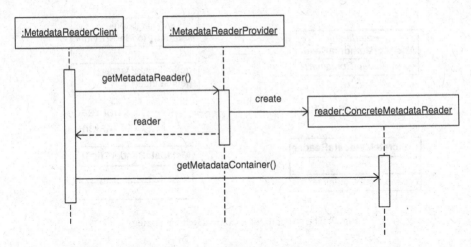

Fig. 8. Sequence of MetadataReaderClient retrieving a Metadata Container

Consequences

- (+) The framework can provide more than one alternative for metadata definition for an application to use.
- (+) The application can provide new approaches for metadata definition, extending the framework metadata reading functionality.
- (+) The `MetadataReaderProvider` can return different readers for different classes in the same application.
- (-) In cases in which one approach for metadata definition is enough, the use of this pattern can over-design the component.
- (-) Additional configurations for the **Metadata Reader Strategy** can complicate the first framework instantiation for beginners.

Known Uses

Early versions of the **Hibernate** framework support metadata definition by only using XML. The class `Configuration` is used to setup the configuration files and create the `SessionFactory` instance. The project Hibernate Annotations is a separate release that gives support to annotations to the framework. Furthermore, the class `AnnotationConfiguration`, which extends `Configuration`, creates the same `SessionFactory` instance by using annotations as the metadata source.

The **ACE framework** supports the mapping of web functionalities to mobile systems. It provides metadata definition by using annotations for new applications and using XML files for legacy applications. As a result, it uses the interface `MetadataFactory` to abstract the metadata reading and has implementations to get it both from annotations and from XML files, respectively `AnnotationMetadataFactory` and `XmlMetadataFactory`.

MentalLink maps ontology instances to objects by using annotations. Natively it does not support other types of metadata definition, but it uses the structure of this pattern to allow for the extension of the metadata reading mechanism by the application. The interface `AdapterFactory` is used to abstract the metadata reading and the class `AnnotationAdapterFactory` implements the annotations reading. A new implementation of `AdapterFactory` can be created by the application and configured in the `AdapterFactoryManager` to be used by the framework.

Running Example

The application that uses the Comparison Component now needs to compare classes from a legacy application whose source code the developers do not have access to modify. One solution to this problem is to provide the Comparison Component with a facility to define metadata by using XML files.

Before implementing the reading from XML files, the framework is refactored to implement the Metadata Reader Strategy. Then, the `ComparisonMetadataReader` class is renamed to `AnnotationComparisonMetadataReader` and an interface, named `ComparisonMetadataReader`, is extracted to generalize the concept of metadata reading.

To provide the current reader implementation to the framework, the `MetadataReaderProvider` class is introduced. It is a Singleton class that returns an instance of the configured `ComparisonMetadatReader`. It has two static methods that encapsulate the access to the singleton instance to set and to get the metadata reader instance. In this case, the metadata factory instance should now be obtained by using this new class in the `Repository`.

After the refactoring, the metadata reading using XML files can be implemented and used by the Comparison Component. Listing 4 presents an example of an XML document for the class metadata definition. For simplicity, the class metadata is considered to be stored in an XML file with the same name of the class.

Listing 4. An example of the metadata definition in XML.

```
<?xml version="1.0" encoding="UTF-8"?>
<comparison>
    <prop name="name"/>
    <prop name="weight" tolerance="0.1" />
    <prop name="address" deep="true" />
</comparison>
```

The `XMLComparisonMetadataReader` source code is presented in Listing 5. It uses JColtrane framework [31], which is based on SAX [50] parsing, to read XML files. JColtrane uses annotations for the SAX event management. Listing 6 exhibits the XML handler that reads metadata and populates the `ComparisonDescriptor`.

Listing 5. The implementation of XMLComparisonMetatadaReader.

```
public class XMLComparisonMetadataReader implements ComparisonMetadataReader{
    @Override
    public ComparisonDescriptor createContainer(Class c) {
        try {
            SAXParser parser= SAXParserFactory.newInstance().newSAXParser();
            File file=new File(c.getSimpleName()+".xml");
            ComparisonXMLHandler handler = new ComparisonXMLHandler();
            parser.parse(file,new JColtraneXMLHandler(handler));
```

```
            return handler.getDescriptor();
        } catch (Exception e) {
            throw new RuntimeException("Can't read metadata",e);
        }
    }
}
```

Listing 6. The handler to interpret XML files using JColtrane framework.

```
public class ComparisonXMLHandler {

    private ComparisonDescriptor descriptor = new ComparisonDescriptor();

    @StartElement(tag="prop")
    public void addProperty(@Attribute("name") String name,
                @Attribute("tolerance") Float tolerance,
                @Attribute("deep") Boolean deep){
        PropertyDescriptor pd = new PropertyDescriptor();
        pd.setName(name);
        if(tolerance != null)
            pd.setTolerance(tolerance);
        if(deep != null)
            pd.setDeepComparison(deep);
            descriptor.addPropertyDescriptor(pd);
    }

    public ComparisonDescriptor getDescriptor() {
        return descriptor;
    }
}
```

Related Patterns
Metadata Reader Strategy provides the flexibility in the achievement of metadata required by other patterns in this pattern language. Both Metadata Reader Chain and Metadata Reader Adapter are patterns based on the fact that it is possible to change the algorithm for metadata reading.

This pattern uses the same structure of Strategy [17] to help to solve the problem of metadata reading. It is also related to Data Mapper [15] and Data Access Object [1], also known as DAO, which are used to encapsulate data access and manipulation in separate layers. By using one of them, it is possible to have different implementations for retrieving data from different data sources.

4.2   Metadata Reader Chain

Also Known as
Composite Metadata Reader, Aggregate Metadata Reader

Context
The code annotations define metadata closer to the application class, making it easier to manage and to maintain this information. The usage of XML is more indicated when the metadata may need to be changed at deploy-time without source code recompilation. However, if a few classes in a system need to be configured at deploy time, that does not justify the use of XML metadata definition for all of them.

Each metadata definition strategy has its applicability and, in some applications, the best solution is a combination of more than one. In this context, to read different metadata sources exclusively is not enough for a framework, because the metadata may need to be dispersed in more than one source. Consequently, the framework should combine metadata from different sources in the reading process.

For instance, the implementations of `ComparisonMetadataReader`, presented in listings 2 and 5, read metadata from respectively annotations and XML files. Despite both metadata formats being supported, their combination is not.

Problem

How to allow for metadata reading to combine information from more than one source?

Forces

- Each kind of metadata definition has its benefits and drawbacks and some applications need to take advantage of the benefits from more than one.
- The use of more than one metadata source requires an organization of the precedence between these sources.
- Some metadata can be retrieved partially from alternative sources, such as metadata from other frameworks, and must be complemented with additional information from other sources.
- An order can be defined for reading metadata from more than one source, but some applications may need to use a different order.
- Code annotations are an easy way to define metadata and can be complemented by an XML document that can be changed at deployment time.

Solution

Metadata Reader Chain proposes combining different metadata readers to compose the framework metadata reading algorithm. Each reader is responsible for retrieving metadata from one source and the metadata should be merged to create the complete Metadata Container. The merging algorithm, which can be implemented inside or outside the readers, should be prepared to deal with redundancy and conflicts.

The framework should provide a Metadata Reader Strategy which coordinates the execution of other readers. During the execution of this Metadata Reader Chain, this implementation is also responsible for passing the Metadata Container instance among the reader implementations or to merge the information contained in the Metadata Container instances returned by them. The precedence is defined by the readers order and by the action taken when the Metadata Container is already populated with some given information.

Structure

Figure 9 shows the class diagram that represents the basic structure of this Metadata Reader Chain. The `CompositeMetadataReader` is a class that uses other readers to compose the metadata reading algorithm. It has the responsibility of coordinating the other readers and returning a `MetadataContainer` populated with metadata combined from all the sources.

One alternative to implement the `CompositeMetadataReader` is to retrieve the `MetadataContainer` from all the `ConcreteMetadataReader` instances and combine merge the metadata in only one `MetadataContainer`. By using this approach, the readers implementation does not need to worry about the metadata from the other readers, however the implementation which coordinates Metadata Reader Chain should be responsible for the merging.

In the other option to implement this pattern, the `AbstractMetadataReader` implementations should have a different approach for reading metadata. Instead of `populateMetadataContainer()` returning a `MetadataContainer` instance, it should receive it as a parameter and populate it. As a result, the reading algorithm of each `ConcreteMetadataReader` should not assume that `MetadataContainer` instance is empty and consider that another reader may have already populated it.

Participants

- `AbstractMetadataReader` - It represents an abstraction of a metadata reader. Any `ConcreteMetadataReader` must implement it.
- `ConcreteMetadataReader` - It is responsible for reading metadata from one source and implementing the interface `AbstractMetadataReader`. It should also consider that `MetadataContainer` might have already been populated by another source.
- `MetadataReaderClient` - It represents a `Repository` or a `FrameworkController`, depending on the component structure. It is the class that needs to directly retrieve metadata from a reader.
- `CompositeMetadataReader` - It represents the reader that uses other `AbstractMetadataReader` implementations to compose the metadata reading algorithm.
- `MetadataContainer` - It is responsible for representing metadata of an application class at runtime. It is created by the `MetadataReaderClient` and populated by metadata readers.

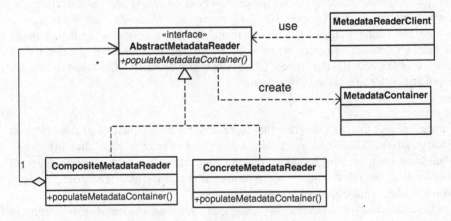

Fig. 9. Structure of Metadata Reader Chain

Dynamics

Figure 10 represents one possible implementation of how CompositeMetadataReader can use other readers to compose the information in MetadataContainer. The MetadataReaderClient is responsible for creating a MetadataContainer instance, which is passed as a parameter to the CompositeMetadataReader. It is noticeable that the CompositeMetadataReader delegates for each reader instance the responsibility to read metadata and populate the MetadataContainer.

Another possible implementation is for the CompositeMetadataReader to retrieve distinct instances of MetadataContainer for each ConcreteMetadataReader. In this scenario, the CompositeMetadataReader should retrieve information from each MetadataContainer and merge them in only one to be returned.

Consequences

- (+) The framework can use simultaneously more than one source of metadata.
- (+) Alternative metadata sources that contain only partial information can be used to complement the metadata reading.
- (+) The order that the readers retrieve metadata can be set in the Metadata Reader Chain.
- (-) The use of more than one source for metadata definition by the framework can slow down the metadata reading.
- (-) The metadata read can be validated only at the end of the reading process, since each source contains only partial information.
- (-) The metadata defined in one source can be inconsistent with other sources and the readers must consider that situation, dealing with it appropriately.

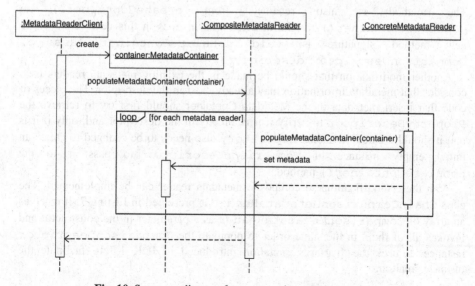

Fig. 10. Sequence diagram for a composite metadata reading

Known Uses

The **ACE framework** supports the metadata definition by using annotations and XML documents. The XML-based definition overrides the annotation-based definition allowing for the configurations to be changed at deployment time. This pattern is used internally by the class `ChainMetadataFactory` to allow for the reading from multiple sources.

In **MetadataSharing**, a repository reads the metadata from many sources and then provides an API for the frameworks to retrieve the information that they need. The metadata reading is implemented as a Chain of Responsibility [17], where the abstract class `MetadataFactory` can have an instance of another factory, which is invoked in sequence. The configuration file `sharing-config.xml` defines the order of the metadata readers.

By using **Hibernate Validator**, release 4.0 alpha, it is possible to override the metadata defined in annotations by the metadata in XML files, but according to the specification this order cannot be changed. For instance, by setting the attribute `ignore-annotations` as `true` in the XML file, it is possible to ignore all the validation annotations defined in the class.

Running Example

After the Comparison Component is deployed with the application, some comparison rules might need to be changed. Based on that requirement, the definition of metadata in XML files is the most appropriate solution, but it is easier and more productive to configure the comparison metadata by using annotations. To solve this conflict, the Comparison Component is refactored to support the definition of metadata by using annotations which can be overridden by definitions conveyed by an XML document.

The first modification to be made is to change the signature of the method that reads metadata to receive a `ComparisonDescriptor` instance as a parameter. The method is also renamed from `createContainer()` to `populateContainer()` to best describe what it does in this new version. The new method signature is: `void populateContainer(Class c, ComparisonDescriptor descriptor)`.

Another modification that should be made in the existing metadata readers is to consider that metadata information may already exist in the descriptor. The pieces of code that insert metadata in the Metadata Container should first try to retrieve the `PropertyDescriptor` to verify if it is already in the descriptor and, only if it is not, it should create a new one. `Repository` also needs to be changed to create an initial empty instance of `ComparisonDescriptor` to pass it to the `populateContainer()` method.

With these modifications, a composite metadata reader can be implemented. The class `ChainComparisonMetadataReader` is presented in Listing 7. It receives an array of `ComparisonMetadataReader` as a parameter in the constructor and invokes all of them in the same order to populate the `ComparisonDescriptor` instance. It uses the "var-args" notation introduced in JDK 1.5 to facilitate the instance creation.

Listing 7. Source code of ChainComparisonMetadataReader.

```
public class ChainComparisonMetatataReader implements ComparisonMetadataReader {

    private List<ComparisonMetadataReader> readers;

    public ChainComparisonMetatataReader(ComparisonMetadataReader... readers) {
        this.readers = new ArrayList<ComparisonMetadataReader>();
        for(ComparisonMetadataReader reader : readers){
            this.readers.add(reader);
        }
    }
    @Override
    public void populateContainer(Class c, ComparisonDescriptor descriptor) {
        for(ComparisonMetadataReader reader : readers){
            reader.populateContainer(c, descriptor);
        }
    }
}
```

Related Patterns

Metadata Reader Chain is important to enable metadata reading from sources that contain only a part of the needed metadata. It is important for the implementation of Metadata Reader Adapter, which uses metadata already obtained from other frameworks to populate the Metadata Container.

Moreover, Metadata Reader Chain uses Composite [17] as part of the solution to enable the creation of a metadata reader composed by other readers. An alternative implementation of this pattern could use other patterns with recursive composition, like Chain of Responsibility [17]. In this case, each reader could represent a handler in the processing chain, invoking the next one after its own metadata reading.

This pattern also presents a similar solution to the Hierarchical Property Loader [58], which provides a Property Loader [58] which handles multiple property storages in a way so that more specific storage values overwrite less specific storage values. The greatest difference to metadata reading is that when more than one metadata source is provided, they usually define metadata in different formats, such as XML and annotations. Consequently, while Hierarquical Propety Loader can use the same reading algorithm for different storages, the Metadata Reader Chain should provide an interface for distinct implementations to be plugged in.

4.3   Metadata Reader Adapter

Also Known as
Metadata Converter, Metadata Transformer

Context
The metadata defined for a framework is additional information about a program element. The information defined for one framework can also be useful to another one. For example, an instance validation framework can provide metadata elements to configure the maximum and minimum value of a numeric field. This information is also useful for a metadata-based framework which creates graphical interfaces, since it can be used to create a graphical component to represent that field.

For frameworks which provide many options for metadata definition, such as using a Metadata Reader Chain, it is not trivial to retrieve the metadata directly. For instance, it can be spread in annotations and XML files. When the metadata is defined in external files, another issue is to obtain the location of these files. Specially when metadata reading is a complex process, it is not desirable for another framework to recreate all this process.

For instance, the Comparison Component could benefit from metadata for object-relation mapping in the Hibernate [2] framework. For instance, it can define the deep comparisons based on which class an entity is mapped to the database. However, Hibernate metadata can be defined in XML files or by using annotations, and the external files can be located in several places.

Problem
How to allow for a framework to retrieve metadata already available in another one?

Forces
- The performance can degrade with two frameworks reading the same information in the same application.
- It is easy to locate metadata of frameworks that support only one source, but this is not true for frameworks that support more than one source.
- It is not possible to predict where the metadata are when the framework provides an extensible metadata reading.
- Metadata defined in external files can be hard to locate when that depends on the other framework configurations.
- The same information can be defined in the metadata formats of two frameworks, but it can lead to inconsistencies and that may reduce productivity.
- Some frameworks provide an API that enables the retrieval of a representation of the metadata already read.

Solution
Metadata Reader Adapter proposes creating a Metadata Reader Strategy which accesses the Metadata Repository from another framework to obtain its Metadata Container. The metadata contained in the other framework container is accessed by the Metadata Reader Adapter and properly inserted in its own Metadata Container. This information is usually not directly applicable, needing to be interpreted to the other framework context.

It is important for the other framework to provide an accessible Metadata Repository which enables the access to its metadata. In cases where the repository is not available, another possibility is to directly access the metadata reader. However, this alternative has the drawback of repeating the metadata reading process.

Since the metadata of the other framework is usually not enough to fulfill all the required metadata, the Metadata Reader Adapter is normally used as part of a Metadata Reader Chain. In this context, it is important to define the metadata source precedence for cases when there are conflicts with the metadata from the other framework.

Structure

Figure 11 presents the structure of this pattern. The class `AdapterMetadataReader` uses a repository from another framework, represented by the class `OtherRepository`, to retrieve its metadata container, represented by the class `OtherMetadataContainer`.

The `AdapterMetadataReader` is an implementation of the `AbstractMetadataReader`. The `CompositeMetadataReader`, which implements Metadata Reader Chain, is also represented in the diagram since the Metadata Reader Adapter usually reads only a piece of metadata. Consequently, the `MetadataContainer` should be complemented with information from other sources read by other `ConcreteMetadataReader`.

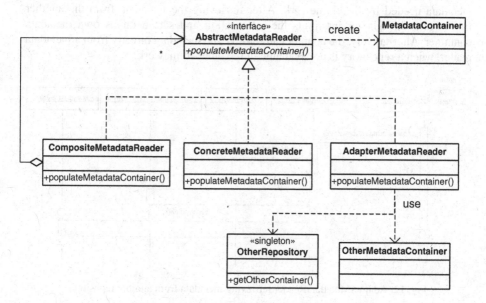

Fig. 11. Structure of Metadata Reader Adapter

Participants

- `AbstractMetadataReader` - It represents an abstraction of a metadata reader.
- `ConcreteMetadataReader` - It is responsible for reading metadata from one source and implementing the interface of `AbstractMetadataReader`.
- `CompositeMetadataReader` - It represents the reader that uses other `AbstractMetadataReader` to compose the metadata reading algorithm.
- `AdapterMetadataReader` - It represents the metadata reader that accesses `OtherRepository` to retrieve instances of `OtherMetadataContainer`. It also converts the information obtained to the `MetadataContainer` format.

- `MetadataContainer` - It is responsible for representing the application class metadata needed by the framework.
- `OtherRepository` - It represents the metadata repository of another framework.
- `OtherMetadataContainer` - It is responsible for representing the application class metadata needed from another framework.

Dynamics

Figure 12 represents the sequence diagram for the method `populateMetadataContainer()` of the class `AdapterMetadataReader`. The `AdapterMetadataReader` is represented being invoked by a `CompositeMetadataReader` since it usually does not provide the entire metadata needed by the framework. After retrieving the metadata from the another framework, the adapter interprets the information and sets it on its own metadata container. Alternatively, the adapter can retrieve the metadata directly from a metadata reader, when a repository is not available in the other framework.

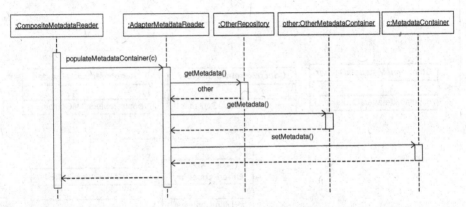

Fig. 12. AdapterMetadataReader retrieving metadata from another repository

Consequences

- (+) The possibility of inconsistencies that might occur with the definition of the same information for the two frameworks is reduced, since the metadata can be defined once and used by both.
- (+) The amount of metadata that should be defined for a class is reduced, since the same metadata can be shared by more than one framework.
- (-) This solution is sensitive to changes in the Metadata Container interface of the other component.
- (-) This solution is only viable when the other component has an API that allows for the access to its Metadata Container.

Known Uses

MetadataSharing has a central repository, implemented in the class `Repository`, used to store metadata read from the configured sources. The components must use a

Metadata Reader Adapter, abstracted by the class `RepositoryAdapter`, to get it from the repository and convert it to the format of its Metadata Container.

Hispagnol [25] proposed a model to unify the models OLTP (Online Transaction Processing), used for persistence, and OLAP (Online Analytical Processing), used for data mining. In the proposed implementation, created in Object Pascal, the OLTP metadata is retrieved and then adapted and complemented to compose the metadata necessary for OLAP.

In Nardon and Silva [42], tips, tricks, and new design patterns are presented in the context of a Java EE application by using the EJB 3 specification [34]. One of the practices described is the use of object-relational metadata retrieved from **Hibernate** `SessionFactory` for its use inside some EJB components. For instance, the id property can be used by other components to identify an entity for auditing purposes.

Running Example

Some applications that use the Comparison Component, may also use the Hibernate [2] in the persistence layer. When a property of a persistent class is also a persistent class, that property is a composed object. For the comparison domain, that means that this property must be deeply compared. In this case, to avoid duplicate configurations and inconsistencies, a Metadata Reader Adapter is created to get this information directly from Hibernate.

The class `AdapterComparisonMetadataReader`, presented in Listing 8, receives in the constructor an instance of `SessionFactory`, namely a Hibernate class with a method that allows for the application to retrieve the class metadata. Based on class metadata, in the method `populateContainer()` searches for properties that are also entities and sets the `deepComparison` to true in the `PropertyDescriptor`.

Listing 8. The AdapterComparisonMetadataReader source code.

```
public class AdapterComparisonMetadataReader implements ComparisonMetadataReader {
    private SessionFactory sessionFactory;

    public AdapterComparisonMetadataReader(SessionFactory sessionFactory) {
        this.sessionFactory = sessionFactory;
    }

    public void populateContainer(Class c, ComparisonDescriptor descriptor) {
        ClassMetadata metadata = sessionFactory.getClassMetadata(c);
        if (metadata != null) {
            for (String prop : metadata.getPropertyNames()) {
                if (metadata.getPropertyType(prop).isEntityType()) {
                    PropertyDescriptor pd = descriptor.
                                              getPropertyDescriptor(prop);
                    if (pd == null) {
                        pd = new PropertyDescriptor();
                        pd.setName(prop);
                        descriptor.addPropertyDescriptor(pd);
                    }
                    pd.setDeepComparison(true);
                }
            }
        }
    }
}
```

Related Patterns
Metadata Reader Adapter assumes that the framework uses Metadata Reader Chain since the metadata from the other framework would rarely have all the needed information. If that is not true, the Metadata Reader Chain does not need to be implemented. The Metadata Repository also needs to be implemented but in another framework. If it is not implemented, an alternative is to retrieve the metadata directly from a metadata reader.

This pattern is related to the Adapter [17] since it invokes the API to access metadata from another framework and adapts the information for the framework context. In Metadata Reader Adapter, it is not the functionality provided that is adapted to another API, but the information provided by the other framework that is used and interpreted in another context.

4.4   Metadata Reader Delegate

Also Known as
Extended Metadata Reader, Metadata Piece Reader

Context
Every metadata-based framework provides a format which defines how its metadata should be created. If metadata is defined in an XML file, this format should be defined in an XML Schema or in a DTD. If the metadata is defined in annotations, this format is the annotations defined by the framework. This format adopted by the framework is called *metadata schema* and a piece of this information, such as an annotation or an XML element, is called *metadata piece*.

Since the framework needs to be adapted to applications, sometimes new kinds of metadata elements are necessary. For instance, if the application extends a Metadata-based Graphical Framework [19] by adding a new component, probably extending the metadata schema would also be necessary. As another example, metadata pieces can also be added to express concepts in an application domain.

If the framework provides only a hotspot for the entire metadata reading algorithm by using Metadata Reader Strategy, it is necessary to create a reader which can handle all the metadata schema to deal with one additional metadata piece. In this context it is important for the framework to provide more fine grained hotspots in the metadata reading to allow for the addition of new metadata pieces.

In the Comparison Component domain, the classes can have attribute types which should have a particular treatment by the framework. For instance, if an application has some properties representing a weight configured with a custom annotation, it should be possible to extend the framework to understand this new metadata piece.

Problem
How to allow for the framework to understand extensions in metadata schema?

Forces
- Sometimes the source code can become clearer if the application expresses the metadata by using domain terms.

- It is possible to read metadata from different schemas by using the Metadata Reader Strategy, but sometimes it is important to extend the reading to add a new metadata piece.
- The frameworks provide metadata for general use, but for some specific domains, some applications could need more specific metadata. For instance, in instance validation domain, metadata schema should enable the extension to allow for the creation of custom validations by the application.
- If the metadata provided by the framework do not fulfill the application requirements, they can limit or prevent their usage.
- The framework behavior extension sometimes cannot be done without the extension of the metadata schema.

Solution

Metadata Reader Delegate proposes delegating metadata pieces reading to other classes. This pattern is applied in a context of a Metadata Reader Strategy and the other existing readers do not necessarily need to implement it. Each metadata piece should be associated to a Metadata Reader Delegate, which should be invoked in the reading algorithm. The Metadata Reader Delegate should interpret the metadata piece and the Metadata Container should be populated with that information.

To enable the extension of the metadata schema, it should be possible to configure the Metadata Reader Delegate associated with a metadata piece. In XML files it can be performed by associating class names to the element types and in annotations an Annotation Reader [18] can be used. Consequently, if the application defines a new metadata piece mapped to a Metadata Reader Delegate, the framework will be able to perform its processing.

Structure

Figure 13 represents the pattern structure. The interface `ReaderDelegate` is an abstraction of the classes that receive a piece of metadata. The `ConcreteMetadataReader` should be able to create the correspondent `ConcreteReaderDelegate` for each metadata piece received. The mapping among the metadata piece and the Metadata Reader Delegate should be configurable to enable the insertion of new metadata pieces.

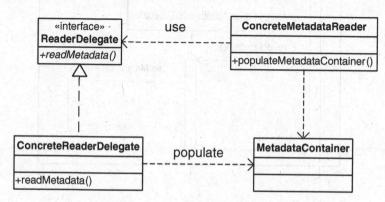

Fig. 13. The structure of Metadata Reader Delegate

A ConcreteReaderDelegate should receive the MetadataContainer as a parameter and populate it based on the metadata piece received. An alternative implementation is the method readMetadata() to return information and the ConcreteMetadataReader is responsible for configuring the MetadataContainer.

Participants

- ConcreteMetadataReader - It represents a class that reads metadata and delegates part of its logic to implementations of ReaderDelegate. It is responsible for instantiating the appropriate ConcreteReaderDelegate for each piece of metadata.
- ReaderDelegate - It is an abstraction of classes that reads and interprets a piece of metadata.
- ConcreteReaderDelegate - It represents a concrete class that implements ReaderDelegate and interprets a specific piece of metadata.
- MetadataContainer - It is responsible for representing the application class metadata needed in the framework.

Dynamics

Figure 14 presents a sequence diagram representing the reading of metadata using the ReaderDelegate. For each piece of metadata found, it creates the respective ConcreteReaderDelegate and delegates the reading of that piece to it. This readMetadata() method receives the MetadataContainer as a parameter and populates it with the metadata contained in that piece. Alternatively, the ConcreteReaderDelegate can return information which should be used by the ConcreteMetadataReader to populate the MetadataContainer.

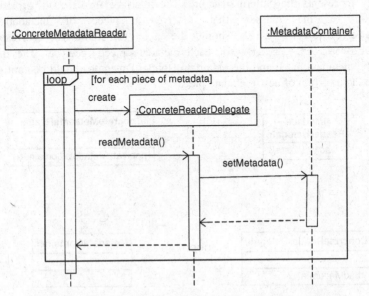

Fig. 14. Metadata reading sequence using Metadata Reader Delegate

Consequences

- (+) The metadata schema can be extended without affecting the concrete class responsible for reading that type of metadata definition.
- (+) The framework metadata schema can be extended by the application.
- (+) The Metadata Reader Delegate can set custom hook classes in the framework structure allowing also for behavior extension.
- (-) Depending on the number of possible different pieces of metadata, there will be many different Metadata Reader Delegates, which are usually small classes.
- (-) In some frameworks, it is difficult to divide metadata into independent pieces, which makes the implementation of this pattern unfeasible.

Known Uses

With the **NHibernate** Validator, new attributes can be created to validate more specific constraints associated to an application domain. When this new attribute contains information, it should receive in the attribute [ValidatorClass] a class which implements the interface IInitializableValidator. This interface has the method initialize() that is used to interpret the metadata.

JColtrane uses annotations to define conditions for each method to be executed. New conditions can be added by creating annotations annotated with @ConditionFactoryAnnotation. This annotation receives the class responsible for reading that annotation, which should implement the interface ElementConditionsFactory.

XapMap provides annotations for converting data among different types and a mechanism for the application to define its own conversion annotations. The mechanism is similar to the ones used in **Hibernate Validator** and **JColtrane**.

Running Example

The Comparison Component in this step is refactored to support annotations created by the application. As a consequence, the application is able to create annotations related to its domain, which can also be used by other frameworks and components.

The interface AnnotationReader is introduced to abstract the reading of an annotation. It contains a method named readAnnotation() that receives as parameters the annotation to be interpreted and the PropertyDescriptor associated to the property where the annotation is found. Each new annotation should be configured with @DelegateReader by indicating the instance of AnnotationReader which should interpret it.

The class AnnotationComparisonMetadataReader, which was the ComparisonMetadataReader renamed presented in Listing 2, must have the method populateContainer() refactored in order to look for annotations with @DelegateReader. For each one that is found, it should create the configured AnnotationReader and subsequently to invoke the readAnnotation() method. Listing 9 presents the piece of source code that needed to be changed in this class. The specific code to read the @Tolerance and @DeepComparison is removed and substituted by a loop that searches for annotations that have the `@DelegateReader` annotation.

Listing 9. The class AnnotationComparisonMetadataReader.

```
for(Annotation an : method.getAnnotations()){
    Class anType = an.annotationType();
    if(anType.isAnnotationPresent(DelegateReader.class)){
        DelegateReader reader =
                (DelegateReader) anType.getAnnotation(DelegateReader.class);
        Class<? extends AnnotationReader> readerClass = reader.value();
        try {
            AnnotationReader anReader = readerClass.newInstance();
            anReader.readAnnotation(an, prop);
        } catch (Exception e) {
            throw new RuntimeException("Cannot instantiate reader",e);
        }
    }
}
```

After the modification in the class that reads comparison metadata using annotations, the `@DelegateReader` must be inserted into the current framework annotations. Listing 10 presents this insertion into `@Tolerance` and the class responsible for reading this annotation and inserting its information in the respective property descriptor. The same must be done for `@DeepComparison`. With this refactoring, new annotations can be created and interpreted by the framework by using the same mechanism.

Listing 10. The definition of @Tolerance annotation with @DelegateReader.

```
@Target({ElementType.METHOD})
@Retention(RetentionPolicy.RUNTIME)
@DelegateReader(ToleranceReader.class)
public @interface Tolerance {
    double value();
}

public class ToleranceReader implements AnnotationReader<Tolerance>{
    @Override
    public void readAnnotation(Tolerance annotation, PropertyDescriptor desc){
        desc.setTolerance(annotation.value());
    }
}
```

Related Patterns

Metadata Reader Delegate is often used with Metadata Processor, allowing the extension of the metadata schema with the extension of the framework logic. Both patterns can be used independently, nevertheless it is more plausible to imagine them being used together.

Annotation Reader [18] is an idiom for the usage of Java annotations. It proposes the usage of an annotation in other annotations to configure the class which the framework should use to interpret it. It can be used to configure the Metadata Reader Delegate if annotations are used to define metadata.

An alternative to a Metadata Reader Delegate when the behavior extension is not required is the use of Annotation Mapping [18]. It proposes the creation of application-specific annotations that are mapped to the framework annotations. By using this solution the framework configurations can be used indirectly in application annotations. To enable this practice, the framework should implement a Metadata Reader Strategy which search for framework annotations inside other annotations.

5   Metadata Processing Patterns

5.1   Metadata Processor

Also Known as
Metadata Executor, Metadata Piece Processor

Context
The flexibility in metadata reading is important to enable metadata schema extension and its reading from different sources and formats. However, despite these hotspots being important to adjust the metadata reading to the application needs, they do not actually change the framework's main logic. An extension in the metadata schema may be motivated by requirements for the insertion of new behavior in the framework.

The insertion of a metadata piece in a programming element usually changes the framework behavior when it is processing this element. In some domains, it is important for the application to extend the framework functionality in the processing of specific elements. Consequently, a new metadata piece defined by the application should be associated to a new behavior also defined by the application. The nonexistence of such mechanism may prevent or limit the framework usage.

As an example, in the `AnnotationComparisonMetadataReader` presented in Listing 9 the metadata reading of annotation is delegated to other classes, however these classes cannot extend the comparison functionality already supported. For instance, it is not possible for only a substring of a property to be considered in a comparison, even when adding a new annotation `@CompareSubstring`.

Problem
How to allow framework behavior extension to process new metadata pieces?

Forces
- Some applications need some more specific behavior than those provided only by the framework metadata configuration.
- Applications can use alternative solutions to implement functionalities not covered by the framework, even though the architecture will have two components with the same responsibility.
- The application developers may change the source code of an open-source framework to change its behavior, but it might make it unfeasible to take advantage of its future versions.
- In some framework domains, such as instance constraint validation, the metadata extension associated to a behavior extension is important to increase reuse.

Solution

Metadata Processor proposes delegating part of the framework main functionality to other classes. These class instances compose the Metadata Container and are created during the metadata reading phase. The Metadata Reader Delegate associated with a metadata piece is usually responsible for the respective Metadata Processor creation. However it can also be created directly by a Metadata Reader Strategy which uses reflection to instantiate them.

During the execution relative to a metadata piece, the framework controller should retrieve the respective Metadata Processor instance from the Metadata Container. Further, the framework delegates its execution for that metadata piece to the Metadata Processor. This solution provides a hotspot which enables the insertion of new behavior in the processing of each metadata piece.

Structure

Figure 15 shows the class diagram for this pattern. The interface `MetadataProcessor` abstracts the processing of a piece of metadata. The `DefaultMetadataProcessor` represents a default implementation for processing and the `ConcreteMetadataProcessor` represents other implementations. In addition, the `MetadataProcessor` implementations may have instance variables to represent part of the metadata obtained during its reading.

The `MetadataProcessor` instances should compose the respective `MetadataContainer`. This structure allows for new implementations of `MetadataProcessor` to carry new attributes and new behavior. The `FrameworkController` can access the `MetadataProcessor` through the `MetadataContainer`.

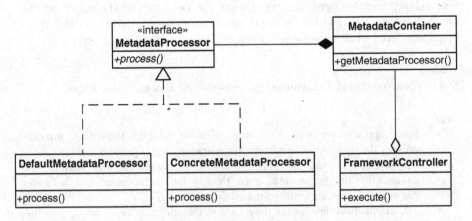

Fig. 15. The structure of Metadata Processor

Participants

- `FrameworkController` - It is the framework entry point. It is responsible for executing the main logic and also for being a controller of other classes. Besides, it retrieves an implementation of the

`MetadataProcessor` from the `MetadataContainer` and executes it as part of the framework logic.

- `MetadataContainer` - It is responsible for representing the application class metadata needed by the framework. It is composed of instances of `MetadataProcessor` implementations.
- `MetadataProcessor` - It is an abstraction of the classes that compose the `MetadataContainer` and is invoked as part of the framework logic by the `FrameworkController`.
- `DefaultMetadataProcessor` - It represents a default implementation of the `MetadataProcessor`.
- `ConcreteMetadataProcessor` - It represents a concrete implementation of the `MetadataProcessor`.

Dynamics

A sequence diagram that represents the use of the processor by the framework is presented in Figure 16. The `FrameworkController` retrieves the `MetadataProcessor` from the `MetadataContainer` and invokes its methods. The `MetadataProcessor` should previously be created by the metadata reading algorithm and inserted in the `MetadataContainer`. Likewise, it is possible to have more than one kind of processor in a framework, depending on the different tasks that it executes and the necessity to make it extensible.

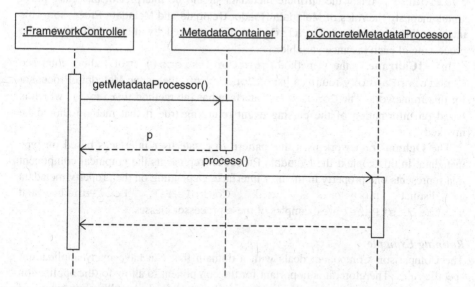

Fig. 16. Sequence diagram representing the use of Metadata Processor

An alternative implementation is to store the metadata in the `MetadataContainer` in a more flexible way, for example by using attribute maps, and then using this information in the `FrameworkController` to create or retrieve the processor. This is recommended when the processor must have heavyweight objects or it cannot be shared between more than one framework entry point instances.

Consequences

- (+) It is possible to extend the framework functionalities by creating more Metadata Processor implementations.
- (+) The Metadata Container uses a more flexible structure, easily allowing for the addition of different information.
- (+) It allows for the application to extend the metadata schema by adding functionality relative to its domain.
- (-) The Metadata Container, whose objective is to store metadata, is composed of instances that also contain framework logic.
- (-) To implement this pattern, the metadata must be divided into pieces that can be processed separately and in some framework domains that is not possible.
- (-) The use of processors in the Metadata Container structure may make it hard for the metadata interpretation when it is retrieved by a Metadata Reader Adapter.

Known Uses

In **NHibernate Validator** new annotations can be defined by using the attribute `[ValidatorClass]` to reference a class that implements the interface `Ivalidator`. When the attribute metadata should be interpreted, this class plays simultaneously the roles of Metadata Reader Delegate and Metadata Processor. This interface has the method `isValid()` that is invoked by the framework for the processing of each instance variable.

In **JColtrane**, the method `getConditions()` of the interface `ConditionFactory` returns a list of `Condition`, that is the Metadata Processor for this framework. The `Condition` interface has the method `verify()`, which is based on information of the parsing event returning true if that method should be invoked.

The **Oghma** framework uses this pattern to create user interfaces based on type metadata. In this context the Metadata Processor represents the graphical component that represents one property in the user interface. Depending on the property metadata, a distinct processor is used. `ComboPanel`, `BoolPanel` and `VirtualListPanel` are examples of these processor classes.

Running Example

The Comparison Component deals with a domain that can have many application-specific rules. Therefore, it is important for the component to allow for the application developers to add new comparison types and associate them with new pieces of metadata. In this section, the Comparison Component is refactored and a new kind of comparison is added.

The interface `ComparisonProcessor` is introduced to abstract the logic of a comparison. The method `compare()` receives the property name and the values to be compared, and then returns null if they can be considered the same or the respective Difference instance. The PropertyDescriptor class is also refactored to contain an instance variable with the respective ComparisonProcessor. In this case, the method getProcessor() returns an instance of RegularProcessor, which represents the default comparison algorithm, if the processor attribute is null.

The tolerance, which is stored as an attribute in the PropertyDescriptor, now is an instance variable of the ToleranceProcessor, introduced in Listing 11. The class responsible for reading the @Tolerance annotation, represented in Listing 12, is also adapted to create the instance of ToleranceProcessor with the correct tolerance value.

The implementation of the class ComparisonComponent should be refactored to get benefit of this new mechanism. In the execution of the comparison of each property, when the property deepComparison is false, the ComparisonProcessor is retrieved from the PropertyDescriptor and is used to compare the values.

Listing 11. The class ToleranceProcessor that processes the tolerance metadata.

```
public class ToleranceProcessor implements ComparisonProcessor {
    private double tolerance;
    public ToleranceProcessor(double tolerance) {
        this.tolerance = tolerance;
    }
    @Override
    public Difference compare(String prop, Object oldValue, Object newValue) {
        double dif = Math.abs(((Double) newValue) - ((Double) oldValue));
        if (dif > tolerance) {
            return new Difference(prop, newValue, oldValue);
        }
        return null;
    }
}
```

Listing 12. The class ToleranceReader that creates the ToleranceProcessor instance.

```
public class ToleranceReader implements AnnotationReader<Tolerance>{
    @Override
    public void readAnnotation(Tolerance annotation,
            PropertyDescriptor descriptor){
        double tolerance = annotation.value();
        ToleranceProcessor processor = new ToleranceProcessor(tolerance);
        descriptor.setProcessor(processor);
    }
}
```

Related Patterns

Metadata Processor is often used in conjunction with Metadata Reader Delegate, allowing for the extension of the metadata schema conveying the extension of the framework logic. Nevertheless, this pattern can also be used with a Metadata Container with a flexible structure, where the processors are created based on the information contained in it.

A Metadata Processor has a structure similar to Command [17], however it is related to a metadata piece. It is also similar to Strategy [17], since each processor can be considered a strategy for executing one piece of metadata.

Associative Annotation [18] proposes the creation of an annotation which receives a class as a parameter. This solution can be used to define which Metadata Processor should the annotation be associated to. By using this solution a more general Metadata Reader Strategy which instantiates this class should be created. It is an alternative to the use of Metadata Reader Delegate to create the Metadata Processor.

5.2   Metadata Processing Layers

Also Known as
Metadata Processing Chain, Metadata Execution Layers

Context
Sometimes it is not possible to divide the metadata-based framework processing into metadata pieces, specially when they need to be related. For instance, a method metadata may contain references for other metadata elements. However, these functionalities which need the entire Metadata Container can usually be divided into independent framework responsibilities.

Metadata Processor proposes a structure that provides flexibility in the processing of different metadata pieces inside the same framework responsibility. However, in some framework domains it is important to enable the application to add new responsibilities that uses the entire metadata schema. These new hotspots should be more coarsely grained than the ones proposed by Metadata Processor.

In the Comparison Component there are some responsibilities in the comparison algorithm, such as the comparison of null values, the comparison by using the metadata processors, and the deep comparison. In the current implementation it is not possible to insert a new kind of comparison or to change its order.

Problem
How to allow for behavior extension that uses the entire metadata schema?

Forces
- Some metadata-based frameworks execute independent tasks based on the same metadata.
- The Metadata Processor enables extension when it is possible to separate the logic by metadata pieces, but when the framework has more than one responsibility it is harder to make this separation.
- The framework may have well defined responsibilities, but the application may need to extend them using the same metadata.
- The framework can provide some functionality which needs to be enabled or disabled depending on the application needs.
- Distinct framework responsibilities implemented in the same class may complicate their maintenance and evolution.

Solution

Metadata Processing Layers proposes dividing framework responsibilities into independent processing layers. These layers can be easily inserted and removed, providing a hotspot which can access and process the information of the entire Metadata Container. Consequently, this improves the framework flexibility, allowing for the application to add more general behaviors.

In the framework processing, part of its execution should be delegated to the Metadata Processing Layers. It is the framework responsibility to coordinate the layers execution. For instance, depending on the framework all the layers should be always executed or it can execute the layers until one gives an expected answer. The framework should also provide ways to manage the existing layers and allow for the application to configure them.

Structure

Figure 17 demonstrates the pattern structure. The FrameworkController is composed of many processing layers with different responsibilities. The FrameworkController is responsible for defining when the layers should be invoked. Moreover, each ConcreteProcessingLayer can access the information in MetadataContainer to use the metadata as the base for its logic. The MetadataContainer instance can be retrieved in the repository by the FrameworkController or directly by each ConcreteProcessingLayer.

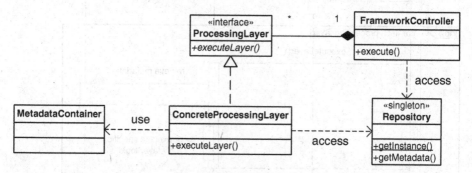

Fig. 17. Structure of Metadata Processing Layers

Participants

- FrameworkController - It is the framework entry point. It is responsible for executing the main logic and for being a controller of the other classes. In order to do so, it contains a list of ProcessingLayer implementations and invokes them in the right order.
- MetadataContainer - It is responsible for representing the application class metadata needed by the framework. Each ProcessingLayer can use it during the logic processing.
- ProcessingLayer - It is an abstraction of the classes that represent a framework processing layer.

- `ConcreteProcessingLayer` - It represents a concrete implementation of the `ProcessingLayer`. It uses the `MetadataContainer` to execute a part of the framework logic.
- `Repository` - It is responsible for managing the metadata reading and storing internally the instances of `MetadataContainer`. Likewise it is a singleton and provides metadata for `FrameworkController` or for each `ConcreteProcessingLayer`.

Dynamics
There are two alternatives for each layer to access the metadata. The `FrameworkController` can retrieve the `MetadataContainer` and pass it as a parameter in each layer, as illustrated in the sequence diagram of Figure 18. The other solution is for each layer to access the `Repository` separately to retrieve the `MetadataContainer`, as represented in Figure 19.

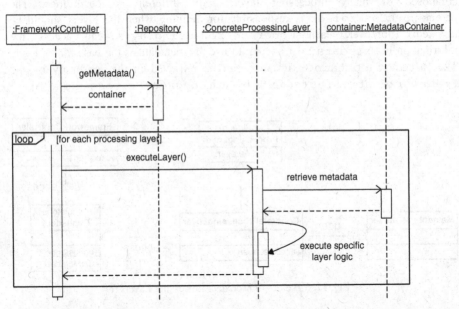

Fig. 18. Sequence of Metadata Processing Layers passing Metadata Container as a parameter

The use of the `Repository` is not mandatory, but it is particularly important when each layer retrieves metadata independently. On the one hand, to hold an instance of `MetadataContainer` to pass through the layers can complicate the framework flow. On the other hand, to retrieve the container for every layer can generate an overhead for locating it many times.

As an alternative, the layers can also be implemented by using Chain of Responsibility [17]. In this implementation, each layer would be responsible for invoking or not the next one. As a result, the `FrameworkController` does not control the layers invocation and only calls the first one.

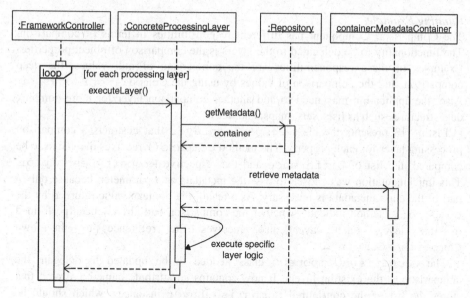

Fig. 19. Sequence of Metadata Processing Layers accessing Repository directly

Consequences

- (+) It is possible to extend the framework functionalities by creating more Metadata Processing Layers.
- (+) The order of layers execution can be customized by the application.
- (+) Metadata Processing Layers can be added, substituted and removed for each framework instantiation instance, enabling different behaviors of the framework in the same application.
- (-) The creation of layers can over-design the framework if it has a well-defined responsibility that rarely can be extended.
- (-) The use of Metadata Processor is more complicated with processing layers since each layer has a different responsibility to execute.

Known Uses

JBoss Application Server supports the EJB 3 specification, which defines that an EJB container must execute many responsibilities, such as transaction management, access control and exception handling. These functionalities are executed based on class metadata implemented in many aspects, using JBoss AOP. In this context, each aspect advice can be considered a processing layer.

SwingBean implements many responsibilities such as validation, form and table creation, and customization of each graphical component. Each responsibility is implemented in a different class, which receives a `FieldDescriptor` instance with the class metadata. In this framework it is not possible to insert new layers in the execution.

Esfinge Framework provides a layered structure that allows layers to be easily created and inserted. Therefore, each layer can use the entity class metadata to customize its behavior. There are layers implemented for logging, remote access, remote notification, and access control.

Running Example

The Comparison Component has different responsibilities in terms of comparison. The functionality to be delegated to the layers is the comparison of object properties. Examples of these responsibilities are the comparison of null values, the deep comparison, and the comparison of values by using the `ComparisonProcessor`. Also, the application may need to add another comparison layer for more complex data structures such as lists, sets, maps, and trees.

Listing 13 presents the class `ComparisonLayer` that abstracts a comparison processing layer for each property. The method `compare()` receives the values to be compared, the list of `Difference` and the respective `PropertyDescriptor`. This implementation was chosen to pass the metadata as a parameter, because only a part of the class metadata is necessary. As a result, the boolean value returned by the `compare()` method indicates whether the comparison had already been performed in that layer. Each layer also receives the reference to the own `ComparisonComponent`.

The `ComparisonComponent` class nedded to be updated to delegate the comparison to the existing layers. It now contains an attribute named `layers` that stores the list of the configured `ComparisonLayer` instances, which should be provided in the constructor. Additionally, in the `compare()` method, the comparison of each property uses each layer comparison until one returns true, meaning that the comparison is already completed.

Listing 13. The ComparisonLayer abstract class.

```
public abstract class ComparisonLayer {
    private ComparisonComponent component;
    public abstract boolean compare(Object oldValue, Object newValue,
                List<Difference> difs, PropertyDescriptor descProp)
                    throws CompareException ;
    public ComparisonComponent getComponent() {
        return component;
    }
    public void setComponent(ComparisonComponent component) {
        this.component = component;
    }
}
```

All the comparison logic was moved to the following layer classes: `NullComparisonLayer`, `DeepComparisonLayer` and `ValueComparisonLayer`. They present the implementation of comparison layers whose functionalities are already included in the earlier version of the Comparison Component. Listing 14 presents the implementation of the `ValueComparisonLayer` as an example of a comparison layer.

Listing 14. ValueComparisonLayer, for comparisons using the ComparisonProcessor.

```
public class ValueComparisonLayer extends ComparisonLayer {
    @Override
    public boolean compare(Object oldValue, Object newValue,
            List<Difference> difs, PropertyDescriptor descProp)
```

```
                throws CompareException {
        ComparisonProcessor processor = descProp.getProcessor();
        Difference dif = processor.compare(descProp.getName(),
                                            oldValue, newValue);
        if(dif != null)
            difs.add(dif);
        return true;
    }
}
```

Related Patterns

Metadata Processing Layer can be combined with Metadata Processor to extend the framework logic in different ways. Yet, the Metadata Processor is usually used in only one layer. The use of this pattern in conjunction with Metadata Repository is recommended, since the metadata can be retrieved independently in each layer.

This pattern can be implemented by using the structure of the Chain of Responsibility [17], in which one layer is responsible for invoking the next one. Besides, in frameworks that implement crosscutting concerns, each layer can be implemented as a different Proxy or Decorator [17]. Additionally, in aspect-oriented frameworks, each advice can represent a layer from the same framework.

6   Related Patterns and Pattern Languages

This section presents patterns and pattern languages related to the one presented in this paper. The following items presents how each one complements and differ from the proposed pattern language:

- Metadata-based Frameworks are clearly related to Reflection [3], which is an architectural pattern that proposes a mechanism for changing structure and behavior of software systems dynamically. The additional domain-specific or application-specific metadata which should be defined for the framework complements the information on the meta level. The use of this metadata is what enables the framework behavior adaptation.

- The **Architectural Patterns for Metadata-based Frameworks Usage** [19] presents a collection of patterns which identifies situations where the usage of a metadata-based framework is appropriate. For a framework developer, the proposed pattern language and these architectural patterns are complementary, since they provide best practices on two distinct perspectives necessary in this kind of development. However, the pattern language can also be considered independent of the architectural patterns, since it focuses on the framework internal structure, metadata reading and metadata processing, which can be done whatever the framework domain.

- The **Idioms for Code Annotations in Java Language** [18] presents a collection of patterns which propose solutions about how to structure metadata in code annotations, considering their limitations in the Java language. These patterns are complementary to the pattern language presented in this paper in situations where code annotations are the strategy chosen for metadata definition. The Metadata Reading Patterns allow for the framework to abstract the metadata definition from the logic processing, decoupling it from the solutions used to structure metadata in code annotations.

- The pattern language described for **Handling Application Properties** [58] provides patterns for loading and reading application properties. Although some of these patterns can be similar to some of the Metadata Reading Patterns, they deal with a different context. Since application properties are configured for each application instance, there can be metadata associated with every programming element. Consequently, metadata are more fine-grained than application properties. Another difference is that the patterns for application properties provide solutions for reading these properties in different contexts, but not for extending the reading mechanism. Since this paper pattern language is focused on frameworks, its patterns concern more on allowing extension of the reading mechanism than in describing more concrete solutions.

- The **Pattern Language for Adaptive Object Models** [11, 57, 61, 62] documents patterns for reading the metadata and building a flexible and adaptive object model at runtime. In this context, the metadata are used to create the whole object model and not only a framework behavior adaptation. Despite all of the Pattern Language for Metadata-based Frameworks known uses reads metadata from a static class model, these patterns could also be used on frameworks created for an adaptive object model context. On the one hand, both pattern languages deal with metadata, but for distinct purposes. On the other hand, they can also be complementary since a framework for an adaptive object model would probably be based on the objects metadata.

7   Conclusion

This paper presents a **Pattern Language for Metadata-based Frameworks** intended to document design best practices for this kind of framework. Many existing frameworks employed in the development of applications apply analogous concepts and this work can help in the development of new frameworks and in the refactoring of existing ones.

The following are the main contributions of this work: (a) The study and analysis of the internal structural solutions of existing open source metadata-based frameworks; (b) The documentation of the best practices found, in the form of a pattern language that includes solutions for the structure, metadata reading, and logic processing of metadata-based frameworks; (c) The creation of a detailed running example that illustrates how to refactor a metadata-based framework to implement each pattern of the presented pattern language.

By observing the running example, Comparison Component, that was functional before implementing any of the patterns, it is possible to verify how it became more flexible and extensible after having used the best practices documented in the presented pattern language. The consolidation of metadata-based frameworks design knowledge is important for generating more mature solutions as to the development of this kind of software. The metadata sharing among different frameworks, for instance, is a hard goal to be accomplished in an architecture based on the structure of many existing frameworks.

In this work, the design patterns are applied to the Comparison Component through refactoring, but in real framework development, its requirements should make some part of the code to be implemented in the first place. A suggestion for future work is to define a methodology for the development of metadata-based frameworks that should include not only the framework design but also activities like metadata modeling.

Acknowledgments. The authors would like to thank all the students who worked in the development of several metadata-based frameworks which became examples and sources of research for this work, like Renzo, Diego, Bruno, Leandro, Gustavo, Jorge, and Ricardo. We also thank the support of PPGAO and LAB-C2 in this research.

Additionally, we thank the PLoP shepherd Ademar Aguiar for the hard work of reviewing this huge pattern language and giving us feedback to improve it. We'd also like to thank all the friends we made at PLoP, especially those who gave us precious feedback at the writers' workshop, like Joseph Yoder, Brian Foote, Rebecca Wirfs-Brock, and James Siddle. Finally, we thank all TPLoP reviewers, whose observations   increased the maturity of this work.

References

1. Alur, D., Malks, D., Crupi, J.: Core J2EE patterns: best practices and design strategies, 2nd edn. Prentice Hall, Upper Saddle River (2003)
2. Bauer, C., King, G.: Hibernate in Action. Manning Publications (2004)
3. Buschmann, F., et al.: Pattern-oriented software architecture - A system of patterns. Wiley (1996)
4. Chen, N.: Convention over configuration, http://softwareengineering. vazexqi.com/files/pattern.html (accessed on December 2010)
5. Costa, B., Figueredo, L.: Uma Arquitetura Baseada em Metadados para Integração entre Aplicações Web e Plataformas Móveis. Technical Report, Aeronautical Institute of Technology (2009)
6. Damyanov, I., Holmes, N.: Metadata driven code generation using .NET framework. In: International Conference on Computer Systems and Technologies, pp. 1–6 (2004)
7. Doucet, F., Shukla, S., Gupta, R.: Introspection in system-level language frameworks: meta-level vs. Integrated. In: Source Design, Automation and Test in Europe, pp. 382–387 (2003)
8. Ernst, M.: Type annotations specification (JSR 308), http://types.cs washington.edu/jsr308/specification/java-annotation-design.pdf
9. Esfinge Framework, http://esfinge.sourceforge.net/ (accessed on July 2011)
10. Fayad, M., Schmidt, D., Johnson, R.: Application frameworks. In: Fayad, M., Schmidt, D., Johnson, R. (eds.) Building Application Frameworks: Object-oriented Foundations of Frameworks Design, ch. 1, pp. 3–27. Wiley, New York (1999)

11. Ferreira, H.: Adaptive Object-Modeling Patterns, Tools and Applications. PhD Thesis, University of Porto, Faculty of Engineering (2010)
12. Foote, B., Yoder, J.: Evolution, architecture, and metamorphosis. In: Pattern Languages of Program Design 2, ch. 13, pp. 295–314. Addison-Wesley Longman, Boston (1996)
13. Forman, I., Forman, N.: Java reflection in action. Manning Publ., Greenwich (2005)
14. Fowler, M.: Inversion of Control Containers and the Dependency Injection Pattern (2004), http://www.martinfowler.com/articles/injection.html (accessed on December 2010)
15. Fowler, M.: Patterns of enterprise application architecture. Addison-Wesley Professional, Boston (2002)
16. Fowler, M.: Using metadata. IEEE Software 19(6), 13–17 (2002)
17. Gamma, E., Helm, R., Johnson, R., Vlissides, J.: Design Patterns: Elements of Reusable Object-Oriented Software. Addison-Wesley (1994)
18. Guerra, E., Cardoso, M., Silva, J., Fernandes, C.: Idioms for Code Annotations in Java Language. In: Proceedings of 8ª Latin American Conference on Pattern Languages of Programming, SugarLoafPLoP 2010, Salvador (2010)
19. Guerra, E., Fernandes, C., Silveira, F.: Architectural Patterns for Metadata-based Frameworks Usage. In: Conference on Patterns Languages of Programs, Reno, vol. 17 (2010)
20. Guerra, E., Fernandes, C.: A Metadata-Based Components Model. In: Proceedings of Doctoral Symposium at 22nd European Conference on Object Oriented Programming, ECOOP 2008, Paphos (2008)
21. Guerra, E., Parente, J., Fernandes, C.: Mapeando Objetos para Entidades de uma Ontologia Utilizando Metadados. In: Proceedings of SIGE - Defense Operational Applications Symposium, São José dos Campos (2008)
22. Guerra, E., Pavão, F., Fernandes, C.: Padrões de Projeto para Frameworks e Componentes Baseados em Metadados. In: Proceedings of 7ª Latin American Conference on Pattern Languages of Programming, SugarLoafPLoP 2008, Fortaleza (2008)
23. Guerra, E., Silva, J., Silveira, F., Fernandes, C.: Using Metadata in Aspect-Oriented Frameworks. In: Proceedings of 2nd Workshop on Assessment of Contemporary Modularization Techniques, AcoM 2008, Nashville (2008)
24. Hibernate Validator, http://www.hibernate.org/412.html (accessed on July 2011)
25. Hispagnol, G.: Modelo multidimensional unificado: integrando domínios OLAP e OLTP. Technical Report, Aeronautical Institute of Technology (2009)
26. Hot Comments (2011), http://c2.com/cgi/wiki?HotComments (accessed on July 2011)
27. Hunt, A., Thomas, D., Hargett, M.: Pragmatic Unit Testing in C# with NUnit, 2nd edn. Pragmatic Bookshelf (2007)
28. JavaBeans(TM) specification 1.01 Final release, http://java.sun.com/javase/technologies/desktop/javabeans/docs/spec.html (accessed on December 2010)
29. JAX-RS: The JavaTM API for RESTful Web Services, http://www.jcp.org/en/jsr/detail?id=311 (accessed on July 2011)
30. JBoss Application Server, http://www.jboss.org/jbossas/ (accessed on December 2010)
31. JColtrane – Better than SAX Alone, http://jcoltrane.sf.net (accessed on December 2010)
32. Johnson, R., Foote, B.: Designing reusable classes. Journal Of Object-Oriented Programming 1(2), 22–35 (1988)

33. JSR 175: A Metadata Facility for the Java Programming Language, http://www.jcp.org/en/jsr/detail?id=175 (accessed on December 2010)
34. JSR 220: Enterprise JavaBeans 3.0, http://www.jcp.org/en/jsr/detail?id=220
35. JSR 222: Java Architecture for XML Binding (JAXB), http://jcp.org/en/jsr/detail?id=222 (accessed on December 2010)
36. JSR 299: Contexts and Dependency Injection for the JavaTM EE platform, http://jcp.org/en/jsr/summary?id=299 (accessed on July 2011)
37. JSR 303: Bean Validation, http://jcp.org/en/jsr/detail?id=303 (accessed on December 2010)
38. JSR 314: JavaServerTM Faces 2.0, http://www.jcp.org/en/jsr/detail?id=314 (accessed on July 2011)
39. Kuaté, P., Bauer, C., King, G., Harris, T.: NHibernate in Action. Manning Publications (2009)
40. Massol, V., Husted, T.: JUnit in action. Manning Publ., Greenwich (2003)
41. Miller, J.: Common Language Infrastructure Annotated Standard. Addison-Wesley, Boston (2003)
42. Nardon, F., Silva, E.: Implementing Java EE applications, using enterprise javabeans (EJB) 3 technology: real-world tips, tricks, and new design patterns, Session TS-4721 (2007), http://developers.sun.com/learning/javaoneonline/2007/pdf/TS-4721.pdf (accessed on December 2009)
43. Newkirk, J., Vorontsov, A.A.: How .NET's Custom Attributes Affect Design. IEEE Software 19, 18–20 (2002)
44. Noble, J.: Classifying Relationships between Object-Oriented Design Patterns. In: Proceedings of the Australian Software Engineering Conference 1998, ASWEC 1998, Adelaide, Australia, pp. 98–109 (1998)
45. Nock, C.: Data Access Patterns: Database Interactions in Object-Oriented Applications. Addison-Wesley Professional (2003)
46. Pree, W.: Hot-spot-driven development. In: Fayad, M., Schmidt, D., Johnson, R. (eds.) Building Application Frameworks: Object-oriented Foundations of Frameworks Design, ch. 16, pp. 379–393. Wiley, New York (1999)
47. Project Lombok, http://projectlombok.org/ (accessed on July 2011)
48. Quinonez, J., Tschantz, M.S., Ernst, M.D.: Inference of reference immutability. In: Vitek, J. (ed.) ECOOP 2008. LNCS, vol. 5142, pp. 616–641. Springer, Heidelberg (2008)
49. Ruby, S., et al.: Agile Web Development with Rails. Pragmatic Bookshelf (2009)
50. SAX Project, http://www.saxproject.org/ (accessed on December 2010)
51. Schwarz, D.: Peeking inside the box: attribute-oriented programming with Java 1.5, http://missingmanuals.com/pub/a/onjava/2004/06/30/insidebox1.html (accessed on December 2010)
52. Silva, J., Okura, R.: Um Modelo para Compartilhamento de Metadados entre Frameworks. Technical Report, Aeronautical Institute of Technology (2009)
53. SwingBean, http://swingbean.sourceforge.net/ (accessed on December 2010)
54. Tansey, W., Tilevich, E.: Annotation Refactoring: Inferring Upgrade Transformations for Legacy Applications. In: The International Conference on Object Oriented Programming, Systems, Languages and Applications, OOPSLA 2008, Nashville (2008)
55. Wada, H., Suzuki, J.: Modeling Turnpike Frontend System: a Model-Driven Development Framework Leveraging UML Metamodeling and Attribute-Oriented Programming. In: Proceedings of the 8th ACM/IEEE International Conference on Model Driven Engineering Languages and Sytems, MoDELS/UML (2005)

110   E. Guerra, J. de Souza, and C. Fernandes

56. Walls, C., Richards, N., Oberg, R.: XDoclet in Action. Manning Publications (2003)
57. Welicki, L., Yoder, J., Wirfs-Brock, R., Johnson, R.: Towards a Pattern Language for Adaptive Object-Models. In: Companion of the 22st ACM SIGPLAN Object Oriented Programming Systems, Languages, and Applications, OOPSLA 2007, Montreal (2007)
58. Wellhausen, T., Wagner, M., Müller, G.: Handling Application Properties - Simplify Application Customization in Different. In: 14th European Conference on Pattern Languages of Programs, EuroPLoP 2009, Bavaria (2009)
59. Wirfs-Brock, R., Johnson, R.: Surveying current research in object-oriented design. Communications Of The ACM 33(9), 104–124 (1990)
60. XapMap - Cross Application Mapping Framework, http://xapmap.sf.net (accessed on December 2010)
61. Yoder, J., Foote, B.: Metadata and Active Object-Models. In: Fifth Conference on Patterns Languages of Programs, PLoP 1998, Monticello (1998)
62. Yoder, J., Johnson, R.: The Adaptive Object-Model Architectural Style. In: IEEE/IFIP Conference on Software Architecture: System Design, Development and Maintenance, vol. 3, pp. 3–27 (2002)

User Interface Patterns for Multimodal Interaction

Andreas Ratzka*

I:IMSK, University of Regensburg, Germany
Andreas.Ratzka@eml.org

Abstract. Multimodal interaction aims at more flexible, more robust, more efficient and more natural interaction than can be achieved with traditional unimodal interactive systems. For this, the developer needs some design support in order to select appropriate modalities, to find appropriate modality combinations and to implement promising modality adaptation strategies. This paper presents first patterns for multimodal interaction and focuses on patterns for "fast input", "robust interaction" and patterns for "flexible interaction". Before these patterns are outlined in detail, an introduction to the field of multimodal interaction is given and the pattern identification process that was the basis of this work is presented.

Keywords: User Interface Patterns, Multimodal Interaction, Speech User Interfaces, Graphical User Interfaces, Mobile Interaction.

1 Introduction

Multimodal systems combine several interaction modalities and channels (such as visual, auditory and tactile modalities) to optimise the overall system usability. According to Oviatt and Kuhn [1] goals of multimodal interaction are

- flexibility and adaptability of the system with respect to users and contexts of use,
- high interaction robustness due to mutual disambiguation of input sources,
- interaction efficiency because of better integration into the work situation, and
- the possibility to interact with the system in a natural way.

Traditional approaches for multimodal interaction design provide implementation and prototyping frameworks [2, 3, 4] and knowledge-based design support for earlier analysis and design phases [5, 6, 7].

The goal of this work is to complement those approaches by identifying patterns for multimodal interaction and, this way, provide design support for rich user interfaces.

---

* Now at European Media Laboratory GmbH, Heidelberg, Germany.

J. Noble et al. (Eds.): TPLOP III, LNCS 7840, pp. 111–167, 2013.
© Springer-Verlag Berlin Heidelberg 2013

Multimodal interaction is a relatively new field which is mostly treated in a research context and by now entered only into few consumer products. This makes it difficult to find proven solutions for interaction problems which is a central claim for pattern identification. Nevertheless, there exists already a corpus of well founded research results and successful system implementations in which recurring patterns can be found [8].

When reading the patterns, you might notice a bias toward speech-based interaction. The attempt is not to replace "traditional" graphical user interfaces by voice interaction but rather to enhance them in a multimodal way. As there already exist a lot of GUI patterns [9, 10, 11, 12], this pattern collection attempts to show, how these existing interface styles – and GUI patterns – can be extended by using elements of speech interaction.

Before presenting the details of the patterns themselves, it is necessary to give some background information about multimodal interaction and to clarify some notions that are used in this context.

1.1 Modality

The research literature frequently treats the notions *modality, channel, mode.* and *medium* ambiguously or even as synonyms [13, p. 4]. To avoid confusion, this section will clarify how these terms are used in this article.

Charwat [14] defines the notion *modality* in a human-centred way as

> Perception via one of the three perception-channels. You can distin-guish the three modalities: visual, auditory, and tactile (physiology of senses) [15, p. 5].

Hedicke defines *modality* from a human-centred perspective, too, and considers both perception and action modalities [16, p. 206, p. 210]. According to the human senses, he distinguishes an *auditory interface*, a *visual interface*, and a *haptic interface*, as well as an *olfactory* and a *gustatory* interface.

Bernsen [17] defines modalities not as *sensory modalities* but as *representa-tional modalities*:

> A modality is a mode or way of representing information to humans or machines in a physically realised intersubjective form, such as in one of the media of graphics, acoustics and haptics [17].

In addition to the interaction medium or the interaction channel Bernsen [17, 18] includes semiotic aspects of the interaction language as part of the modality, so that you can distinguish between speech output, signal tones, pictures, written text, tables etc. as different modalities.

In contrast to the before mentioned human-centric definitions of *modality* Nigay and Coutaz [19, 20] define modality from a system-centred point of view as a compound of the communication channel and *device* on the one hand and the manner of perception and expression i.e. the *interaction language* on the other hand.

This article claims, similar to the definitions by Bernsen [18] and Nigay and Coutaz [19, 20], that the term *modality* comprises both *sensory* (interaction channel) and *semiotic* (interaction language) aspects.

1.2   Process Model of Man-Machine Interaction

The process model of man-machine interaction [15, p. 1 ff.] distinguishes the processes of *control* and *perception*. The perception process consists of *human input channels* (HIC) and *computer output media* (COM). The control process comprises *human output channels* (HOC) and *computer input modalities* (CIM).

In addition to this extrinsic loop of the information flow, the process model contains a loop of intrinsic feedback, which is needed e.g. for eye-hand coordination (or cursor-mouse-coordination). This back-channel plays an important role for the enactive nature [21] of direct manipulation interfaces, where users can try out actions and receive immediate feedback [22, p. 234]. But also speech communication requires such a feedback loop: According to the *speech-chain model* [23], people have problems to talk fluently without receiving acoustic feedback of their own voice.

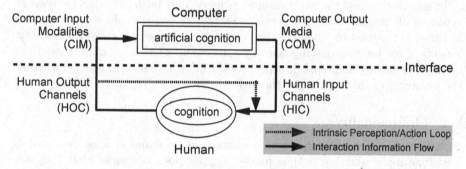

Fig. 1. Process Model of Man-Machine Interaction by Schomaker et al. [15, p. 2]

This process model allows to view modalities both from a system-centred view (as input and output modalities) and from a human-centred view (as perception and action modalities)

1.3   Modality, Mode, Medium, Channel

To avoid confusion, this work distinguishes the notions *mode* and *modality*, although they are used in some texts as synonyms. In general, *mode* is used for a system state, where user operations may have context-specific consequences, or where only specific user operations are enabled. That is, the mode determines how user actions and information input by the user are interpreted by the system [19].

The unix editor *vi* can be essentially in one of two modes (not modalities), the *edit* mode or the *command* mode. A key press has very different consequences depending on in which mode you are.

Graphical user interfaces know *modal* dialogs, where all actions except the dialog actions are blocked until the user answers this dialog.

Speech dialog systems are modal in this sense, too, since they usually restrict the speech recognition vocabulary that is active at the time to a context-specific subset.

According to Raskin [24] these modes may lead to confusion because the user might miss that the system changed or remained in a mode different from what she expects. Thus, in many cases, mode-less interaction should be preferred to modal interaction.

The notion *medium* is ambiguous, too. Bernsen [18] defines medium as "physical realisation of some presentation of information". This corresponds to the notion of *perception medium* [25, p. 10 ff.]. Multimedia technology [cf. 25, p. 10 ff.] distinguishes further between *representation media* (i. e. data formats such as text, images, audio, video), *presentation media* (input and output devices), *storage media* (paper, hard discs, DVD-ROM, etc.), *transmission media* (wire, air, water etc.) and *information exchange media* (union of storage media and transmission media).

In similar contexts the word channel is used. This term is frequently used as synonym of *transmission medium, information exchange medium* or *perception medium*. In contrast to *modality*, the notion channel does not cover the semiotic aspects of the interaction language. This article uses the word *channel* to focus on the articulatory and sensoric aspects of the information exchange, i.e. whether the auditory, visual, haptic etc. channels are used.

1.4   Multimodality

Although each form of man-machine interaction combines at least two modalities (one input and one output modality), this does not mean that they are multimodal: command languages, graphical menus, spoken dialog systems etc. are usually considered as unimodal interaction styles. According to Bouchet et al. [26, p. 37] multimodality means that there are at least two modalities either at the input or at the output side of the system [cf. also 15, p. 6 f.]. In contrast to multimedia systems, which record and play back multimedia content, multimodal systems interpret input coming from various modalities as user commands and generate multimodal output for interaction feedback.

2   Steps to Identify User Interface Patterns

The pattern collection presented here is based on a thorough literature review of multimodal interaction in industrial and research projects. The process of pattern identification consisted of both top-down and bottom-up aspects. The following questions helped to find an adequate categorisation of question-solution pairs and provided thus a basis for pattern mining [cf. 27, 28]:

- Top-down aspects:
    - When should certain interaction modalities (speech input or pointing input, speech output or graphic output) be used?
    - How can modalities be selected to fit best to the context of use (user, environment, or situation)?
    - How should multiple interaction modalities (speech and pointing, speech and graphics etc.) be combined?
- Bottom-up aspects:
    - In which concrete interaction scenarios is multimodal interaction being applied?

The top-down aspects provided a means of structuring and categorising the patterns, whereas the bottom-up aspects helped to find patterns from concrete usage scenarios.

2.1 Modality Selection Rules

For selecting appropriate interaction modalities, the designer can resort to existing work such as *modality theory* and *modality properties* [29], which cover roughly following aspects [29]:

- Interaction Channel:
  Spoken language is transmitted acoustically whereas written text is transmitted visually.
- Saliency:
  Auditory signals attract the user's attention more effectively than visual signals.
- Directedness:
  Visual signals are perceived only, when the user's visual attention is directed to the display area.
- User Control:
  The pace of spoken language output is controlled by the computer. When presenting visual text instead, the user can read and process it at his own pace.
- Learning Efforts:
  Arbitrary modalities, i.e. interaction languages that are based on domain or application specific conventions require more learning effort than the ones that are based on well known concepts.
- Expressiveness:
  Analoguous modalities such as graphic pictures are especially suited for transmitting spatial information whereas linguistic modalities such as text are more suited for presenting conceptual information such as numbers, facts, concrete instructions etc. in a more abstract way.

Using these modality properties, concrete rules for modality selection according to task properties can be formulated.

2.2 Modality Selection Based on Interaction Constraints: Accessibility and Adaptation

An important issue for the design of user interfaces, web sites and consumer products is accessibility or universal design [30, 31, 32, 33, 34], i.e. to make them accessible to people with disabilities.

A notable amount of research on multimodal interaction is devoted to this [35]. Examples are speech interaction for blind people [36, 37], special design requirements for elderly users [38, 39], multimodal feedback for elderly people [40], especially for visually impaired users [41, 42, 43, 44], speech-based [45] or haptic [46] interaction for motor impaired people.

In addition to disabilities, an important challenge for the development of modern products and user interfaces is to build systems that can be used by different users, in different environments, situations and with different devices. Obrenović et al. [7, p. 86] sketch a metamodel of accessibility and distinguish between *device constraints*, *environmental constraints*, *user constraints* and *social constraints* that affect human computer interaction. Noisy environments, deaf users, bad microphones etc. complicate the application of auditory output and speech input. In crowded environments, bystanders might feel annoyed by people talking with an interactive system. Blind users, mobile users, environments with bad lighting etc. impede the use of graphical and pointing-based interaction.

While an adaptation to the current context of use could be done by the user via switching the interaction style or system configuration, a notable amount of research is devoted to so-called *plastic user interfaces* [47, 48, 49], i.e. user interfaces that adapt themselves to a new platforms, users, environments etc. "while retaining usability" [50].

Such adaptive multimodal systems require an appropriate architecture. The Arch-Model [51, 52] and other multi-tier architecture models [53, p. 14 ff.] provide means to separate the abstract dialogue state and the current user interface components.

In addition to this multi-layered architecture, a so-called adaptation module is required, which analyses the context of use (logged in user, device identification, sensor data) and adapts the interaction according to the respective user, platform and environment models [48, 49, 54, 4].

The aspects of user-initiated and system-driven adaptation are reflected in the patterns *Multiple Ways of Input*, *Context Adaptation* and *Global Channel Configuration*.

2.3 Modality Combination

Modalities are combined in order to minimse task interferences, to maximise interaction speed, to maximise input robustness, to optimise saliency of output information, to assure communication across channel limitations and to provide "natural interactivity" [1]. Following paragraphs will outline this in more detail.

Minimising Task Interference. According to the *multiple resource theory* [55, 56] each perception and action modality are assigned separate cognitive resources. Double-task experiments revealed that an appropriate partitioning of parallel tasks to different modalities can reduce task interferences. This fact is being exploited for driver assistance systems [57, 58, 59, 60, 61] and applications for the mobile industrial worker [6].

Maximising Interaction Speed. If it is true that different modalities are assigned separate cognitive resources, the multimodal presentation (visual images and audio text) of output can increase the amount of information presented to the user effectively in a fixed amount of time. This has been shown in experiments on multimedia learning [62].

At the same time, information input rates can be improved if the user is able to select and combine different modalities such as pointing and speaking in a way that best fits the data to be conveyed to the system [cf. 63].

Mutual Disambiguation of Input Information. When identical information is transmitted via several distorted channels, the recovery chances are higher than if only one channel is used. Audiovisual speech recognisers combine the analysis of the acoustic speech signal with the analysis of visual data representing the lip forms [13, 64]. This way, speech recognition in loud environments becomes more robust. Other modality combinations such as voice and face recognition for identification are subject of research, too [65, 66]. This is the central idea of the multimodal pattern *Redundant Input.*

Optimising the Saliency of Output Information. Important and urgent information is more likely to be perceived by the user when several channels are used. Reaction times can be reduced by about 30% when redundant (visual, acoustic, haptic) signals are used [67]. This fact is the motivation of Tidwell's user interface pattern *Important Message* [11].

Assuring Interaction across Channel Restrictions. When it is not clear from the beginning, which interaction channels are likely to work (because of background noise, lighting conditions, deaf or visually impaired users), channel redundancies should be used, to maximise the probability, that the information is being perceived by the user.

In this context, research on multimodal text output for elderly and visually impaired people is to be mentioned [41, 42, 43, 44].

It has been proven that, especially in noisy environments, persons understand spoken language better when they can look at the face of their interlocutor [68, 69, 70, 71, 72]. Talking heads and embodied conversational agents in systems such as PPP [73], NUMACK [74], COMIC [75], SmartKom ["Smartakus" 76] consider this and display animated lip movements while they play back spoken language.

These aspects – maximising the probability that a user perceives and understands the information conveyed by the system – are covered by the pattern *Redundant Output.* In fact, this pattern is a generalisation of Tidwell's pattern *Important Message* [11], which focuses on the maximisation of saliency.

Achieving Natural Interactivity. A lot of research on multimodal interaction is motivated by the vision of *natural interactivity*. The system is designed to simulate "perceptive" and "expressive abilities" similar to those of human beings. This way, the user can interact with the system in a similar way as with a human. There is no need to input information that the system can derive from verbal and non-verbal user actions [77].

In this context, research on affective computing needs to be mentioned, which addresses human emotion understanding and expression [cf. 78, 79, 80, 81]. According to empirical studies human emotions can be determined most reliably from facial expressions and gestures [82, 81]. Lisetti and Nasoz [83, p. 163] present an overview over the research and list the following approaches:

- recognition of facial expressions [84, 85, 86, 87, 88]
- analysis of prosodic signals [89, 90, 91]
- analysis of touch (pressure, dither, skin moisture) and biosignals [92, 93, 94, 95, 96, 97]
- analysis of the language content (syntax, formulations) [98]

In human-computer interaction emotional cues are used to detect frustration and interaction failure and appropriately react upon them [cf. 99].

To increase the robustness of emotion detection, recent research combines several emotional cues [83], such as facial expressions and prosody [100, 101], facial and body gestures [102], prosody and gesture recognition [103] or gaze direction in combination with other emotional cues [cf. 104]. This are further examples for the pattern *Redundant Input*.

In addition to the recognition of emotion, there is a significant amount of research on the simulation of an emotional system. Embodied conversational agents, *talking heads* [cf. Smartakus – 76] etc. which represent human-like agents may play an important role for future e-commerce applications [105].

2.4   Pertinent Multimodal Interaction Scenarios

Patterns are based on recurring solutions. In contrast to prescriptive templates and design rules, patterns are rather descriptive – they describe, how a solution has been solved several times successfully. Thus, it is not sufficient to derive design rules from theoretical considerations. Patterns should be rather identified in pertinent interaction scenarios. Typical cases where multimodal interaction is applied cover dual-task and map-based scenarios, graphic design applications, and mobile systems.

This section discusses which existing user interface patterns – i.e. those that are not primarily related to multimodal interaction but come rather from a GUI context – can be applied in these interaction scenarios and how multimodality may help to simplify interaction. Multimodal interaction techniques which recur in several projects are identified as new multimodal user interface patterns. Previously published (mostly GUI-centred) user interface patterns that are mentioned in the following discussions are shortly outlined in section 7.

Double-Task Scenarios. Applications for the mobile industrial worker (view [6] for some examples) as well as driver assistance systems such as MoTiV-MMI [57], CarMMI [58], SIMBA-IABA [59, 60] and in-car infotainment systems such as SAMMIE [61] deal with situations, where the user's hands are involved in other tasks (the primary task) than the one supported by the interactive device (the secondary task).

In this case, system output has to be organised in a task-appropriate way. Whereas important and urgent notifications (probably necessary to avoid accidents) have to attract the user's attention, status information should not disrupt the user during his work. In the first case Tidwell's pattern *Important Message* [11] can be used. This pattern combines several output channels to attract the user's attention. It is a specialisation of the more general multimodal pattern *Redundant Output*, which combines several output channels in order to maximise the probability that the user perceives and is able to understand the information to be conveyed. In the second case, Tidwell's GUI pattern *Status Display* [11] is used, which displays static status information at a consistent place without disrupting the user.

Map-Based Tasks. Map-based systems are one of the most wide-spread interaction scenarios in the research on multimodal interaction. Systems like CUBRI-CON [106], QuickSet [107], SmartKom mobile [108], MATCH [109, 110] and MUST [111] are well-known examples.

These systems allow the user to combine mouse-based, pen-based or touch-screen gestures with spoken input such as "zoom in here", "fix this region", or "show cheap italian restaurants in this neighbourhood". This interaction style can be found in almost all of the above mentioned projects. That is, why it is identified as a multimodal user interface pattern which is called *Gesture-enhanced Speech Command*.

Graphic Design Applications

GUI Patterns for Graphic Editors

Graphic applications allow the user to edit pictures using various tools. These applications are built using the pattern *Canvas plus Palette* [12]. This means, that the user can select the desired tool from a toolbar (the palette) and apply this tool to the graphic elements displayed on the canvas.

As the selection of palette tools usually changes the mode, i.e. the behaviour, of the application, they are used in combination with the pattern *Mode Cursor* [10]: That means, that a meaningful icon is used as mouse cursor to make the mode of the system (the selected tool) evident to the user. This helps the user to predict system behaviour and the implications of his own input actions.

Systems based on *Canvas plus Palette* force the user to move the mouse cursor between canvas and toolbar forth and back which may slow down interaction. This can be circumvented by the pattern *Helping Hands* [112]: The user uses one hand to input keyboard shortcuts for tool selection, and the other hand to perform drawing and manipulation actions.

With a growing number of commands, this approach reaches its limits. Not every command and tool can be mapped onto an meaningful and unambiguous key code. Consequently, some shortcut keys are too cryptic to be remembered by the user or too complex for one-handed input.

The pattern *Contextual Menu* [10] can help to reduce the need of mouse movements for command input. However, context menus can mask parts of the working surface while still requiring tedious mouse movements.

Multimodal Patterns for Graphic Editing

Multimodal design applications such as VoicePaint [113], S-tgif [114], or Speak'n'Sketch [115] make use of spoken commands. Speech input avoids repeated mouse movements and is more convenient than keyboard shortcuts. This approach to enrich the pattern *Canvas plus Palette* with spoken interaction is called in this paper *Speech-enabled Palette*.

Speech recognition should only be active, as long as (or during a short time window after) the user holds down for instance the right mouse button or the context menu key of the keyboard. This way, false positive recognition errors caused by background noise can be avoided. This is an application of the Tidwell's pattern *Spring-loaded Mode* (or *One-off Mode*) [12] to multimodal interaction.

Other graphic applications, such as those for mobile and tablet-based systems use pen or touch screen input and do not display a tool palette because of place restrictions. Furthermore, pen- or touch-based input implies that no mouse cursor and hence no *Mode Cursor* is displayed. Hence, the user would not know whether e.g. the rectangle or the polygon tool is selected. To circumvent problems like this, these systems apply a different, sketch-based paradigm [116, 117]: The user inputs raw sketches, which are transformed by a recogniser into geometrical primitives. To give the recogniser more information – e.g. to make clear that the sketch should be transformed into a square, the user can input embellishing commands.

Systems such as TAPAGE [118], QuickSet [107] or DPD [119] allow the user to combine pen-based sketches with speech-based embellishing commands using the pattern *Gesture-enhanced Speech Command*.

TAPAGE [118] and QuickSet [107] support special editing gestures such as crossing out for deleting an object. These editing gestures combine two information sources: the location of the gesture (i.e. the object on the surface the gesture is referred to) and the form of the gesture (the command such as delete). This interface pattern is called in this paper *Location-sensitive Gesture*.

Mobile Systems. Multimodal mobile systems comprise personal assistants for email and web access such as MiPad [120, 121, 122] and Personal Speech Assistant [123], tourist guides and city information systems such as SmartKom mobile [108], MATCH [109, 110], MUST [111] and COMPASS [124].

Up-to-date *smartphones* use frequently speech commands – that is the pattern *Voice-based Interaction Shortcut* – to circumvent the deep menu navigation imposed by place limitations. Simple speech commands can be used to start programs, place telephone calls etc.

Voice-Based Interaction Shortcut for Starting Programs

The pattern *Hub and Spoke* [12] is one way to start applications on mobile systems with limited screen space: Each one of the most important applications is easily reachable from the main page. When an application is closed, the system returns to this main page. This way, orientation may be preserved despite place restrictions.

In addition, some mobile devices offer so-called *quick launch buttons* that allow the user to start the four/five most important applications when pushed.

As an alternative, speech input, i.e. the pattern *Voice-based Interaction Short-cut* can be used. This pattern allows the user to start the desired application whithout the need that the current screen is displaying a direct link to it. Deep menu navigation and scrolling in long lists can be avoided.

Voice-Based Interaction Shortcut for List Selection

The selection of elements from very large lists can be simplified when the pattern *Continuous Filter* [10] is applied. While the user is inputting some characters, the systems filters the selection list. When the size of the list is reduced to a size that fits onto the screen, the user can continue with pointing-based list selection.

As an alternative, the pattern *Voice-based Interaction Shortcut* can be used. Instead of scrolling through lists or to operate a tiny on-screen keyboard for filtering the list, the user can speak the name of the desired list element.

Input of Structured Text

GUI Patterns. The input of text can be simplified by applying the pattern *Autocompletion* [12]. The user has to enter simply some letters until the system proposes a list that contains the desired element.

In some cases such as web forms or e-mail messages, structured text has to be input. Such applications usually apply the pattern *Form* [11]: The user selects an input field and types the text subsequently. Text input can be alleviated using the pattern *Autocompletion* [12], as mentioned above. Some input fields can be combined with *Dropdown Choosers* [12] to allow list selection in addition to text input.

Multimodal Patterns. These *Dropdown Choosers*, but also ordinary text fields, can be combined with the pattern *Voice-based Interaction Shortcut*. A combination of *Forms* [11] with *Voice-based Interaction Shortcut* results in the multimodal pattern *Speech-enabled Form*.

Speech-enabled Form is used by the multimodal organiser MiPad [120, 121, 122]. This system allows the user to create email messages by combining pen gestures with speech input: When the user activates the receiver field, a recognition vocabulary consisting of address book entries is selected and activated. When the text field for the subject or the message is selected, an unconstrained vocabulary is activated.

When the size of the active vocabulary increases, speech recognition works less and less reliable. When using this pattern, only a context specific vocabulary needs to be activated at the time (i.e. when the receiver field is selected, only the receiver vocabulary is activated etc.). This helps to avoid speech recognition errors.

The speech recogniser is activated only, when the user is tapping onto the respective entry field. This is important, because speech recognition should not be active all the time. Otherwise, especially during free text input, background noise might be interpreted as input. This problem can be avoided when the recogniser is activated after the user has tapped onto the form field and deactivated after user input or after a certain amount of time. In this case, the pattern *Speech-enabled Form* uses Tidwell's pattern *One-off Mode* [12].

Beyond MiPad and other mobile assistants, interaction techniques based on the pattern *Speech-enabled Form* are enforced by implementation techniques present in XHTML+VoiceXML [125, 126].

Error Handling and Avoidance. Mobile messaging systems such as *Chatter* [127] and driver assistance systems such as CarMMI [58] have to deal with large and partially problematic speech recognition vocabularies.

After recognition errors, these systems allow the user not only to re-speak the misrecognised word. Instead, the user is given the possibility to select from a list of the *n* best recognition hypotheses, since the correctly recognised word might have been classified as the second or third most probable hypothesis. This selection can be done via pointing gestures, naming the row number or re-speaking the item plus some additional features such as "London with L O". This change of the input technique helps to avoid endless loops of error correction caused by acoustic similarity.

This pattern is called *Multimodal N-best Selection*. The n-best list can be displayed using a *Dropdown Chooser* [12].

In addition, these systems allow the user to type or dictate the first letters. This way, similar to the pattern *Continuous Filter* [10], the selection list is filtered so that the speech recognition vocabulary can be reduced. With this smaller vocabulary, the speech recogniser works more reliably. The resulting pattern *Spelling-based Hypothesis Reduction* is thus a combination of *Continuous Filter* and *Voice-based Interaction Shortcut*. Both *Multimodal N-best Selection* and *Spelling-based Hypothesis Reduction* are special cases of the generalised pattern *Redundant Input*.

3   Pattern Overview

This article focuses on user interface patterns for fast, robust, and flexible multimodal interaction. Three pattern groupings are presented. The first one, *Fast Input*, focuses on the potential of multimodal interaction to accelerate user input. By giving the user the possibility to input information using task-appropriate modalities, the interaction speed can be maximised. *Voice-based Interaction Shortcut* enables the user to simply utter a speech command instead of navigating through menus, scrolling through lists etc. For the input of structured

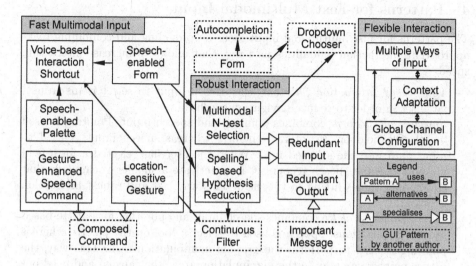

Fig. 2. Pattern Map

text, the pattern *Speech-enabled Form* ist presented. The pattern *Speech-enabled Palette* accelerates tool selection in typical graphic applications. Furthermore, the pattens *Gesture-enhanced Speech Command* and *Location-sensitive Gesture* are used for more convenient input of composed commands.

The second pattern grouping *Robust Interaction* focuses on avoiding and handling recognition errors as well as assuring communication between user and system. It contains the two generic patterns *Redundant Input* and *Redundant Output*. Tidwell's pattern *Important Message* [11, view section 7 in this paper] can be seen as a specific case of *Redundant Output*. The patterns *Multimodal N-best Selection* and *Spelling-based Hypothesis Reduction* are specialisations of the pattern *Redundant Input*. They can be used in connection with the pattern *Speech-enabled Form*, a specialisation of the pattern *Form* [11] which can be itself combined with the patterns *Dropdown Chooser* and *Autocompletion* [12]. The patterns *Dropdown Chooser* [12] and *Continuous Filter* [10] are used to implement *Multimodal N-best Selection* and *Spelling-based Hypothesis Reduction* respectively.

The third grouping, *Flexible Interaction,* focuses on accessibility and cross-context usability. The abstract principle lying behind these patterns is giving the user the possibility to select appropriate interaction modalities according to context factors. In order to achieve this goal, this pattern group has to make use of suitable adaptation strategies which are described in the patterns *Multiple Ways of Input, Context Adaptation* and *Global Channel Configuration.*

A short outline of patterns referenced in this paper but described elsewhere can be found in section 7.

4   Patterns for Fast Multimodal Input

The patterns for fast multimodal input focus on providing and combining task-appropriate interaction modalities in a way that allows to increase interaction speed.

- *Voice-based Interaction Shortcut* uses speech input to select items from a large set in order to reduce navigation overhead.
- *Speech-enabled Form* combines pointing and speech input. Pointing is used to select a field on an interaction form whereas speech input is used to input data into the selected field. When the user has selected a form field via pointing, the speech recogniser may activate a smaller vocabulary that covers only values fitting to this field. This way fast and robust interaction is possible.
- *Speech-enabled Palette* combines speech input and pointing for palette-based graphic applications. Speech is used to select a tool on the palette whereas pointing is used to perform the graphic manipulation task. This way, the mouse pointer can stay in the manipulation area (the canvas) and need not be moved repeatedly to the palette and back.
- *Gesture-enhanced Speech Command* combines speech input with gestures or pointing actions. Speech input is used to specify the desired action (or query) along with some easy to pronounce parameters, whereas pointing is used to select the interaction object the action is to be performed on, as well as further parameters (such as the destination of a copying action). Although this pattern might be seen as a mere combination of *Voice-based Interaction Shortcut* with some pointing or gesturing actions, this pattern covers explicitly the combination of more complex speech and gesture commands and to build a multimodal command language.
- *Location-sensitive Gesture* combines drawn symbols (iconic gestures) with an implicit pointing action. Pointing is used to select an interaction object, the drawn symbol expresses an action that is to be performed on this object (such as a cross for deleting this object). Pointing is implicit in this case because the pointing location is deduced from the onset and offset location of the drawing action.

4.1   Voice-Based Interaction Shortcut

Context. The user has to select items from a large set. Consider selecting an action from a menu or selecting a list item from a drop-down chooser. In this case, this pattern is frequently used as an enhancement of *Contextual Menu* [10] or *Dropdown Chooser* [12].

Either the number of choices is quite large or screen size is scarce such that the items cannot be displayed all at once.

The interaction device is supporting speech input.

Problem. Which interaction style allows the user to quickly select the desired item without having to perform tedious navigation and scrolling actions?

Forces

- Selection via pointing requires almost no learning effort. But if the selection options are numerous and cannot be presented simultaneously on screen they have to be arranged into scrolling lists or hierarchical menu structures. Menu navigation and list scrolling may slow the user down.
- Shortcut keys are a valid alternative for menu/command selection. However, it is difficult to assign shortcut characters that are easy to remember to a wide range of commands or menu options. Thus, some shortcut keys seem arbitrary and require a certain learning effort.
- Typing meaningful words is easier to learn than shortcut or function keys. The users even might not need to type the whole word, because the list can be pre-filtered on the first few characters. However, typing is not always appropriate: Not all users are skilled typers. Typing with mobile devices is very awkward and slow and thus inappropriate for accelerating interaction.

Solution. Design the system to support speech input to speed up interaction. The user should be able to select the desired action or data object by naming it. Especially frequent users to whom the commands, options, parameters and item names are well known can profit from speech input.

When there are more than one appropriate alternative wording for the desired action, the designer should check which synonyms should be included into the speech recognition grammar. User tests, including tests with simulated speech functionality[1] might be useful to elicit familiar wordings for some system functionality.

Even when the designer has elicited familiar wordings, it is not guaranteed that especially first time and occasional users are able to anticipate them, too.

For this, menus and lists should not disappear from the system. *Voice-based Interaction Shortcut* should instead coexist with these and be one of *Multiple Ways of Input*. The wordings used in the visual menus and drop-down lists should be identical to the respective speech commands such that the user's learning efforts can be reduced to a minimum.

After the user has uttered a speech command the system should update the visual display in the same way as it would do after menu or list selection. In addition, it might be appropriate to provide spoken system feedback, as it cannot be taken for sure that the user is looking at the screen when using speech. In this case the system adapts its output strategy according to the user behaviour (cf. the pattern *Context Adaptation*).

Speech recognisers return recognition results based on statistical calculations. Sometimes the actual user utterance does not match the best estimate by the recogniser but one among the five or ten best hypotheses. The pattern *Mutimodal N-best Selection* handles these cases by displaying the n-best list. The user can select from this (smaller) list via pointing.

---

[1] cf. Wizard of Oz tests: A human agent, the *wizard*, simulates the user interface functionality [128, 129, 130, 131].

With problematic (very large) sets of options, speech recognition is likely to fail. Using the pattern *Spelling-based Hypothesis Reduction* might help: When the user inputs a few letters, the list can be filtered and reduced. It might still be too large for being displayed as a whole in a selection list, but the speech recognition vocabulary could be now small enough for reliable speech recognition.

To avoid that background noise or private speech is interpreted as input, a push-to-talk button might be needed. This way, speech input is activated only while the user is holding down the button (cf. Tidwell's pattern *Spring-loaded Mode* [12]) or during a certain time window after (cf. Tidwell's pattern *One-off Mode*). When *Voice-based Interaction Shortcut* is used in combination with *Context Menu* [10], the right mouse button or the context menu key of the keyboard can serve as push-to-talk button.

Consequences

- Screen clutter and the need of menu navigation can be minimised by enabling speech input.
- There is no more need for the user to remember arbitrary action-key-mappings or to obey to strict menu hierarchies.
- Typing can be reduced to a minimum.
- If the selection set is large, speech recognition performance may deteriorate, especially when there are similar sounding words. Even worse: some wordings might be ambiguous within the application context. If this cannot be avoided, the application has to provide clarification dialogs. In the worst case, all speed advantages might be lost.
- The users might actually not learn the exact wording of the items they probably would like to select in the future. That's why menus or dropdown selectors, which provide the visual context, should remain available as an alternative interaction strategy.

Rationale. Users prefer speech input to input descriptive data, or to select objects among large or invisible sets [132, 133]. This counts especially when the list is large and the users know exactly the wording of the item they want to select.

Known Uses. NoteBook is a multimodal notebook implemented on NeXT. The user can edit textual notes, and browse the created notes. Content editing is only supported via typing. Browsing, deleting and creating notes can be done via button clicks or voice input alternatively [19].

VoiceLauncher from Treoware enables speech input for Treos, Centro, and Tungsten/T3 devices [134].

Microsoft Voice Command can be used to enable speech input for Windows Mobile based smartphones (such as HP's iPAQ 514 [135]) Using this software extension, the user can bring up the calendar or contact details in one interaction step [136].

Related Patterns. This pattern can be used as an alternative or complement to van Welie's *Continuous Filter, Context Menu* [10], Tidwell's *Autocompletion, Dropdown Chooser, Hub and Spoke* etc. [12]. In the same way as *Dropdown Choosers* are used in *Forms* [11] *Voice-based Interaction Shortcuts* are used to implement *Speech-enabled Forms.*

To adapt the system feedback to the user behaviour, the pattern *Context Adaptation* might be used. In addition, *Voice-based Interaction Shortcut* should not be used as the only but as one of *Multiple Ways of Input.*

For error handling and avoidance this pattern can be combined with *Multimodal N-best Selection* and *Spelling-based Hypothesis Reduction.* To control recogniser activation either Tidwell's [12] pattern *Spring-loaded Mode* or *One-off Mode* can be used.

4.2   Speech-Enabled Form

Context. The user has to input structured data which can be mapped to some kind of *form* consisting of a set of atomic *fields.*

Devices such as PDAs do not provide a keyboard for comfortable string input.

In other situations the device may support keyboard input but the user has only one hand available for interacting with the system.

Problem. How to simplify string input in form filling applications, especially in mobile scenarios and with small devices, when there is no comfortable keyboard?

Forces

- Selecting areas in 2D-space is accomplished very comfortably with a pointing device but string input via pointing (with on-screen keyboards) is very awkward.
- Values for some form items (academic degree, nationality etc.) are restricted and can be input by using drop-down choosers (comboboxes). But this may lead to screen clutter and additional navigation and scrolling.
- Speech recognition is very comfortable for selecting invisible items but the input of unconstrained text suffers from recognition errors. Speech recognition works more reliably with smaller input vocabularies.

Solution. Let the user select the desired form field via pointing and dictate the content subsequently. The speech input vocabulary can be simplified. Only the vocabulary of the respective form field plus some generic commands need to be activated at the time and recognition errors can be avoided.

Whereever possible, determine acceptable values for each form field to reduce the input vocabulary to a context-specific subset. As alternative to speech input, support value selection via *Dropdown Choosers* and *Autocompletion.*

To avoid that the speech recogniser interprets background noise etc. as input, the speech recogniser should be activated only when the user is performing input.

One possibility is, to activate the speech recogniser only as long as the user is holding down the pen or mouse button over the desired form field (cf. the pattern *Spring-loaded Mode* [12]). Another approach is to activate the recogniser during a certain time window after the user has selected the form field (cf. the pattern *One-off Mode* [12].

Consequences

- The user can combine pointing input via pen, touch-screen or mouse (for selecting an input field) and speech input to fill in this form field. Text input via on-screen keyboards can be avoided.
- Navigation and scrolling in drop-down lists can be avoided.
- Constraining the speech recognition vocabulary to context-specific data for the selected input field helps to avoid speech recognition errors.
- Speech recognition errors might occur anyway. In case of poor recognition performance, all speed advantages might be lost due to the need of error handling.

Rationale. Users prefer speech input to input descriptive data, or to select objects among large or invisible sets [137, 132, 133].

According to Oviatt et al. [138], a structured (form-like) presentation of the interface reduces speech utterance length and the amount of information input per utterance. Thus, the variability of user utterances is reduced, which helps to make speech recognition more robust.

Known Uses. Mobile Systems such as Microsoft's MiPad [120, 121, 122] and IBM's Personal Speech Assistant [123] are good examples.

In MiPad the user can create e-mail messages via *Tap And Talk* [121]. When the user selects the receiver field the speech recognition vocabulary is constrained to address book entries. If the user selects the subject or message field an unconstrained vocabulary is activated so that the user can input unconstrained text.

The multimodal facilities offered by X+V (XHTML and VoiceXML) and supported by the Opera Browser are heavily focused on this *Speech-enabled Form* paradigm [125, 126, 139, 140].

Related Patterns. This pattern is a multimodal extension of *Form* [11] and the speech-based *Form Filling* [141, 142]. It is implemented using the pattern *Voice-based Interaction Shortcut* in the same way as *Forms* are implemented using patterns such as *Dropdown Chooser* and *Autocompletion*.

Tidwell's [12] patterns *Spring-loaded Mode* and *One-off Mode* can be used to control recogniser activation. For error handling, consider to use *Multimodal N-Best-Selection* and *Spelling-based Hypothesis Reduction*.

4.3   Speech-Enabled Palette

Context. Direct manipulation with graphic applications allows the user to edit visually presented objects directly. In order to manipulate these objects the user has to select sometimes special tools. In this context, the patterns *Canvas plus Palette* [12], *Contextual Menu* [10] and *Mode Cursor* [10] are used.

This means that the user has to move the mouse out of the manipulation area (the canvas) in order to select the desired tool from the palette and then reenter the manipulation area in order to proceed the manipulation action. This might be very annoying, especially in drawing applications.

Problem. How to enable the user to select tools from the palette without having to deplace the mouse between canvas and palette or the hand between mouse and keyboard?

Forces

- Both graphic manipulation tasks and selecting tools from a palette are accomplished very comfortably via pointing. But performing both subtasks alternately several times as is needed in design applications is very annoying and time-consuming.
- Using context menus which are opened on right clicks may reduce but not avoid totally lengthy cursor movements. Additionally the context menu (unless transparent) obscures the main manipulation area.
- Using the keyboard instead of the mouse for selecting commands may solve this problem in some cases. However, there might arise a new one: The user has to change his right hand between mouse and keyboard which is time-consuming as well.
- Another solution would be to assign graphic manipulation tasks to the right hand, which controls the mouse, and action/menu selection tasks to the left hand, which remains on the keyboard and presses shortcut keys to select the necessary tools.[2] But the user would have to remember awkward key mappings and possibly to look down to the keyboard to find the desired key.

Solution. Allow the user to select tools using speech input. The palette itself should remain visible and allow the user to explore the interface. Each tool on the palette should have a meaningful name which is made obvious to the user e.g. via tooltip hints. These tool names should be used for the respective speech commands to reduce the learning effort for the user.

To control recogniser activation, Tidwell's [12] patterns *Spring-loaded Mode* or *One-off Mode* might be needed: Speech recognition should be activated only after the user has pressed or while the user holds down e.g. the right mouse button. This way, the system is prevented from interpreting background noise as speech input.

---

[2] This kind of solution is proposed in Welie's pattern *Helping Hands*.

Consequences

- The user can select the desired tool via voice input without the need to replace the mouse cursor between tool palette and manipulation area.
- The screen and especially the main manipulation area is not obscured by popup windows or menus.
- The right hand can stay on the mouse and need not be replaced between keyboard and mouse.
- There is no need to remember awkward key mappings or to look down to the keyboard.
- As users are able to use the motor and vocal channels simultaneously, combining spoken commands and pointing speeds up interaction significantly.
- Speech recognition errors might occur. In case of poor recognition performance, some speed advantages might be lost due to the need of error handling.

Rationale. Studies conducted by Ren et al. [143] have revealed that the combination of pointing devices such as pen or mouse with speech input is fruitful in both CAD systems and map-based interfaces. This way, interaction performance can be increased.

Positive results were also found in experiments with S-tgif [114]. This graphic design application offers the user keyboard and voice shortcuts for system commands as alternatives to pointing gestures.

Known Uses. Graphic applications such as VoicePaint [113], S-tgif [114] and Speak'n'Sketch [115] are examples of systems which allow the user to select a tool from the palette via speech without removing the mouse cursor from the graphics manipulation area.

Related Patterns. This pattern makes use of *Canvas plus Palette* [12], *Mode Cursor* [10] and *Voice-based Interaction Shortcut*.

To control recogniser activation, Tiwell's [12] pattern *Spring-loaded Mode* or *One-off Mode* can be used.

This pattern is an alternative to van Welie's *Helping Hands* [144].

4.4   Gesture-Enhanced Speech Command

Context. Some applications require the input of composed commands consisting of several parameters.

Consider copying one object to another location which consists of inputting *the command*, *the object to be selected* and *the destination*.

Consider setting up an email message: Input *the command*, input *receivers of the message*.

Consider searching a location in a map-based application: Input *the command*, input *area constraints* (square C 5), input *keywords* (italian restaurants).

Problem. How to enable the user to quickly input composed commands consisting of several parameters of different data types (spatial, conceptual, numerical data)?

Forces

- Complex commands can be input efficiently via typed or spoken command languages. But consindering some parameters such as file names, directory locations, positions on a city map, users rather remember where these are than how these are named internally. This might lead to typing errors. When speech interaction is used, users might not know how to pronounce these (partly cryptical) filenames or they would pronounce them in a way that cannot be handled by the speech recogniser.
- Inputting spatial parameters or selecting objects displayed on the screen is most easily done via pointing. But inputting actions or textual parameters would lead to one or more additional interaction steps (button clicks, navigation in menus, scrolling through drop-down lists) or screen clutter.
- Early systems[3] combined pointing gestures with typed natural language input. This way, the user was able to select objects directly via pointing and input commands and queries with the keyboard. However, the user has to move his hands repeatedly between keyboard and pointing devices which slows down interaction.

Solution. Let the user interact via spoken language and provide pointing gestures to specify locations or interactive objects. Consider folllowing cases:

- The user selects a file, says "copy this file there" and selects the target location.
- The user draws a rectangle onto a map and says "are there any supermarkets?"
- The user clicks the button *create mail* and says "to Margret Smith".

At a first glance, this seems to be simply an application of the pattern *Voice-based Interaction Shortcut*. But in the case of *Gesture-enhanced Speech Command* the single interaction steps are seen in the context of a multimodal command language: Appropriate gestures and speech commands – which themselves might already consist of several parts – are combined into composed commands.

This requires the application of multimodal recognition technology and grammar formats for defining multimodal command languages such as MM-DCG [149] and prototyoing frameworks [150, 151, 152] as well as data collection and training frameworks for multimodal recognisers [153].

First time users need a way to explore the interface. That's why *Gesture-enhanced Speech Command* should not be a replacement for alternative interaction styles such as direct manipulation but rather be intergrated into them.

---

[3] cf. Shoptalk [145, 146] and XTRA [147, 148].

Consequences

- Commands and textual data can be input as text.
- Parameters such as file or directory names, locations on a map etc. can be input directly via pointing. There is no need to invent and remember cryptic names.
- Typing and recognition errors can be reduced as pointing replaces the input of the information parts that are hard to formulate as text.
- The user is able to utter simultaneously spoken language queries and pointing gestures: This way, inputting spatial parameters and selecting objects can be done using pointing devices. At the same time, the input of textual data can be done via spoken language. The user need not change his hands between different input devices.
- Screen clutter, i.e. the need of drop-down menus and popup dialogs which would obscure the potentially scarse screen space can be minimised when combining pointing with spoken natural language input. There is no need of additional buttons, dropdown menus, popup dialogs.
- Even if user input can be accelerated this way, recognition errors might compromise this advantage. Clarification and error handling dialogs have to be designed with care. This is especially true when "natural" speech input is supported. The system should find a stable way of error handling without discouraging the user to make use of efficient interaction styles in future.

Rationale. Users prefer speech input to input descriptive data. Pointing devices are preferred for inputting spacial or sketch-based data [132, 133].

Combining direct manipulation with written natural language was shown to be plausible for some tasks [146, 154, 155]. A comparison of direct manipulation and the multimodal pen- and speech-based interface of QuickSet revealed multimodal interaction to be faster [63].

Known Uses. This is one of the patterns found in the first multimodal systems. Bolt [156] describes a voice- and gesture-based interface which combines pointing with natural language. The title of Bolt's article outlines this pictorially: "Put that there".

HOME [157] provides a multimodal interface for home appliances, which takes into account special needs of elderly and disabled users and attempts to provide more natural communication consisting of speech and free gestures. The user can interact by using the touch screen, free gestures and spoken language. These input modalities can be combined:

```
  User: Switch the light on.
System: Which light?
  User: This lamp? <points to the lamp>
System: <switches the lamp on>
```

The map-based system GEORAL allows the user to input spoken multi-token natural language utterances while pointing to the relevant position on the map [158]. The user can select a place or an area (by pointing to a single point or encircling a zone) while asking questions such as *Are there any beaches in this locality?*, *Where are the campsites?* or *Show me the castles in this zone.*

Further examples are CUBRICON [145], QuickSet [107], MVIEWS [159], MATCH [110, 109], SmartKom [160, 161], ARCHIVUS [162], COMPASS2008 [124], RASA [163] and DAVE_G [164].

Related Patterns. This pattern is together with *Location-sensitive Gesture* a specialisation of *Composed Command* [11].

There are similarities to *Voice-based Interaction Shortcut* but *Gesture-enhanced Speech Command* explicitly supports the semantic integration of gestures and speech. Furthermore *Gesture-enhanced Speech Command* combines speech commands and gestures that might themselves be already composed of several parts.

4.5 Location-Sensitive Gesture

Context. Some devices support pointing actions being performed with so-called *direct pointing devices* such as graphic tablets and pens.

There is no keyboard available or the user has only one hand free for interaction and this hand controls the pointing device.

Speech input is not supported or not appropriate due to context factors.

Problem. How to enable the user to input easily and quickly standard commands (such as deleting, moving etc.) consisting of selecting items and performing actions on them?

Forces

- Commands can be input efficiently textually or via speech. Command parameters such as the selected files can be mapped onto text, too. But when neither keyboard nor speech input is available annoying on-screen keyboards have to be used.
- Selecting areas or objects displayed on the screen can be done easily via pointing. Inputting commands via pointing is possible, too. But this would lead to at least one additional interaction step (clicking on buttons, navigating through menus, scrolling etc.) and to cluttered screens.

Solution. Let the user interact with the system as he would do with paper: draw meaningful symbols / pen gestures onto the object of interest – encircle items or cross them out, draw arrows and the like. A pattern recogniser transforms the gesture into a command. Onset and offset pen positions can be interpreted as positional parameters, i.e. they are used to relate the painted command gesture to the respective interaction object.

Pen gestures have to be thoroughly planned. One aspect is that different gestures should be designed in a way that they are not too similar and too likely to be confused by the system. It might be necessary to restrict the amount of available gestures to a few ones, to allow reliable recognition. Furthermore, toolkit-based design support might be needed [cf. 165].

Consequences

- There is no more need to find an awkward textual representation for items displayed on the screen. The user does not have to remember strange names, to type them in, or to try to pronounce them. He has simply to recognise the desired object displayed on the screen.
- There is no need to require keyboard or speech input.
- Screen clutter, scrolling and menu navigation can be avoided.
- The user can input a complex action in one simple step: Drawing a meaningful gesture onto an object displayed on the screen leads to opening, copying, deleting and the like. In usual graphic user interfaces, the user would have to select the object first and then select an action. This would require more steps.
- The user has to learn and remember a series of gestures. But some users might prefer commands instead. The system should provide a command interface as an alternative.
- Gesture recognition is not always fully reliable because of the high variability of human gestures. Pen gestures can be misinterpreted: The system can miss user input or recognise some, where there is none.
- Slips of pen can be misinterpreted as gestures and lead to unwanted actions.
- Although gestures should be designed to be meaningful, first time users will require some time of training before mastering the interfaces with all its advantages.
- When the system supports a wider range of (distinct) gestures, the user is forced to remain within a very narrow range of variations for each one of the standardised gestures. This increases the learning effort as well as the cognitive load during usage.

Rationale. Gestures are easy to learn and additionally provide a means of *terse and powerful interaction*, because both position and movement patterns can be exploited to convey information [166].

Known Uses. QuickSet [107, 63] allows the user to place military units via drawing military icons directly onto a map. The form of the icon designates the type of military base and the drawing position corresponds to the desired target location. Furthermore QuickSet supports specific editing gestures such as for *crossing out* (deleting) objects on the map.

Further examples can be found in TAPAGE [118] and the systems described by Fiore et al. [167] and Ou et al. [168].

Related Patterns. This pattern is, besides *Gesture-enhanced Speech Command*, a specialisation of *Composed Command* [11].

Variant. A variant of this pattern uses handwriting instead of gestures, as with handwriting you can simultaneously input spatial and linguistic information, too. However, to input spacial data more precisely, it is better to combine a separate pointing gesture with subsequent (and not parallel) handwriting. Such a combined input is supported by map-based systems such as PAVE [169] and MATCH [110, 109].

5   Patterns for Robust Multimodal Interaction

This subcollection comprises a set of four patterns: two more generic ones and two concrete specialisations. Both generic patterns *Redundant Output* and *Redundant Input* address the mutual disambiguation of redundant signals. Whereas the pattern *Redundant Output* is used to present redundant data to the user such that the user is more likely to understand or at least perceive the information conveyed by the system, the pattern *Redundant Input* fuses user input coming from several channels in order to reduce recognition and interpretation errors.

These two generic patterns play a central role in multimodal interaction and also in related fields such as affective computing [78, 81] and might provide an extension point for this pattern collection in the future.

The pattern *Redundant Output* has no specialisation within this collection. Tidwell's pattern *Important Message* [11] can be seen as a specific case of this one: It suggests the usage of several modalities (visual and auditory signals) to attract the user's attention and to convey urgent information.

For the pattern *Redundant Input* two refining patterns are presented:

- *Multimodal N-best Selection* combines several interaction modalities for input and disambiguation dialogs. The user first utters a word or command. The speech recogniser returns as a result the best guess among several statistical hypotheses. In cases where the actual user input does not match the best guess by the recogniser but one of the other hypotheses, it is better to present the user a list of the n best recognition hypotheses instead of cancelling the failed input attempt. The user can now directly select from this list e.g. via pointing. When the user wants to select the n-best item via speech input, alternatives to simply re-speaking the item are needed. The user might be prompted for repeating the number of the item he wants to select. This avoids endless loops of repeated errors, especially when the n hypotheses sound similar.
- *Spelling-based Hypothesis Reduction* combines several input modalities to reduce recognition errors. Speech recognition works more reliable with smaller

vocabularies. To reduce the size of the active recognition vocabulary, the user may first input some letters via typing so that the list of alternatives can be filtered. After that, the user speaks the desired entry which can be properly recognised by the system. Spelling can be done after spoken input, too. Then the previously recorded user utterance is processed by the speech recogniser again using a smaller recognition vocabulary.

These patterns can be used in conjunction with *Voice-based Interaction Shortcut* and *Speech-enabled Form* which can be combined with *Continuous Filter* [10], *Form* [11], *Autocompletion* [12] and *Drop-down Chooser* [12]. Furthermore the patterns *Dropdown Chooser* and *Continuous Filter* are used to implement *Multimodal N-best Selection* and *Spelling-based Hypothesis Reduction*.

5.1   Redundant Output

Context. Communication channels might be unpredictably distorted or blocked due to bad lighting conditions, background noise, technical (network) problems or disabilities such as speech, motor or perception disorders.

Public systems that are supposed to be accessible for everybody should use this pattern, especially during the first interaction steps when it is not clear which interaction channels are appropriate for the current user.

The user's attention may not be focused on the interaction device in situations when urgent information has to be conveyed by the system.

Problem. How to assure information output when communication channels are distorted in an unforseeable way or the user is currently not paying attention to system output?

Forces

- The system can be configured or adapted to output information using modalities that are less affected by channel disorders. However, in some cases several interaction channels are distorted to some degree. Examples are:
  - Visually impaired or illiterate people who want to interact in loud environments.
  - Deaf people that want to interact in bad lighting conditions or while moving around.
- Potential channel distortions might be circumvented by selecting alternative interaction channels. However, if the potentially distorted channel were otherwise the best candidate, abandoning this channel cannot be justified.
- The system can use those modalities that are most appropriate in the current environmental context. However, when the user's attention does not fit to the situation he might miss important notifications. When the system provides for instance only visual output due to a high background noise level but the user's visual attention is focused elsewhere, the system fails to notify the user.

Solution. Combine several output channels in order to make use of redundancy. Information should be output both visually and acoustically and possibly even in a haptic way (e.g. using vibration) to raise the probability that it is perceived and can be understood by the user.

Consequences

- The use of several channels raises the probability that the user is able to perceive the information conveyed to him by the system. Visually impaired people in loud environments or deaf people in bad lighting conditions can process more data when output is presented redundantly to them.
- You don't need to abandon an output channel totally, only because it might be distorted. Visually impaired people might have problems reading a text and recognise each letter. After hearing the spoken variant and knowing what the text is about, the visual representation can be used as memory hook. The same might be true for dark environments or mobile scenarios, when it is difficult to fix visual attention to the text.
- It is more likely to attract the user's attention when information is output via several channels, e.g. both audio and sight, than when only one output modality is used.

Rationale. Important and urgent information is more likely to be perceived by the user when several channels are used. Reaction times can be reduced by about 30% when redundant (visual, acoustic, haptic) signals are used [67].

Independent distortions of different channels rarely affect the same aspects of the content.

Multi-channel feedback of written and spoken text has proven to be effective for elderly [40] and visually impaired users [41, 42, 43, 44].

Plosives ([p], [t], [k], [b], [d], [g]) sound similar and are likely to be confused when sound quality is low. At the same time these phones have distinctive lip shapes such as open lips (in the case of [g] and [k]) vs. initially closed lips (in the case of [b] and [p]). Lip shapes may differ for some similar sounding vowels, too.

In the context of language understanding, it has been proven that people understand spoken language better when they can look at the lips of their interlocutor while listening [68, 69, 70, 71, 72, 170, 15], especially in loud environments.

Known Uses. Systems that display a talking head such as *PPP* [73], *NUMACK* [74], *COMIC* [75] and *SmartKom* ["Smartakus" 76] can exploit the advantages of audiovisual language understanding [13].

Mobile phones combine visual (blinking), auditory (ringing) and haptic (vibrating) signals in order to notify the user about phone calls or incoming short text messages. Visual and auditory cues are combined to remind the user to plug in his laptop or mobile phone so that the batteries are charged.

Related Patterns. Tidwell's *Important Message* [11] is a concretisation of this pattern. The focus of Tidwell's *Important Message* is on handling cases where the user's attention might not be directed to the interactive device. The pattern *Redundant Output* is more generic and addresses additionally comprehension problems caused by context factors such as bad light or background noise.

5.2 Redundant Input

Context. Communication channels might be unpredictably distorted due to bad lighting conditions, background noise, technical (network) problems or disabilities such as speech or motor disorders.

Problem. How to assure input when communication channels are distorted in an unforseeable way?

Forces

- The system can be configured or adapted to recognise and interpret the modality that is less affected by channel disorders, but in some cases all available interaction channels are distorted to some degree.
  - In loud environments users with motor disabilities or illiterate people have problems to interact with the system.
  - In dark environments or in hands-free scenarios (e.g. while carrying a bag, wandering around, driving a car) people with speech disorders have problems to input data.
  - In extreme conditions – e.g. while carrying out an exhausting primary task, both speech input and pen gestures are problematic.
- Interaction can be alleviated if modalities for implicit data input (gaze input, free gestures) or authentication (voice recognition, face recognition) are used. However, these interaction channels are error prone so that they cannot be applied directly.

Solution. Combine several interaction channels in order to make use of redundancy. Input coming from several channels (visual: e.g. lip movements, auditory: e.g. the speech signal) should be interpreted in combination in order to reduce liability to errors.

Consequences

- The use of several channels raises the probability that the system is able to recognise and interpret the information input by the user in the desired way.
- Even if several channels are distorted the distortion rarely affects exactly the same pieces of information. Fusion mechanisms allow for reconstructing of at least some part of the input information.
- "Imperfect", error prone interaction channels can be combined to mutually disambiguate recognition errors.

Rationale. Independent distortions of different channels rarely affect the same aspects of the content. That's why for instance audio-visual speech recognition, which combines acoustic and visual (lip movement analysis) signals, leads to better recognition performance than unimodal speech recognition in loud environments [cf. 13, p. 24 f.]:

Plosives ([p], [t], [k], [b], [d], [g]) sound similar and are likely to be confused when sound quality is low. At the same time these phones have distinctive lip shapes such as open lips (in the case of [g] and [k]) vs. initially closed lips (in the case of [b] and [p]). Lip shapes may differ for some similar sounding vowels, too. Channel distortions rarely affect both the recognition of a specific phoneme in the acoustic signal and of the corresponding viseme in the visual signal in the same way. Fusion algorithms allow to combine sound pieces of information from several channels such that some distorted parts can be reconstructed [13].

Studies conducted by Oviatt [171] revealed that an appropriate recogniser architecture that combines gesture and speech recognition can reduce recognition errors. This was shown for non-native speakers, in loud environments [172, 173, 174] and for cases where the users were carrying out an exhausting task in parallel [175].

Known Uses. This pattern is manifested in very different application areas including data input (audio-visual speech recognition), scene analysis [176], person identification [177, 65, 66, 178, 179], affective computing and emotion recognition [180, 83, 100, 102, 101] and the like. Following modality combinations are used:

- virtual reality and speech [181],
- gaze direction and speech [182, 183, 184, 185],
- lip-reading in loud environments [64], e.g. to filter out simultaneous speakers [186],
- speech and gesture [187, 188],
- voice, ink and touchtone [189],
- biometrics, voice and face to identify persons [65, 66].

Related Patterns. *Spelling-based Hypothesis Reduction* as well as *Multimodal N-best Selection* are refinements of this pattern.

5.3 Multimodal N-best Selection

Context. This pattern can be used in multimodal systems that offer speech input of unconstrained text or speech-based selection of items from very large sets such as timetable or navigation systems.

Problem. Speech recognition is based on statistical processes. The recognition of input phrases results in a set of several recognition hypotheses. Usually the recogniser returns the best match as "the result". It is frequently the case that the original user input does not match this "best guess" but is included in the list of n best hypotheses returned by the recogniser.

Forces

- When a speech input attempt fails, the user can be prompted to repeat or to switch to another interaction modality. But it is inefficient to throw away input data which has failed the goal just by a hair.
- Playing back the n best recognition hypotheses, prompting for (spoken) selection and reducing the speech recognition vocabulary to this reduced list of n items can correct the error in just one further interaction step. However, items contained in the n-best list are likely to have some acoustic similarity so that they might be mixed up repeatedly by the recogniser.
- Playing back just the item on top of the n best recognition hypotheses and prompting for accepting or rejecting may resolve this problem in a few steps, but if the desired item is only the fifth (sixth, seventh ...) best recognition hypothesis five (six, seven ...) error correction steps are needed.

Solution. Provide the user a means of selecting the correct result from a set of recognition hypotheses via pointing or key presses.

The number of alternatives should be restricted to a manageable size so that the system remains easy to control.

In order to satisfy cases where the desired item cannot be found in the n-best list there has to be a way of explicitly leaving the list selection dialog and to start over the input attempt.

Disabled users or users in restricted environments might want to use speech input as well for this. In order to circumvent recognition problems that arise because the vocabulary contains similar sounding words, the list should be presented in a standardised way and contain line numbers in addition to the item wordings. The user should then be encouraged to speak the line number plus the item name so that the system can distinguish better between alternative hypotheses.

Consequences

- Imperfect recognition results are not thrown away but reused in subsequent interaction steps.
- Instead of re-speaking the misrecognised item, the user can point to the item displayed in the list. By changing the input strategy, recurring recognition problems are avoided.
- Frequently, instead of endless error correction loops, this pattern helps to correct recognition errors in just one additional interaction step.

Rationale. Suhm et al. [190] point out that re-speaking the same word or phrase after recognition failure is not the most promising form of error recovery in interactive systems, although this might seem to the user to be the most obvious strategy. Changing the input modality to list selection seems to be more promising [191, 192].

Known Uses. Directory assistance, timetable information systems, speech-based driver assistance systems, office applications such as *MedSpeak* [193] and *Human-Centric Word Processor* [194, 195] support n-best selection.

Related Patterns. This pattern can be used in conjunction with *Speech-enabled Form*, *Drop-down Chooser* [12] and *Autocompletion* [12] to alleviate error handling in speech-enhanced input forms.

This pattern and *Spelling-based Hypothesis Reduction* are refinements of *Redundant Input*. *Multimodal N-best Selection* may display the *n* best recognition hypotheses in a *Drop-down Chooser* [12].

Variant. The solution described in this pattern is not restricted to multimodal interaction in a narrower sense. Speech-only systems provide similar speech-based approaches of selecting the desired item from a list of hypotheses.

If n-best selection via speech is supported, it is important to offer input modifications to avoid repeated errors. The user should be given the possibility to select the desired option via speaking the line number or re-speaking the item plus some distinctive features such as the first letter(s).

In these cases, the user has to be prompted in a way that reveals alternative selection strategies apart from simple re-speaking, e.g.: "Did you mean *one* Jonathan Smith, *two* John Griffith, *three* Joseph Reddish or *new input*".

While the list is being read out the user should have the possibility to interrupt the playback. In full-duplex systems with cleanly separated channels for audio input and output, barge-in can be used. That means that system playback is stopped when the user starts speaking. In half-duplex systems, the user should be able to interrupt system playback using a push-to-talk button. In the cases of both barge-in and push-to-talk, the time information when speech output was interrupted can be used as a further information source to identify the selected item [196, 197].

5.4   Spelling-Based Hypothesis Reduction

Context. Examples where this pattern can be used are systems that offer speech input of unconstrained text or speech-based selection of items from very large sets such as timetable or navigation systems. Errors are particularly likely in cases, when the user has to select from lists with similar sounding words or words with inconsistent pronunciation such as foreign names.

Problem. Large recognition vocabularies entail error-prone speech recognition, especially when many similar sounding words have to be distinguished or a wider range of pronunciation variants has to be supported.

Forces

- Speech input can be used for selecting items from a list that cannot be displayed completely on a small screen, but if the list is too large for speech recognition or includes several similar sounding or problematic words, speech recognition is likely to fail. Problem areas are names in directory assistance systems as well as album and song titles in entertainment systems.

- In the case of recognition failures, the user can switch to text input (typing), but in some applications such as driver assistance systems only unhandy (if any) string input facilities are available.
- Typing the first letters can reduce the size of the selection list so that pointing is possible again, but in some applications such as navigation systems, a lot of characters need to be input (using an impractical input device) before the list can reduced to a size feasible for display and list selection.
- Some speech recognisers, especially those for small devices, have only restricted resources such that only small vocabularies e.g. for number recognition or for recognising letters of the alphabet are supported. But operating applications this way provides only little added value in contrast to using a small keypad, especially since some letters sound similar and are likely to be confused by the recogniser.

Solution. Offer the user to type the first few letters of the word or list item before speaking it. Use this substring to filter the list of selectable alternatives, i.e. to reduce the size of the active speech recognition vocabulary. With this smaller vocabulary, speech recognition is more reliable.

Alternatively, record speech input attempts and keep this recording available for a disambiguation step. When recognition fails, the user should be encouraged to input the first (few) character(s) e.g. via typing. Now the list of alternatives is filtered and the size of the active vocabulary is reduced. The speech recogniser can then be re-run with the previous recording and the smaller vocabulary.

Consequences

- By inputting quite few letters, the set of alternatives can be reduced to a size that – although still unsuited for pointing-based list selection – allows robust speech recognition.
- The user needs to input only a few letters. This is important in cases where typing is inconvenient.
- There is no need to navigate and scroll through lists.
- Recognition of names, song titles and other problematic words becomes more robust.
- This technique of reducing speech recognition vocabularies simplifies speech recognition on platforms with limited resources.

Rationale. With an increasing amount of words or phrases activated, speech recognition accuracy decreases. By reducing the active speech recognition vocabulary the recognition performance can be improved significantly.

Known Uses. Marx and Schmandt [127] describe the messaging system *Chatter* which allows the user to input contact names via voice spelling, touch-tone spelling and speech-based naming in a combined fashion.

The prototype of the multimodal driver assistance system *CarMMI* [58] allows the user to input the first letters using a rotary knob mounted on the centre console, so that the speech recognition vocabulary can be reduced.

Similar examples can be found in Suhm et al. [190] and Tan et al. [183].

Related Patterns. This pattern can be used in conjunction with *Speech-enabled Form, Drop-down Chooser* [12] and *Autocompletion* [12] to alleviate error handling in speech-enabled input forms.

This pattern and *Multimodal N-best Selection* are refinements of *Redundant Input. Spelling-based Hypothesis Reduction* uses (or is) some kind of variant of *Continuous Filter* [10]. Instead of filtering the items of a selection list, the recognition vocabulary is reduced according to the letters input by the user.

Variant Some systems allow the user to dictate (i.e. speak) characters (voice spelling) to reduce the active recognition vocabulary [127]. The recognised spellings are expanded by using a so-called confusability matrix to avoid that misrecognised characters reduce the list of input alternatives too much.

In addition, phonetic alphabets can be used to reduce recognition failures. But this is only feasible if the target user group is expected to be proficient in that phonetic alphabet.

When a phonetic alphabet is supported the user is not proficient in, this might result in spontaneous wordings such as *Motel* instead of *Mike* or *October* instead of *Oscar*. This way, recognition errors might even increase.

6   Patterns for Flexible Multimodal Interaction

The patterns for flexible interaction focus on accessibility and usability across changing situations, environmental and other context factors. The three patterns described here provide each one different runtime modality adaptation strategies, i.e. ways of dynamically allocating interaction modalities:

- *Multiple Ways of Input* offers the user several alternative interaction techniques. The user is free to select the interaction modality that is most appropriate in the current context. He need not perform additional configuration steps.
- *Context Adaptation* requires the system to evaluate the interaction history and environment data to adapt system behaviour accordingly.
- *Global Channel Configuration* provides several interaction profiles with each different configurations of input and output channels. This way, the system can be tailored to typical contexts of use. The user can switch the interaction profile in just one interaction step using an always-on-top widget or function button. Thus, the user can switch on/off audio output or speech recognition when appropriate.

The abstract principle behind these patterns is to provide several alternative modalities for each atomic task. This way, following forces can be resolved:

- Typing is powerful for a lot of tasks but if the target user group includes typing-unskilled or even illiterate people other alternatives have to be used.
- Speech input is well suited for both text input and item selection. But in loud environments, speech recognition will be very error prone because the background noise masks the proper signal or is interpreted as input where there is none.
- Mechanical input via keyboards or pointing devices is widely applicable. But if the user's hands are occupied, wet, or dirty, there is no way to operate the systems.
- Graphic output and feedback is useful in a lot of situations but cannot be perceived in bad lighting conditions or by blind people. At the same time, speech output might be difficult to understand or even be overheard in loud environments.
- Speech output and input can make mobile interaction more comfortable. But confidential data must not be read out loudly in public environments.
- Environmental factors can be controlled via special installations such as specially mounted lamps, enclosed areas (e.g. phone booths, kiosks etc.), directional speakers, earphones etc., but these measures are not viable in every case such as mobile interaction.

These patterns may be used in conjunction: For the input side, the pattern *Multiple Ways of Input* provides maximal user freedom and flexibility. The user might start from an obvious interaction technique such as direct manipulation or menu navigation. This way he can explore the interface and learn about the scope of the system functionality. Later on, he might try alternative input strategies which are suggested in system hints, tooltips etc.

System output may start from a reasonable default configuration and then adapt automatically based on how the user inputs data into the system (*Context Adaptation*): On manual input, the system may stay quiet and provide only graphical output. When the user utters speech commands the system plays back spoken language in addition to graphical output. If the user does not want the system to adapt its behaviour automatically or simply wants to have more verbose or more terse spoken output he may indicate this by changing the settings (*Global Channel Configuration*).

6.1 Multiple Ways of Input

Context. Context factors are not always predictable. This holds especially for mobile interaction in changing environments or public information kiosks that should be usable for quite different user groups.

Problem. How can input modalities be adapted to the context of use without burdening the user with additional configuration tasks?

Forces

- The user should be able to interact with the system using preferred and task appropriate interaction styles. However, disabilities or changing environmental conditions such as lighting or background noise may affect the usability and robustness of task-optimised interaction modalities.
- If background noise is low, speech input and output provide a valid interaction style. However, in public environments, bystanders might feel annoyed by persons conversing with an interactive system.
- Environmental factors can be controlled by using special installations:
  - Specially mounted lamps help to overcome bad lighting conditions.
  - Enclosed areas (e.g. phone booths, kiosks etc.) reduce background noise and help to assure privacy.

  But these measures are not viable in every case such as mobile interaction. ⋅
- Users might differ according to preferences, language, reading, typing skills etc. The system can provide alternative interaction styles and adapt to the user. However, the system is not able to predict precisely which input modalities are most likely to be selected by the user in the current situation.

Solution. Enable the user to trigger each system function by using one of several alternative interaction modalities, be it speech, typing or pointing. The alternative modalities should be active and ready to use all the time without further configuration needs.

The system has to be designed in a way, that the user can choose alternative modalities wherever sensible, even for single interaction steps of a more complex task.

Labels, help messages, prompts, console and speech commands should share a uniform wording in order to minimise learning efforts and confusion for the user, when he wants to sidestep to another modalitiy.

Consequences

- By providing several alternative interaction styles, the system can be used by physically disabled or illiterate people.
- As the user can choose among several modalities which are each differently affected by environmental factors, the system can be used in varying environmental conditions.
  - In loud or public environments the users can simply sidestep to pointing or text input.
  - When background noise is low users can opt for speech interaction.
- Expert users can estimate whether speech input or pointing gestures are possible or desirable at the current moment.
- It is up to the users to select their preferred interaction style. They do not need to wait for the system to automatically adapt. Instead, they gain self-confidence since they are controlling the system which leads to higher user satisfaction.

- First time users might not know which interaction styles are available at all. The system must provide effective help and prompting strategies that reveal alternative interaction modalities.
- The more flexible a system is, the more planning, testing and reviewing is needed during design since the number of error sources increases rapidly with system complexity.

Rationale. According to user characteristics, preferences, environment and situation, different interaction modalities are preferable [133, 6, 7].

Users can judge better than the system, which interaction modality and style is appropriate, e.g. whether background noise or bad lighting impedes the use of speech or graphics, whether surrounding people might feel annoyed because of spoken interaction or whether private information is being conveyed.

Ibrahim and Johansson [198] have shown for their multimodal TV guide, that users prefer, when they can choose to use direct manipulation and speech either unaccompanied or combined in order to adapt to the current context of use.

Users learn to estimate and select the most context-appropriate modality. After recognition errors, users tend to switch the interaction modality [133, 199, 200, 171].

Known Uses. SmartKom [161] allows the user to interact either via pen or speech.

Mobile systems such as Microsoft's MiPad [120, 121, 122] and IBM's Personal Speech Assistant [123] are good examples for systems that allow users to flexibly select input modalities. The same holds for driver assitance systems such as the ones decribed by Neuss [58] and Pieraccini et al. [201].

Further examples of this pattern can be found in the interactive TV guide by Ibrahim and Johansson [198], and MICASSEM [202].

Related Patterns. This pattern is on the one hand an alternative to *Global Channel Configuration* and *Context Adaptation*. On the other hand these patterns can be combined.

Whereas *Global Channel Configuration* requires an additional interaction step to select the input / output profile of the system, *Multiple Ways of Input* keeps all input modalities activated so that they can be used without additional configuration steps. In contrast to *Global Channel Configuration*, this pattern is restricted to the adaptation of user input.

That's why this pattern should be used together with *Context Adaptation*. This way, system output can be adapted according to the user's input behaviour.

In contrast to system-driven *Context Adaptation*, *Multiple Ways of Input* offers, similarly to *Global Channel Configuration*, user-driven system adaptation.

6.2   Context Adaptation

Context. Examples for this pattern can be found in interactive devices that support different alternative and complementary interaction channels such as audio output and input, typing and graphic manipulation.

Problem. How can interaction (input and output) be adapted to the current situation, environment and user without the user having to perform additional interaction steps?

Forces

- Redundant output via several channels can assure information perception by users. However, superfluous spoken output might disrupt or slow down the user's secondary task or annoy third persons.
- Alternatively, one could let the user configure system input and output according to the current context of use. But, as long as sufficient information is available to the system, additional configuration steps should be avoided.
- Letting the user configure the system himself seems not to be a problem at first. But the user might not be able to remember the current configuration state of the system and to reconfigure the system at each situation change.

Solution. The system should analyse as much assured context information as available to setup system configuration autonomously. One information source that can be used is the interaction history:

- If the user interacts via speech, it is not clear where the user looks. In this case speech output should complement display updates.
- If the user does not want to annoy surrounding people, he will avoid speech interaction.
- If the user is currently typing or using a pointing device – might be in order not to annoy surrounding people – he is usually looking at the display such that speech output is superfluous.

Other aspects of system state can be exploited for adaptation, too: A driver assistance system should disable touch screen input while the user is driving – the driver should keep his hands on the steering wheel. Smartphones should disable touch screen input during a telephone call – the ear of the user should not lead to unwanted actions.

In addition to these situational aspects, the system can adapt system output according to the user expertise level. For first time users, more verbose speech output prompts are necessary. When the user already has proven to use a system function successfully several times, shorter prompts are sufficient [203, 197].

Systems that can be used by several users need a user identification mechanism (e.g. a log-in facility) to keep a specific user model available for future interaction sessions with this user.

The system should not be prematurely adapted based on statistical assumptions with low confidence scores, but only after enough context information has been analysed. In order to keep adaptation predictable for the user, it should take place in a transparent way that can be undone easily.

Consequences

- Information output can be restricted according to the context of use.
- The user does not need to reconfigure the system repeatedly where this can be done by the system itself.
- The user need not remember configuration states and reconfigure the system at each situation change.
- Automatic adaptation can fail or be unappropriate. That's why the user should always have the possibility to carry over control and perform interaction configuration himself.

Rationale. So-called *plastic user interfaces* adapt automatically to the context of use. For this, they analyse comprehensive context information [47, 50, 48, 49] and require an appropriate runtime architecture [54, 4].

Known Uses. SmartKom [161] allows the user to interact either via pen or speech. System feedback is adapted in a way that fits to the user's attention: The TV-guide subsystem of SmartKom presents the TV-program usually as a listing. But when the user query has been done by voice input spoken feedback is played back. When the user is watching TV, the system presents the program list verbally, too, because it supposes that the visual channel is occupied.

Driver assistance system such as the ones decribed by Neuss [58] and Pieraccini et al. [201] offer the user to interact using speech or manual input devices. System output is adapted accordingly.

Smartphones disable touch screen input during telephone calls.

Related Patterns. This pattern is an alternative to *Global Channel Configuration* and *Multiple Ways of Input* but may be used complementarily to those ones. In contrast to those user-driven adaptation strategies, *Context Adaptation* implements a system-initiated adaptation strategy.

This pattern can be used as complement to *Multiple Ways of Input* in order to adapt the system output according to the user input.

In addition to *Context Adaptation*, *Global Channel Configuration* should be supported to give the user control over the system.

6.3   Global Channel Configuration

Context. Interactive devices that offer several alternative and complementary interaction channels such as audio input and output, typing and graphic manipulation have to be adapted to the context of use.

Problem. How can interaction (input and output) be adapted to the current context of use, while giving the user control over the system without burdening him with too much configuration tasks?

Forces

- One can keep several input channels active and leave it up to the user to select the interaction modality that is most appropriate for the current context. However, the system might try to interpret input from unused distorted channels. This might lead to situations where the system misinterprets background noise as input.
- Redundant output via several channels can assure information perception by users. However, in public environments, bystanders might feel annoyed by persons conversing with an interactive system. In the same way, it is not desirable, that private data be read out loudly by the system.
- The system may analyse interaction behaviour, lighting conditions, background noise, movement and position changes and adapt to the user and context of use. However, the system does not find out as fast as the user does which interaction modalities are most appropriate in the current context of use or for the current user.
- Even if automatic adaptation works quite well, many users will prefer being able to control the system.

Solution. Provide several interaction profiles with input and output channel configurations tailored to each context of use. Enable the user to select the interaction profile of the system (speech input, audio output, verbosity level of speech output etc. or, for example, the notification profile of a mobile phone such as ringing, vibrating, mute) with only one additional interaction step.

For this, display for instance always on top buttons or widgets with self explaining icons or provide physical *push-to-talk* and *mute* buttons.

Systems that are used by several users require an identification (log-in) mechanism to keep the profile lastly selected by a specific user available for future interaction sessions.

Consequences

- The user can quickly react to context changes and reconfigure the system accordingly in one interaction step:
  - Input channels such as speech input can be deactivated when necessary (in loud environments) by simply clicking the respective button.
  - In order not to disturb bystanders in public environments, the user can deactivate audio output with one click.
- Users feel better when exercising control over the system instead of being delivered to non-predictive system adaptation.
- Users have to do at least one additional interaction step, which might be annoying anyway.

- Users might by fault select an inappropriate interaction profile.
- The users might not be able to rembember the current configuration state of the system and forget to reconfigure it at each situation change.

Rationale. According to user preferences, abilities, environment and situation, different interaction modalites are appropriate and preferred [133, 6, 7]. Users learn to estimate and select the most context-appropriate modality. After recognition errors, users tend to switch the interaction modality [133, 199, 200, 171].

Known Uses. The multimodal map-based system *SmartKom Mobile* covers the usage scenarios of pedestrian and automotive navigation as well as map-based queries [108] and allows the user to switch between several interaction modes [cf. 204, p. 59]:

- *Default*: All input and output modalities are supported.
- *Listener*: Speech and graphics are supported for output, for input only pen gestures are possible.
- *Silent*: Only graphics for output and pen gestures for input are supported.
- *Speech Only*: Only speech interaction is active.

Some mobile phones – e.g. *Nokia E71* – offer the user to select profiles such as *office* or *home*. In addition to different startup screens, these profiles can be set to an appropriate context-dependent notification mode (ringing, vibrating).

Some desktop applications, operating system environments, and multimedia applications provide an audio icon in the system tray for setting the system's audio characteristics. With some restrictions, these can be seen as examples for this pattern, too.

Related Patterns. This pattern is an alternative to *Multiple Ways of Input* and *Context Adaptation* but can be used in combination with them, too.

In contrast to *Multiple Ways of Input*, which offers the user to select among several alternative input modalities without having to perform additional configuration actions, this pattern requires one additional interaction step. In addition to *Multiple Ways of Input* this pattern also addresses the adaptation of system output.

7 Related Patterns from Other Collections

User interface patterns were published for diverse problem domains, such as:

- task modelling [205, 206],
- prototyping [207],
- internationalisation [208],
- graphical user interfaces [9, 10, 11, 12],
- web sites [209],

- multimedia [210, 211, 212],
- auditory (speech-based) user interfaces [141, 142],
- speech user interfaces for elderly users [38],
- *ubiquitous computing* [213].
- interactive TV applications [214]

The following table summarises patterns referenced in this article.

Name Reference	Problem	Solution
Important Message [11]	How should the artefacts convey this information to the user?	Interrupt whatever the user is doing with the message, using both sight and sound if possible.
Status Display [11]	How can the artefacts best show the state information to the user?	Choose well-designed displays for the information to be shown. [...] emphasize[s] the important things, [...] do[es]n't hide or obscure anything, and prevent[s] confusion of information [...]
Canvas plus Palette [12]	You're designing any kind of graphical editor [... that allows] creating new objects and arranging them on some virtual space.	Place an iconic palette next to a blank canvas; the user clicks on the palette buttons to create objects on the canvas.
Mode Cursor [10]	The user is creating or modifying an object and needs to know which edit function is selected.	Show the interface state in the cursor.
Helping Hands [112]	Users need to enter many different types of [graphical] objects.	Use one hand to enter the data while the other hand is used to switch modes (e.g. to select the appropriate tool from the palette).
Contextual Menu [10]	At any point in time, users need to know what their possibilities are in order to decide what to do.	Put the choices in a menu. Show a list of all functions that are available in the current context. Make the functions accessible in one action.
Hub and Spoke [12]	Your UI contains several discrete tasks, sub-applications, or content elements, [...]. You don't want to connect each of them to all the others [...].	Isolate the sections of the app into mini-applications, each with one way in (from the main page) and one way out (back to the main page).
Continuous Filter [10]	The user needs to find an item in an ordered set.	Provide a filter component with which the user can in real time filter only the items in the data that are of interest.
Form [11]	The user must provide structural textual information to the application. The data to be provided is logically related.	Provide users with a form containing the necessary elements. Forms contain basically a set of input interaction elements and are a means of collecting information [...].

Auto-completion [12]	The user types something predictable, such as a URL, the user's own name or address, today's date, or a filename [...].	With each additional character that the user types, the software quietly forms a list of the possible completions to that partially entered string [...].
Drop-down Chooser [12]	The user needs to supply input that is a choice from a set [...], a date or time, a number, or anything other than free text typed at a keyboard. [...].	For the Drop-down Chooser control's 'closed' state, show the current value of the control in either a button or a text field. To its right, put a down arrow. [...] A click on the arrow (or the whole control) brings up the chooser panel, and a second click closes it again [...].
Spring-loaded Mode [12]	One of the big problems with modes is that a user can forget what mode he's in.	Let the user enter a mode by holding down a key or a mouse button. When the user releases it, leave the mode and go back to the previous one.
One-off Mode [12]	Users will find it annoying to switch into a mode, do one little thing, and then explicitly switch out of that mode again.	When a mode is turned on, perform the operation once. Then switch back automatically into the default or previous mode.
Composed Command [11]	How can the artifact best present the actions that the user may take?	Provide a way for the user to directly enter the command, such as by speech or by typing it in.
Form Filling [142]	How to collect structured information from the user [in the context of speech-based applications]?	Identify a short description or label of the field to be filled in and prepare a variable to store the entered information. Use comprehensive instructions for the label using a consistent, brief, and clear terminology with which the user is familiar [...] Present the label to the user, followed with an optional input prompt and silence to let the user enter the data, as if she were filling out a form [...].

8 Conclusion

This paper outlines a pattern collection for multimodal interaction which is far from being complete. Explorative user tests on desktop- and PDA-based e-mail prototypes [215], which implemented a subset of the patterns presented here, revealed the plausibility of *Voice-based Interaction Shortcut*, *Speech-enabled Form* and *Multiple Ways of Input* [216, 217]. Further research is necessary to cover a wider range of usage scenarios, contexts and patterns.

User interface research on affective computing [78, 79, 80, 81], ambient intelligence [218, 219], ubiquitous computing [213, 220], tangible user interfaces [221, 222], virtual and augmented reality [223, 224] is highly related and has to be covered in future work. The patterns *Redundant Output* and *Redundant Input* may provide an extension point for this pattern collection.

Despite the research history of over twenty years, multimodal interaction is still a research-centric field. It begins to reach some dissemination in the fields of automotive, industrial and mobile applications. New research results and innovative consumer products may contribute to this pattern collection: New patterns might be identified, existing patterns might become obsolete.

An interesting question is, how can patterns be used in several steps of the usability engineering lifecycle [225] i.e. requirements analysis, work reengineering, design standards, detailed design and implementation. Do they play merely an educative role in teaching user interface designers or can they be integrated into software tool chains to facilitate the user interface code generation and, at the same time, the documentation of the design rationale?

In this context, the integration of model-driven and pattern-based approchaes [206, 226, 227] seems to be a promising step in that direction. But there is, nevertheless, a lot of work to be done to understand all the benefits and implications of those techniques [cf. 228, 229, 230].

Acknowledgements. The patterns described here were presented at previous PLoP-conferences [231, 232]. I would like to thank my shepherds Allan Kelly and Michael vanHilst and the members of the workshop groups at VikingPLoP 2007 and EuroPLoP 2008 for their numerous suggestions and valuable feedback.

Furthermore I would like to thank Professor Rainer Hammwöhner, Professor Christian Wolff, Dr. Ludwig Hitzenberger and all my former colleagues at the University of Regensburg who supported me and made possible this work.

References

1. Oviatt, S.L., Kuhn, K.: Referential features and linguistic indirection in multimodal language. In: Proceedings of the International Conference on Spoken Language Processing, vol. 6, pp. 2339–2342. ASSTA (1998)
2. Niedermaier, F.B.: Entwicklung und Bewertung eines Rapid-Prototyping Ansatzes zur multimodalen Mensch-Maschine-Interaktion im Kraftfahrzeug. PhD thesis, Fakultät für Elektrotechnik und Informationstechnik der Technischen Universität München (2003)
3. Dragičević, P.: Un modèle d'interaction en entrée pour des systèmes interactifs multi-dispositifs hautement configurables. PhD thesis, Université de Nantes, école doctorale sciences et technologies de l'information et des matérieaux (March 2004), http://www.dgp.toronto.edu/~dragice/these/html/memoire_dragicevic.html
4. Duarte, C., Carriço, L.: A conceptual framework for developing adaptive multimodal applications. In: IUI 2006: Proceedings of the 11th International Conference on Intelligent User Interfaces, pp. 132–139. ACM, New York (2006)
5. Bernsen, N.O.: Multimodality in language and speech systems - from theory to design support tool. Lectures at the 7th European Summer School on Language and Speech Communication (ESSLSC) (July 1999), http://www.nis.sdu.dk/~nob/stockholm.zip (checked: June 20, 2008)
6. Bürgy, C.: An Interaction Constraints Model for Mobile and Wearable Computer-Aided Engineering Systems in Industrial Applications. PhD thesis, Department of Civil and Environmental Engineering, Carnegie Mellon University, Pittsburgh, Pennsylvania, USA (2002)

7. Obrenović, Z., Abascal, J., Starčević, D.: Universal accessibility as a multimodal design issue. Commun. ACM 50(5), 83–88 (2007)
8. Ratzka, A., Wolff, C.: A pattern-based methodology for multimodal interaction design. In: Sojka, P., Kopeček, I., Pala, K. (eds.) TSD 2006. LNCS (LNAI), vol. 4188, pp. 677–686. Springer, Heidelberg (2006)
9. Coram, T., Lee, J.: Experiences – a pattern language for user interface design (1996), http://www.maplefish.com/todd/papers/experiences/ Experiences.html (checked: June 20, 2008)
10. van Welie, M., Trætteberg, H.: Interaction patterns in user interfaces. In: Proceedings of the Seventh Pattern Languages of Programs Conference, Monticello, Illinois, USA (2000), http://www.cs.vu.nl/~martijn/patterns/PLoP2k-Welie.pdf (checked: June 20, 2008)
11. Tidwell, J.: Common ground: A pattern language for human-computer interface design (1999), http://www.mit.edu/~jtidwell/common_ground.html (checked: June 20, 2008)
12. Tidwell, J.: Designing Interfaces: Patterns for Effective Interaction Design. O'Reilly (2005)
13. Benoît, C., Martin, J.C., Pelachaud, C., Schomaker, L., Suhm, B.: Audio-visual and multimodal speech systems. In: Gibbon, D. (ed.) Handbook of Standards and Resources for Spoken Language Systems - Supplement (1998)
14. Charwat, H.J.: Lexikon der Mensch-Maschine-Kommunikation. Oldenbourg (1992)
15. Schomaker, L., Nijtmans, J., Camurri, A., Lavagetto, F., Morasso, P., Benoît, C., Guiard-Marigny, T., Goff, B.L., Robert-Ribes, J., Adjoudani, A., Defée, I., Münch, S., Hartung, K., Blauert, J.: A taxonomy of multimodal interaction in the human information processing system. Technical report (February 1995)
16. Hedicke, V.: Multimodalität in mensch-maschine schnittstellen. In: Timpe, K.P., Kolrep, H. (eds.) Mensch-Maschine-Systemtechnik, Konzepte, Modellirung, Gestaltung, Evaluation, Symposion, pp. 203–232 (2002)
17. Bernsen, N.O.: A reference model for output information in intelligent multimedia presentation systems. In: Faconti, G.P., Rist, T. (eds.) ECAI 1996 Workshop: Towards a Standard Reference Model for Intelligent Multimedia Systems (1996)
18. Bernsen, N.O.: A toolbox of output modalities: Representing output information in multimodal interfaces (1997), http://www.nis.sdu.dk/publications/papers/ toolbox_paper/ (checked: June 20, 2008)
19. Nigay, L., Coutaz, J.: A design space for multimodal systems: concurrent processing and data fusion. In: Proceedings of INTERCHI 1993 Conference on Human Factors in Computing Systems, pp. 172–178. ACM Press (1993), http://iihm.imag.fr/ publs/1993/InterCHI93_DataFusion.pdf (checked: June 20, 2008)
20. Nigay, L., Coutaz, J.: A generic platform for addressing the multimodal challenge. In: CHI 1995: Proceedings of the SIGCHI Conference on Human Factors in Computing Systems, pp. 98–105. ACM Press / Addison-Wesley Publishing Co., New York (1995)
21. Varela, F., Thompson, E., Rosch, E.: The embodied mind: Cognitive science and human experience. MIT Press, Cambridge (1991)
22. Shneiderman, B., Plaisant, C.: Designing the User Interface. Strategies for Effective Human-Computer Interaction. Person Addison-Wesley, Boston (2005)
23. Denes, P., Pinson, E.: The Speech Chain: The Physics and Biology of Spoken Language, 2nd edn. W.H. Freeman and Company, New York (1993)
24. Raskin, J.: The humane interface: new directions for designing interactive systems. ACM Press / Addison-Wesley Publishing Co., New York (2000)

25. Steinmetz, R.: Multimedia-Technologie: Einführung und Grundlagen. Springer (1993)
26. Bouchet, J., Nigay, L., Balzagette, D.: ICARE: approche à composants pour l'interaction multimodale. In: Mobilité & Ubiquité / UbiMob 2004: Proceedings of the 1st French-speaking Conference on Mobility and Ubiquity Computing, pp. 36–43. ACM Press, New York (2004)
27. Ratzka, A.: Identifying user interface patterns from pertinent multimodal interaction use cases. In: Herczeg, M., Kindsmüller, M.C. (eds.) Mensch & Computer 2008 – 8. fachübergreifende Konferenz für interaktive und kooperative Medien – Viel Mehr Interaktion, Lübeck, Oldenburg Wissenschaftsverlag, pp. 347–356 (September 2008)
28. Ratzka, A.: Steps in Identifying Interaction Design Patterns for Multimodal Systems. In: Forbrig, P., Paternò, F. (eds.) HCSE/TAMODIA 2008. LNCS, vol. 5247, pp. 58–71. Springer, Heidelberg (2008)
29. Bernsen, N.O.: Multimodality in language and speech systems – from theory to design support tool. In: Granström, B. (ed.) Multimodality in Language and Speech Systems. Kluwer, Dordrecht (2001), http://www.nis.sdu.dk/demos/multimodality/multimodality.pdf (checked: June 20, 2008)
30. UDC: Universal designers & consultants, http://www.universaldesign.com/ (checked: November 6, 2010)
31. Erlandson, R.F.: Universal and Accessible Design for Products, Services, and Processes. CRC Press, Boca Raton (2008)
32. W3C: Web content accessibility guidelines 1.0. W3c recommendation, W3C (May 1999), http://www.w3.org/TR/WAI-WEBCONTENT/ (checked: June 20, 2008)
33. Thatcher, J.: Constructing Accessible Web Sites. Glasshaus, Birmingham (2002)
34. Kannengiesser, I., Prickartz, B.: Web-Ergonomie und Barrierefreiheit im Internet. Ferger, Bergisch Gladbach (2006)
35. Glinert, E.P.: Ensuring access for people with disabilities to the national information infrastructure and multimedia computing. SIGCAPH Comput. Phys. Handicap. (59), 10–16 (1997)
36. Bellik, Y., Burger, D.: Multimodal interfaces: new solutions to the problem of computer accessibilty for the blind. In: CHI 1994: Conference Companion on Human Factors in Computing Systems, pp. 267–268. ACM Press, New York (1994)
37. Uzan, G., Teixeira, A.: Speech-based interaction as seen by blind users: from services evaluation to the evaluation of an interaction model. In: IHM 2003: Proceedings of the 15th French-speaking Conference on Human-Computer Interaction / 15ème Conférence Francophone sur l'Interaction Homme-Machine, pp. 174–181. ACM Press, New York (2003)
38. Zajicek, M.: Patterns for encapsulating speech interface design solutions for older adults. In: CUU 2003: Proceedings of the 2003 Conference on Universal Usability, pp. 54–60. ACM Press, New York (2003)
39. Zajicek, M., Morrissey, W.: Multimodality and interactional differences in older adults. Universal Access in the Information Society 2(2), 125–133 (2003)
40. Emery, V.K., Edwards, P.J., Jacko, J.A., Moloney, K.P., Barnard, L., Kongnakorn, T., Sainfort, F., Scott, I.U.: Toward achieving universal usability for older adults through multimodal feedback. In: CUU 2003: Proceedings of the 2003 Conference on Universal Usability, pp. 46–53. ACM Press, New York (2003)
41. Vitense, H.S., Jacko, J.A., Emery, V.K.: Multimodal feedback: establishing a performance baseline for improved access by individuals with visual impairments. In: Assets 2002: Proceedings of the Fifth International ACM Conference on Assistive Technologies, pp. 49–56. ACM Press, New York (2002)

42. Jacko, J.A., Scott, I.U., Sainfort, F., Barnard, L., Edwards, P.J., Emery, V.K., Kongnakorn, T., Moloney, K.P., Zorich, B.S.: Older adults and visual impairment: what do exposure times and accuracy tell us about performance gains associated with multimodal feedback? In: CHI 2003: Proceedings of the SIGCHI Conference on Human Factors in Computing Systems, pp. 33–40. ACM Press, New York (2003)

43. Jacko, J.A., Barnard, L., Kongnakorn, T., Moloney, K.P., Edwards, P.J., Emery, V.K., Sainfort, F.: Isolating the effects of visual impairment: exploring the effect of amd on the utility of multimodal feedback. In: CHI 2004: Proceedings of the SIGCHI Conference on Human Factors in Computing Systems, pp. 311–318. ACM Press, New York (2004)

44. Edwards, P.J., Barnard, L., Emery, V.K., Yi, J.S., Moloney, K.P., Kongnakorn, T., Jacko, J.A., Sainfort, F., Oliver, P.R., Pizzimenti, J., Bade, A., Fecho, G., Shallo-Hoffmann, J.: Strategic design for users with diabetic retinopathy: factors influencing performance in a menu-selection task. In: Assets 2004: Proceedings of the 6th International ACM SIGACCESS Conference on Computers and Accessibility, pp. 118–125. ACM Press, New York (2004)

45. Manaris, B., Harkreader, A.: Suitekeys: a speech understanding interface for the motor-control challenged. In: Assets 1998: Proceedings of the Third International ACM Conference on Assistive Technologies, pp. 108–115. ACM Press, New York (1998)

46. Hwang, F., Keates, S., Langdon, P., Clarkson, P.J., Robinson, P.: Perception and haptics: towards more accessible computers for motion-impaired users. In: PUI 2001: Proceedings of the 2001 Workshop on Perceptive user Interfaces, pp. 1–9. ACM Press, New York (2001)

47. Thevenin, D., Coutaz, J.: Plasticity of user interfaces: Framework and research agenda. In: Sasse, A., Johnson, C. (eds.) Human-Computer Interaction – INTERACT 1999 , IFIP TC, vol. 13. IOS Press (1999)

48. Calvary, G., Coutaz, J., Thevenin, D., Limbourg, Q., Bouillon, L., Vanderdonckt, J.: A unifying reference framework for multi-target user interfaces. Interacting with Computers 15(3), 289–308 (2003)

49. Calvary, G., Dâassi, O., Balme, L., Demeure, A.: Towards a new generation of widgets for supporting software plasticity: The "Comet". In: Feige, U., Roth, J. (eds.) EHCI-DSVIS 2004. LNCS, vol. 3425, pp. 306–324. Springer, Heidelberg (2005)

50. Jabarin, B., Graham, T.C.N.: Architectures for widget-level plasticity. In: Jorge, J.A., Jardim Nunes, N., Falcão e Cunha, J. (eds.) DSV-IS 2003. LNCS, vol. 2844, pp. 124–138. Springer, Heidelberg (2003)

51. Bass, L., Faneuf, R., Little, R., Mayer, N., Pellegrino, B., Reed, S., Seacord, R., Sheppard, S., Szezur, M.R.: Arch, a metamodel for the runtime architecture of an interactive system. uims tool developers workshop. SIGCHI Bulletin 24(1) (1992)

52. Coutaz, J.: Software architecture modeling for user interfaces. In: Marciniak, J.J. (ed.) Encyclopedia of Software Engineering, pp. 38–49. Wiley, Chichester (1994)

53. Frankel, D.S.: Model Driven Architecture^{TM}. Applying MDA^{TM} to Enterprise Computing. OMG Press, Wiley, Indianapolis, Indiana (2003)

54. Coutaz, J., Crowley, J.L., Dobson, S., Garlan, D.: Context is key. Commun. ACM 48(3), 49–53 (2005)

55. Wickens, C.D.: The structure of attentional resources. In: Nickerson, R.S. (ed.) Attention and Performance VIII, pp. 239–257. Lawrence Erlbaum, Hillsdale (1980)

56. Wickens, C.D.: Engineering Psychology and Human Performance. Harper Collins, New York (1992)

57. Bengler, K., Geutner, P., Steffens, F.: „eyes free – hands free" oder „zeit der stille". ein demonstrator zur multimodalen bedienung im fahrzeug. In: Gärtner, K.P. (ed.) Multimodale Interaktion im Bereich der Fahrzeug- und Prozessführung. DGLR-Bericht 200-02, München, Deutsche Gesellschaft für Luft- und Raumfahrttechnik d.V (DGLR), pp. 299–307 (2000)

58. Neuss, R.: Usability Engineering als Ansatz zum Multimodalen Mensch-Maschine-Dialog. PhD thesis, Fakultät für Elektrotechnik und Informationstechnik, Technische Universität München (2001)

59. Salmen, A., Großmann, P., Hitzenberger, L., Creutzburg, U.: Dialog systems in traffic environment. In: Proceedings of ESCA: Tutorial and Research Workshop on Interactive Dialogue in Multi-Modal Systems, Kloster Irsee (1999)

60. Salmen, A.: Multimodale Menüausgabe im Fahrzeug. PhD thesis, Lehrstuhl für Informationswissenschaft, Philosophische Fakultät IV, Universität Regensburg (2002)

61. Becker, T., Blaylock, N., Gerstenberger, C., Korthauer, A., Perera, N., Pitz, M., Poller, P., Schehl, J., Steffens, F., Stegmann, R.: D5.3: In-car showcase based on talk libraries. Deliverable 5.3, Universität des Saarlandes (2007)

62. Mayer, R.E., Moreno, R.: split-attention effect in multimedia learning: Evidence for dual processing systems in working memory. Journal of Educational Psychology 90(2), 312–320 (1998)

63. Cohen, P.R., McGee, D., Clow, J.: The efficiency of multimodal interaction for a map-based task. In: Proceedings of the Sixth Conference on Applied Natural Language Processing, pp. 331–338. Morgan Kaufmann Publishers Inc., San Francisco (2000), http://www.aclweb.org/anthology-new/A/A00/A00-1046.pdf (checked: June 20, 2008)

64. Saenko, K., Darrell, T., Glass, J.R.: Articulatory features for robust visual speech recognition. In: ICMI 2004: Proceedings of the 6th International Conference on Multimodal Interfaces, pp. 152–158. ACM Press, New York (2004)

65. Yang, J., Zhu, X., Gross, R., Kominek, J., Pan, Y., Waibel, A.: Multimodal people id for a multimedia meeting browser. In: MULTIMEDIA 1999: Proceedings of the Seventh ACM International Conference on Multimedia (Part 1), pp. 159–168. ACM Press, New York (1999)

66. Hazen, T.J., Weinstein, E., Park, A.: Towards robust person recognition on handheld devices using face and speaker identification technologies. In: ICMI 2003: Proceedings of the 5th International Conference on Multimodal Interfaces, pp. 289–292. ACM Press, New York (2003)

67. Selcon, S.J., Taylor, R.M.: Integrating multiple information sources: Using redundancy in the design of warnings. Ergonomics 38(11), 2362–2370 (1995)

68. Sumby, W.H., Pollack, I.: Visual contribution to speech intelligibility in noise. Journal of the Acoustical Society of America 26, 212–215 (1954)

69. Neely, K.K.: Effect of visual factors on the intelligibility of speech. Journal of the Acoustical Society of America 28, 1275–1277 (1956)

70. Binnie, C.A., Montgomery, A.A., Jackson, P.L.: Auditory and visual contributions to the perception of consonants. Journal of Speech & Hearing Research 17, 619–630 (1974)

71. Erber, N.P.: Interaction of audition and vision in the recognition of oral speech stimuli. Journal of Speech & Hearing Research 12, 423–425 (1969)

72. Erber, N.P.: Auditory-visual perception of speech. Journal of Speech & Hearing Disorders 40, 481–492 (1975)

73. André, E., Muller, A.J., Rist, T.: The ppp persona: A multipurpose animated presentation agent. In: et al (ed.): Advanced Visual Interfaces, pp. 245–247. ACM Press (1996)
74. Kopp, S., Tepper, P., Cassell, J.: Towards integrated microplanning of language and iconic gesture for multimodal output. In: ICMI 2004: Proceedings of the 6th International Conference on Multimodal Interfaces, pp. 97–104. ACM Press, New York (2004)
75. Foster, M.E., White, M., Setzer, A., Catizone, R.: Multimodal generation in the comic dialogue system. In: ACL 2005: Proceedings of the ACL 2005 on Interactive Poster and Demonstration Sessions, pp. 45–48. Association for Computational Linguistics, Morristown (2005)
76. Wahlster, W., Reithinger, N., Blocher, A.: Smartkom: Towards multimodal dialogues with anthropomorphic interface agents. In: Wolf, G., Klein, G. (eds.) Proceedings of International Status Conference: Lead Projects Human-Computer-Interaction, Saarbrücken, Projektträger des BMBF für Informationstechnik: Deutsches Zentrum für Luft- und Raumfahrttechnik (DLR) e.V., pp. 23–32 (2001)
77. Bernsen, N.O.: What is natural interactivity. In: Dybkjær (ed.) Proceedings of the Workshop From Spoken Dialogue to Full Natural Interactive Dialogue. Theory, Empirical Analysis and Evaluation, pp. 34–37. European Language Resources Association, Athen (2000)
78. Picard, R.W.: Perceptual user interfaces: affective perception. Commun. ACM 43(3), 50–51 (2000)
79. Picard, R.W.: Affective Computing. MIT Press, Cambridge (2000)
80. Brave, S., Nass, C.: Emotion in human-computer interaction. In: Jacko, J.A., Sears, A. (eds.) The Human-Computer Interaction Handbook. Fundamentals, Evolving Technologies, and Emerging Applications, pp. 81–96. Lawrence Erlbaum Assoc., Mahwah (2003)
81. Pantic, M., Sebe, N., Cohn, J.F., Huang, T.: Affective multimodal human-computer interaction. In: MULTIMEDIA 2005: Proceedings of the 13th Annual ACM International Conference on Multimedia, pp. 669–676. ACM Press, New York (2005)
82. Ambady, N., Rosenthal, R.: Thin slices of behavior as predictors of interpersonal consequences: A meta-analysis. Psychological Bulletin 2, 256–274 (1992)
83. Lisetti, C.L., Nasoz, F.: Maui: a multimodal affective user interface. In: MULTIMEDIA 2002: Proceedings of the Tenth ACM International Conference on Multimedia, pp. 161–170. ACM Press, New York (2002)
84. Essa, I., Darrell, T., Pentland, A.: Tracking facial motion. In: Proceedings of the IEEE Workshop on Nonrigid and Articulate Motion (1994)
85. Black, M., Yakoob, Y.: Recognizing faces showing expressions. In: Proceedings of the International Workshop on Automatic Face and Gesture Recognition. IEEE Press (1995)
86. Black, M., Yacoob, Y.: Tracking and recognizing rigid and non-rigid facial motions using local parametric models of image motion. In: Proceedings of the International Conference on Computer Vision, pp. 374–381 (1995)
87. Terzopoulos, D., Waters, K.: Analysis and synthesis of facial images using physical and anatomical models. In: Proceedings of the International Conference on Computer Vision, pp. 727–732 (1990)
88. Kearney, G., McKenzie, S.: Machine interpretation of emotion: Design of a memory-based expert system for interpreting facial expressions in terms of signaled emotions. Cognitive Science 17 (1993)

89. Murray, I., Arnott, J.: Toward the simulation of emotion in synthetic speech: A review of the literature on human vocal emotion. Journal Acostical Society of America 93(2), 1097–1108 (1993)
90. Kompe, R.: Prosody in Speech Understanding Systems. LNCS, vol. 1307. Springer, Heidelberg (1997)
91. Batliner, A., Buckow, A., Niemann, H., Nöth, E., Warnke, V.: The prosody module. In: Wahlster, W. (ed.) Verbmobil: Foundations of Speech-to-Speech Translations, pp. 106–121. Springer, Berlin (2000)
92. Picard, R.: Affective Computing. MIT Press, Cambridge (1997)
93. Healey, J., Picard, R.: Smartcar: Detecting driver stress. In: Proceedings of ICPR 2000, Barcelona, Spanien (2000)
94. Ark, W., Dryer, D., Lu, D.: The emotion mouse. In: Bullinger, H.J., Ziegler, J. (eds.) Human-Computer Interaction: Ergonomics and User Interfaces, pp. 818–823. Lawrence Erlbaum Assoc. (1999)
95. Crosby, M.E., Auernheimer, B., Aschwanden, C., Ikehara, C.: Physiological data feedback for application in distance education. In: PUI 2001: Proceedings of the 2001 Workshop on Perceptive user Interfaces, pp. 1–5. ACM Press, New York (2001)
96. Qi, Y., Reynolds, C., Picard, R.W.: The bayes point machine for computer-user frustration detection via pressuremouse. In: PUI 2001: Proceedings of the 2001 Workshop on Perceptive User Interfaces, pp. 1–5. ACM Press, New York (2001)
97. Mentis, H.M.: Using touchpad pressure to detect negative affect. In: ICMI 2002: Proceedings of the 4th IEEE International Conference on Multimodal Interfaces, p. 406. IEEE Computer Society, Washington, DC (2002)
98. O'Rorke, P., Ortony, A.: Explaining emotions. Cognitive Science 18(2), 283–323 (1994)
99. Holzapfel, H., Fuegen, C.: Integrating emotional cues into a framework for dialogue management. In: ICMI 2002: Proceedings of the 4th IEEE International Conference on Multimodal Interfaces, p. 141. IEEE Computer Society, Washington, DC (2002)
100. Busso, C., Deng, Z., Yildirim, S., Bulut, M., Lee, C.M., Kazemzadeh, A., Lee, S., Neumann, U., Narayanan, S.: Analysis of emotion recognition using facial expressions, speech and multimodal information. In: ICMI 2004: Proceedings of the 6th International Conference on Multimodal Interfaces, pp. 205–211. ACM Press, New York (2004)
101. Zeng, Z., Tu, J., Liu, M., Zhang, T., Rizzolo, N., Zhang, Z., Huang, T.S., Roth, D., Levinson, S.: Bimodal hci-related affect recognition. In: ICMI 2004: Proceedings of the 6th International Conference on Multimodal Interfaces, pp. 137–143. ACM Press, New York (2004)
102. Gunes, H., Piccardi, M., Jan, T.: Face and body gesture recognition for a vision-based multimodal analyzer. In: VIP 2005: Proceedings of the Pan-Sydney Area Workshop on Visual Information Processing, pp. 19–28. Australian Computer Society, Inc., Darlinghurst (2004)
103. Shi, R.P., Adelhardt, J., Zeissler, V., Batliner, A., Frank, C., Nöth, E., Niemann, H.: Using speech and gesture to explore user states in multimodal dialogue systems. Technical Report 36, Lehrstuhl für Mustererkennung, Institut für Informatik, Friedrich Alexander Universität Erlangen, Martensstraße 3, 91058 Erlangen (June 2003)
104. Rudmann, D.S., McConkie, G.W., Zheng, X.S.: Eyetracking in cognitive state detection for hci. In: ICMI 2003: Proceedings of the 5th International Conference on Multimodal Interfaces, pp. 159–163. ACM Press, New York (2003)

105. Lindner, C. (ed.): Avatare. Digitale Sprecher für Business und Marketing. Springer, Berlin (2003)
106. Neal, J.G., Thielman, C.Y., Dobes, Z., Haller, S.M., Shapiro, S.C.: Natural language with integrated deictic and graphic gestures. In: HLT 1989: Proceedings of the Workshop on Speech and Natural Language, pp. 410–423. Association for Computational Linguistics, Morristown (1989)
107. Cohen, P.R., Johnston, M., McGee, D., Oviatt, S., Pittman, J., Smith, I., Chen, L., Clow, J.: Quickset: multimodal interaction for distributed applications. In: MULTIMEDIA 1997: Proceedings of the Fifth ACM International Conference on Multimedia, pp. 31–40. ACM Press, New York (1997)
108. Malaka, R., Häußler, J., Aras, H.: Smartkom mobile: intelligent ubiquitous user interaction. In: IUI 2004: Proceedings of the 9th International Conference on Intelligent user Interface, pp. 310–312. ACM Press, New York (2004)
109. Johnston, M., Bangalore, S., Vasireddy, G., Stent, A., Ehlen, P., Walker, M., Whittaker, S., Maloor, P.: Match: an architecture for multimodal dialogue systems. In: ACL 2002: Proceedings of the 40th Annual Meeting on Association for Computational Linguistics, pp. 376–383. Association for Computational Linguistics, Morristown (2002)
110. Hastie, H.W., Johnston, M., Ehlen, P.: Context-sensitive help for multimodal dialogue. In: ICMI 2002: Proceedings of the 4th IEEE International Conference on Multimodal Interfaces. IEEE Computer Society, Washington, DC (2002), http://www.research.att.com/~johnston/papers/hastieh_mmhelp.pdf (checked: June 20, 2008)
111. Almeida, L., Amdal, I., Beires, N., Boualem, M., Boves, L., den Os, E., Filoche, P., Gomes, R., Knudsen, J.E., Kvale, K., Rugelbak, J., Tallec, C., Warakagoda, N.: Implementing and evaluating a multimodal and multilingual tourist guide. In: Proceedings of the International CLASS Workshop on Natural, Intelligent and Effective Interaction in Multimodal Dialogue Systems, Copenhagen, Denmark (2002)
112. van Welie, M.: Task-based User Interface Design. PhD thesis, Dutch Graduate School for Information and Knowledge Systems, Vrije Universiteit Amsterdam (2001)
113. Gourdol, A., Nigay, L., Salber, D., Coutaz, J.: Two case studies of software architecture for multimodal interactive systems: Voicepaint and a voice-enabled graphical notebook. In: Larson, J., Unger, C. (eds.) Proceedings of IFIP TC3/WG2.7: Working Conference on Engineering for Human Computer Interaction, pp. 271–284. North Holland Publications (1992)
114. Nishimoto, T., Shida, N., Kobayashi, T., Shirai, K.: Improving human interface in drawing tool using speech. In: Proceedings of 4th IEEE International Workshop on Robot and Human Communication, ROMAN 1995, Tokyo, Japan, pp. 107–112 (1995)
115. Sedivy, J., Johnson, H.: Multimodal tool support for creative tasks in the visual arts. Knowledge-Based Systems 13(7-8), 441–450 (2000)
116. Sezgin, T.M., Stahovich, T., Davis, R.: Sketch based interfaces: early processing for sketch understanding. In: PUI 2001: Proceedings of the 2001 Workshop on Perceptive user Interfaces, pp. 1–8. ACM Press, New York (2001)
117. Forbus, K.D., Ferguson, R.W., Usher, J.M.: Towards a computational model of sketching. In: IUI 2001: Proceedings of the 6th International Conference on Intelligent user Interfaces, pp. 77–83. ACM Press, New York (2001)
118. Poirier, F., Julia, L., Rossignol, S., Faure, C.: Tapage: édition de tableaux sur ordinateur à stylo vers une désignation naturelle. In: Proc. IHM 1993 (1993)

119. Milota, A.D.: Modality fusion for graphic design applications. In: ICMI 2004: Proceedings of the 6th International Conference on Multimodal Interfaces, pp. 167–174. ACM Press, New York (2004)
120. Microsoft: Mipad: Speech powered prototype to simplify communication between users and handheld devices, http://www.microsoft.com/presspass/features/2000/05-22mipad.asp (checked: June 20, 2008) Microsoft
121. Microsoft: Your pad or mipad, http://research.microsoft.com/srg/mipad.aspx (checked: June 20, 2008) Microsoft
122. Huang, X., Acero, A., Chelba, C., Deng, L., Duchene, D., Goodman, J., Hon, H., Jacoby, D., Jiang, L., Loynd, R., Mahajan, M., Mau, P., Meredith, S., Mughal, S., Neto, S., Plumpe, M., Wang, K., Wang, Y.: Mipad: A next generation pda prototype. In: ICSLP, Peking (2000), http://research.microsoft.com/srg/papers/2000-xdh-icslp.pdf (checked: June 20, 2008)
123. Comerford, L., Frank, D., Gopalakrishnan, P., Gopinath, R., Sedivy, J.: The ibm personal speech assistant. In: Proc. of IEEE ICASSP 2001, DARPA, pp. 319–321 (2001)
124. Aslan, I., Xu, F., Uszkoreit, H., Krüger, A., Steffen, J.: COMPASS2008: Multimodal, multilingual and crosslingual interaction for mobile tourist guide applications. In: Maybury, M., Stock, O., Wahlster, W. (eds.) INTETAIN 2005. LNCS (LNAI), vol. 3814, pp. 3–12. Springer, Heidelberg (2005)
125. IBM: Developing X+V Applications Using the Multimodal Toolkit and Browser (October 2002)
126. IBM Pervasive Computing: Developing Multimodal Applications using XHTML+Voice (January 2003)
127. Marx, M., Schmandt, C.: Putting people first: specifying proper names in speech interfaces. In: UIST 1994: Proceedings of the 7th Annual ACM Symposium on User Interface Software and Technology, pp. 29–37. ACM Press, New York (1994)
128. Gould, J.D., Conti, J., Hovanyecz, T.: Composing letters with a simulated listening typewriter. Commun. ACM 26(4), 295–308 (1983)
129. Womser-Hacker, C.: Statistical experiments on computer talk. In: First International Comference on Quantitative Linguistics, pp. 251–263. Kluwer, Dordrecht (1993)
130. Hitzenberger, L., Womser-Hacker, C.: Experimentelle untersuchungen zu multimodalen natürlichsprachlichen dialogen in der mensch-computer-interaktion. SDV – Sprache und Datenverarbeitung 19(1), 51–61 (1995)
131. Coutaz, J., Salber, D., Carraux, E., Portolan, N.: Neimo, a multiworkstation usability lab for observing and analyzing multimodal interaction. In: CHI 1996: Conference Companion on Human Factors in Computing Systems, pp. 402–403. ACM Press, New York (1996)
132. Grasso, M.A., Ebert, D.S., Finin, T.W.: The integrality of speech in multimodal interfaces. ACM Trans. Comput.-Hum. Interact. 5(4), 303–325 (1998)
133. Oviatt, S., Cohen, P., Wu, L., Vergo, J., Duncan, L., Suhm, B., Bers, J., Holzman, T., Winograd, T., Landay, J., Larson, J., Ferro, D.: Designing the user interface for multimodal speech and pen-based gesture applications: State-of-the-art systems and future research directions. Human Computer Interaction 15(4), 263–322 (2000)
134. Treoware: Voicelauncher, http://treoware.com/voicelauncher.html (checked: June 20, 2008) Treoware

135. CallMagazin: Hps erstes smartphone: Der ipaq 514 hört aufs wort. CallMagazin (February 16, 2007), http://www.call-magazin.de/handy-mobilfunk/handy-mobilfunk-nachrichten/hpserstes-smartphone-der-ipaq-514-hoert-aufs-wort_20628.html (checked: June 20, 2008)

136. Microsoft: Microsoft voice command, http://www.microsoft.com/windowsmobile/voicecommand/features.mspx(checked: June 20, 2008) Microsoft

137. Grasso, M.A., Finin, T.W.: Task integration in multimodal speech recognition environments. Crossroads 3(3), 19–22 (1997)

138. Oviatt, S., Cohen, P.R., Wang, M.Q.: Toward interface design for human language technology: modality and structure as determinants of linguistic complexity. Speech Commun. 15(3-4), 283–300 (1994)

139. IBM: Multimodal Application Design Issues (December 2003)

140. IBM: XHTML+Voice Programmer's Guide. Version 1.0 edn. (February 2004)

141. Schnelle, D., Lyardet, F., Wei, T.: Audio Navigation Patterns. In: Proceedings of EuroPLoP 2005, pp. 237–260 (July 2005)

142. Schnelle, D., Lyardet, F.: Voice User Interface Design Patterns. In: Proceedings of 11th European Conference on Pattern Languages of Programs, EuroPlop 2006 (2006)

143. Ren, X., Zhang, G., Dai, G.: An experimental study of input modes for multimodal human-computer interaction. In: Tan, T., Shi, Y., Gao, W. (eds.) ICMI 2000. LNCS, vol. 1948, pp. 49–56. Springer, Heidelberg (2000), http://www.springerlink.com/content/wj970gnlyqam67du/fulltext.pdf (checked: June 20, 2008)

144. van Welie, M.: Gui design patterns (2003), http://www.welie.com/patterns/gui/ (checked: May 16, 2007)

145. Oviatt, S.L.: Multimodal interfaces. In: Jacko, J., Sears, A. (eds.) The Human-Computer Interaction Handbook: Fundamentals, Evolving Technologies and Emerging Applications, pp. 286–304. Lawrence Erlbaum Assoc., Mahwah (2003)

146. Cohen, P.R., Dalrymple, M., Moran, D.B., Pereira, F.C., Sullivan, J.W.: Synergistic use of direct manipulation and natural language. SIGCHI Bull. 20(SI), 227–233 (1989)

147. Kobsa, A., Allgayer, J., Reddig, C., Reithinger, N., Schmauks, D., Harbusch, K., Wahlster, W.: Combining deictic gestures and natural language for referent identification. In: Proceedings of the 11th Coference on Computational Linguistics, pp. 356–361. Association for Computational Linguistics, Morristown (1986)

148. Wahlster, W.: User and discourse models for multimodal communication. In: Sullivan, J.W., Tyler, S.W. (eds.) Intelligent User Interfaces, pp. 45–67. ACM Press (1991)

149. Shimazu, H., Arita, S., Takashima, Y.: Multi-modal definite clause grammar. In: COLING 1994, pp. 832–836 (1994)

150. Shimazu, H., Takashima, Y.: Multi-modal-method: A design method for building multi-modal systems. In: COLING 1996, pp. 925–930 (1996)

151. Bui, T., Rajman, M.: Rapid dialogue prototyping methodology. Technical Report 200401 IC/2004/01, Swiss Federal Institute of Technology (EPFL), Lausanne (January 2004)

152. Rajman, M., Bui, T., Rajman, A., Seydoux, F., Quarteroni, S.: Assessing the usability of a dialogue management system designed in the framework of a rapid dialogue prototyping methodology. In: Acta Acustica united with Acustica 2004 (2004)

153. Vo, M.T.: A Framework and Toolkit for the Construction of Multimodal Learning Interfaces. PhD thesis, School of Computer Science, Computer Science Department, Carnegie Mellon University (1998)
154. Cohen, P.R.: The role of natural language in a multimodal interface. In: UIST 1992: Proceedings of the 5th Annual ACM Symposium on User Interface Software and Technology, pp. 143–149. ACM Press, New York (1992)
155. Huls, C., Bos, E.: Studies into full integration of language and action. In: Proceedings of the International Conference on Cooperative Multimiodal Communication (CMC 1995), Eindhoven, pp. 161–174 (1995)
156. Bolt, R.A.: „Put-that-there": Voice and gesture at the graphics interface. In: SIGGRAPH 1980: Proceedings of the 7th Annual Conference on Computer Graphics and Interactive Techniques, pp. 262–270. ACM Press, New York (1980)
157. Bekiaris, E., Machate, J., Burmester, M.: Towards an intelligent multimodal and multimedia user interface providing a new dimension of natural hmi in the tele-operation of all home appliances by e&d users. In: Proceedings of Interfaces 1997, Montpellier, pp. 226–229 (1997)
158. Siroux, J., Guyomard, M., Multon, F., Remondeau, C.: Modeling and processing of oral and tactile activities in the georal system. In: Bunt, H., Beun, R.-J., Borghuis, T. (eds.) CMC 1995. LNCS (LNAI), vol. 1374, pp. 101–110. Springer, Heidelberg (1998)
159. Cheyer, A.: Mviews: Multimodal tools for the video analyst. In: International Conference on Intelligent User Interfaces (IUI 1998), pp. 55–62. ACM Press, New York (1998), http://www.adam.cheyer.com/papers/iui98.pdf (checked: June 20, 2008)
160. Portele, T., Goronzy, S., Emele, M., Kellner, A., Torge, S., te Vrugt, J.: Smartkom-home – an advanced multi-modal interface to home entertainment. In: EUROSPEECH 2003, pp. 1897–1900 (2003)
161. Reithinger, N., Alexandersson, J., Becker, T., Blocher, A., Engel, R., Löckelt, M., Müller, J., Pfleger, N., Poller, P., Streit, M., Tschernomas, V.: Smartkom: adaptive and flexible multimodal access to multiple applications. In: ICMI 2003: Proceedings of the 5th International Conference on Multimodal Interfaces, pp. 101–108. ACM Press, New York (2003)
162. Lisowska, A., Rajman, M., Bui, T.H.: archivus: A System for Accessing the Content of Recorded Multimodal Meetings. In: Bengio, S., Bourlard, H. (eds.) MLMI 2004. LNCS, vol. 3361, pp. 291–304. Springer, Heidelberg (2005)
163. McGee, D.R., Cohen, P.R.: Creating tangible interfaces by augmenting physical objects with multimodal language. In: IUI 2001: Proceedings of the 6th International Conference on Intelligent user Interfaces, pp. 113–119. ACM Press, New York (2001)
164. Rauschert, I., Agrawal, P., Sharma, R., Fuhrmann, S., Brewer, I., MacEachren, A.: Designing a human-centered, multimodal gis interface to support emergency management. In: GIS 2002: Proceedings of the 10th ACM International Symposium on Advances in Geographic Information Systems, pp. 119–124. ACM Press, New York (2002)
165. Long, A.C., Landay, J.A., Rowe, L.A.: "'those look similar!"' issues in automating gesture design advice. In: PUI 2001: Proceedings of the 2001 Workshop on Perceptive user Interfaces, pp. 1–5. ACM Press, New York (2001)
166. Baudel, T., Beaudouin-Lafon, M.: Charade: remote control of objects using free-hand gestures. Commun. ACM 36(7), 28–35 (1993)

167. Di Fiore, F., Vandoren, P., Van Reeth, F.: Multimodal interaction in a collaborative virtual brainstorming environment. In: Luo, Y. (ed.) CDVE 2004. LNCS, vol. 3190, pp. 47–60. Springer, Heidelberg (2004), http://research.edm.uhasselt.be/~fdifiore/research/CDVE2004/CDVE2004.pdf

168. Ou, J., Fussell, S.R., Chen, X., Setlock, L.D., Yang, J.: Gestural communication over video stream: supporting multimodal interaction for remote collaborative physical tasks. In: ICMI 2003: Proceedings of the 5th International Conference on Multimodal Interfaces, pp. 242–249. ACM Press, New York (2003)

169. Cheyer, A., Julia, L.: Multimodal maps: An agent-based approach. In: Bunt, H., Beun, R.-J., Borghuis, T. (eds.) CMC 1995. LNCS (LNAI), vol. 1374, pp. 111–121. Springer, Heidelberg (1998), http://www.springerlink.com/content/cafux7f8f2ymykkw/fulltext.pdf (checked: June 20, 2008)

170. Summerfield, A.Q.: Use of visual information for phonetic perception. Phonetica 36, 314–331 (1979)

171. Oviatt, S.L.: Mutual disambiguation of recognition errors in a multimodal architecture. In: CHI 1999: Proceedings of the SIGCHI Conference on Human Factors in Computing Systems, pp. 576–583. ACM, New York (1999)

172. Oviatt, S.L.: Multimodal signal processing in naturalistic noisy environments. In: Yuan, B., Huang, T., Tang, X. (eds.) Proceedings of the 6th International Conference on SPoken Language Processing (ICSLP), vol. 2, pp. 696–699. Chinese Friendship Publishers, Peking (2000)

173. Oviatt, S.L.: Multimodal system processing in mobile environments. In: UIST 2000: Proceedings of the 13th Annual ACM Symposium on User Interface Software and Technology, pp. 21–30. ACM Press, New York (2000)

174. Oviatt, S.L.: Taming recognition errors with a multimodal interface. Commun. ACM 43(9), 45–51 (2000)

175. Kumar, S., Cohen, P.R., Coulston, R.: Multimodal interaction under exerted conditions in a natural field setting. In: ICMI 2004: Proceedings of the 6th International Conference on Multimodal Interfaces, pp. 227–234. ACM Press, New York (2004)

176. Wachsmuth, S.: Multi-modal Scene Understanding Using Probabilistic Models. PhD thesis, Technischen Fakultät, Universität Bielefeld (2001)

177. Yang, J., Stiefelhagen, R., Meier, U., Waibel, A.: Visual tracking for multimodal human computer interaction. In: CHI 1998: Proceedings of the SIGCHI Conference on Human Factors in Computing Systems, pp. 140–147. ACM Press / Addison-Wesley Publishing Co., New York (1998)

178. Jain, A.K.: Multimodal user interfaces: who's the user? In: ICMI 2003: Proceedings of the 5th International Conference on Multimodal Interfaces, p. 1. ACM Press, New York (2003)

179. Snelick, R., Indovina, M., Yen, J., Mink, A.: Multimodal biometrics: issues in design and testing. In: ICMI 2003: Proceedings of the 5th International Conference on Multimodal Interfaces, pp. 68–72. ACM Press, New York (2003)

180. Nasoz, F., Ozyer, O., Lisetti, C.L., Finkelstein, N.: Multimodal affective driver interfaces for future cars. In: MULTIMEDIA 2002: Proceedings of the Tenth ACM International Conference on Multimedia, pp. 319–322. ACM Press, New York (2002)

181. Kaiser, E., Olwal, A., McGee, D., Benko, H., Corradini, A., Li, X., Cohen, P., Feiner, S.: Mutual disambiguation of 3d multimodal interaction in augmented and virtual reality. In: ICMI 2003: Proceedings of the 5th International Conference on Multimodal Interfaces, pp. 12–19. ACM Press, New York (2003)

182. Zhang, Q., Imamiya, A., Go, K., Mao, X.: Overriding errors in a speech and gaze multimodal architecture. In: IUI 2004: Proceedings of the 9th International Conference on Intelligent User Interface, pp. 346–348. ACM Press, New York (2004)
183. Tan, Y.K., Sherkat, N., Allen, T.: Error recovery in a blended style eye gaze and speech interface. In: ICMI 2003: Proceedings of the 5th International Conference on Multimodal Interfaces, pp. 196–202. ACM Press, New York (2003)
184. Tanaka, K.: A robust selection system using real-time multi-modal user-agent interactions. In: IUI 1999: Proceedings of the 4th International Conference on Intelligent User Interfaces, pp. 105–108. ACM Press, New York (1999)
185. Campana, E., Baldridge, J., Dowding, J., Hockey, B.A., Remington, R.W., Stone, L.S.: Using eye movements to determine referents in a spoken dialogue system. In: PUI 2001: Proceedings of the 2001 Workshop on Perceptive user Interfaces, pp. 1–5. ACM Press, New York (2001)
186. Patterson, E., Gowdy, J.: An audio-visual approach to simultaneous-speaker speech recognition. In: Proceedings of ICASSP, IEEE International Conference on Acoustics, Speech and Signal Processing, vol. 5, pp. 780–783 (2003)
187. Holzapfel, H., Nickel, K., Stiefelhagen, R.: Implementation and evaluation of a constraint-based multimodal fusion system for speech and 3d pointing gestures. In: ICMI 2004: Proceedings of the 6th International Conference on Multimodal Interfaces, pp. 175–182. ACM Press, New York (2004)
188. Chai, J.Y., Qu, S.: A salience driven approach to robust input interpretation in multimodal conversational systems. In: HLT 2005: Proceedings of the Conference on Human Language Technology and Empirical Methods in Natural Language Processing, pp. 217–224. Association for Computational Linguistics, Morristown (2005)
189. Trabelsi, Z., Cha, S.H., Desai, D., Tappert, C.: A voice and ink xml multimodal architecture for mobile e-commerce systems. In: WMC 2002: Proceedings of the 2nd International Workshop on Mobile Commerce, pp. 100–104. ACM Press, New York (2002)
190. Suhm, B., Myers, B., Waibel, A.: Multimodal error correction for speech user interfaces. ACM Trans. Comput.-Hum. Interact. 8(1), 60–98 (2001)
191. Ainsworth, W.A., Pratt, S.R.: Feedback strategies for error correction in speech recognition systems. Int. J. Man-Mach. Stud. 36(6), 833–842 (1992)
192. Murray, A.C., Frankish, C.R., Jones, D.M.: Data-entry by voice: Facilitating correction of misrecognitions. In: Baber, C., Noyes, J. (eds.) Interactive Speech Technology: Human Factors issues in the Application of Speech Input/Output to Computers, pp. 137–144. Taylor and Francis, Bristol (1993)
193. Lai, J., Vergo, J.: Medspeak: Report creation with continuous speech recognition. In: Proceedings of the Conference on Human Factors in Computing (CHI 1997), pp. 431–438. ACM Press (1997)
194. Papineni, K.A., Roukos, S., Ward, R.T.: Feature-based language understanding. In: Proceedings of the 5th European Conference on Speech Communication and Technology, vol. 3, pp. 1435–1438. European Speech Communication Association, Rhodes (1997)
195. Vergo, J.: A statistical approach to multimodal natural language interaction. In: Proceedings of the AAAI 1998 Workshop on Representations for Multimodal Human-Computer Interaction, pp. 81–85. AAAI Press (1998)
196. Balentine, B.: Re-engineering the speech menu. In: Gardner-Bonneau, D. (ed.) Human Factors and Voice Interacive Systems, pp. 205–235. Kluwer Akademic Publishers, Norwell (1999)

197. Balentine, B., Morgan, D.P.: How to Build a Speech Recognition Application. A Style Guide for Telephony Dialogues. EIG Press (2001)

198. Ibrahim, A., Johansson, P.: Multimodal dialogue systems: A case study for interactive tv. In: Proceedings of 7th ERCIM Workshop on User Interfaces for All, Chantilly, France, pp. 209–218 (2002)

199. Oviatt, S., van Gent, R.: Error reslution during multimodal human-computer interaction. In: Proc. of the International Conference on Spoken Language Processing, vol. 2, pp. 204–207 (1996)

200. Oviatt, S., Bernard, J., Levow, G.: Linguistic adaptation during error resolution with spoken and multimodal systems. Language and Speech (special issue on Prosody and Conversation) 41(3-4), 415–438 (1999)

201. Pieraccini, R., Dayanidhi, K., Bloom, J., Dahan, J.G., Phillips, M., Goodman, B.R., Prasad, K.V.: Multimodal conversational systems for automobiles. Commun. ACM 47(1), 47–49 (2004)

202. McCaffery, F., McTear, M.F., Murphy, M.: A multimedia interface for circuit board assembly. In: Bunt, H., Beun, R.-J., Borghuis, T. (eds.) CMC 1995. LNCS (LNAI), vol. 1374, pp. 213–230. Springer, Heidelberg (1998)

203. Yankelovich, N.: How do users know what to say? Interactions 3(6), 32–43 (1996)

204. Wasinger, R.: Multimodal Interaction with Mobile Devices: Fusing a Broad Spectrum of Modality Combinations. PhD thesis, Naturwissenschaftlich-Technische Fakultät I der Universität des Saarlandes, Saarbrücken (2006)

205. Breedvelt-Schouten, I., Paternò, F., Severijns, C.A.: Reusable structures in task models. In: Harrison, H., Torres, J. (eds.) Design, Specification and Verification of Interactive Systems, pp. 115–238. Springer, New York (1997)

206. Sinnig, D.: The complicity of patterns and model-based engineering. Master thesis, Department of Computer Science. Concordia University, Montreal (2004)

207. Stimmel, C.: Hold me, thrill me, kiss me, kill me: Patterns for developing effective concept prototypes. In: Manolescu, D., Wolf, B. (eds.) Proceedings Pattern Languages of Programs, Monticello (1999)

208. Mahemoff, M.J., Johnston, L.J.: The planet pattern language for software internationalisation. In: Manolescu, D., Wolf, B. (eds.) Proceedings of Pattern Languages of Programs (1999), http://jerry.cs.uiuc.edu/~plop/plop99/proceedings/Mahemoff/planet.pdf (checked: June 20, 2008)

209. Duyne, D.K.V., Landay, J., Hong, J.I.: The Design of Sites: Patterns, Principles, and Processes for Crafting a Customer-Centered Web Experience. Addison-Wesley Longman Publishing Co., Inc., Boston (2002)

210. Sutcliffe, A., Dimitrova, M.: Patterns, claims and multimedia. In: Sasse, M.A., Johnson, C. (eds.) Proc. Human-Computer Interaction: Interact 1999. IFIP, pp. 329–335. IOS Press, Amsterdam (1999)

211. Cybulski, J., Linden, T.: Composing multimedia artifacts for reuse. In: Harrison, N., Foote, B., Rohnert, H. (eds.) Pattern Languages of Program Design 4, pp. 461–488. Addison-Wesley Longman (2000)

212. Wolff, C.: Media design patterns. In: Womser-Hacker, C., Wolff, C. (eds.) Designing Information Systems, Konstanz, UVK, pp. 209–217 (2005)

213. Chung, E.S., Hong, J.I., Lin, J., Prabaker, M.K., Landay, J.A., Liu, A.L.: Development and evaluation of emerging design patterns for ubiquitous computing. In: DIS 2004: Proceedings of the 2004 Conference on Designing Interactive Systems, pp. 233–242. ACM Press, New York (2004)

214. Kunert, T.: User-Centered Interaction Design Patterns for Interactive Digital Television Applications. Springer (2009)

215. Ratzka, A.: A wizard-of-oz setting for multimodal interaction. an approach to user-based elicitation of design patterns. In: Osswald, A., Stempfhuber, M., Wolff, C. (eds.) Open Innovation. Proc. 10th International Symposium for Information Science, pp. 159–170. Universitätsverlag Konstanz, Köln (2007)

216. Ratzka, A.: Explorative studies on multimodal interaction in a pda- and desktop-based scenario. In: Proceedings of the International Conference on Multimodal Interfaces 2008. ACM Press (2008)

217. Ratzka, A.: Patternbasiertes User Interface Design für multimodale Interaktion. PhD thesis, Lehrstuhl für Informationswissenschaft, Universität Regensburg (2009/2010)

218. Riva, G. (ed.): Ambient Intelligence. The Evolution of Technology, Communication and Cognition Towards the Future of Human-Computer Interaction. Emerging Communication, vol. 6. IOS Press, Amsterdam (2005)

219. Weber, W. (ed.): Ambient Intelligence. Springer, Berlin (2005)

220. Nylander, S., Bylund, M., Waern, A.: Ubiquitous service access through adapted user interfaces on multiple devices. Personal Ubiquitous Comput. 9(3), 123–133 (2005)

221. Ishii, H., Ullmer, B.: Tangible bits: towards seamless interfaces between people, bits and atoms. In: Proceedings of CHI 1997 Conference on Human Factors in Computing Systems, pp. 234–241. ACM Press (1997)

222. Cohen, P.R., McGee, D.R.: Tangible multimodal interfaces for safety-critical applications. Commun. ACM 47(1), 41–46 (2004)

223. Vince, J.A.: Virtual Reality Systems. Addison Wesley (1995)

224. Sharman, W.R., Craig, A.B.: Understanding Virtual Reality. Morgan Kaufman, San Francisco (1995)

225. Mayhew, D.J.: The Usability Engineering Lifecycle. Morgan Kaufmann, San Francisco (1999)

226. Sinnig, D., Gaffar, A., Reichart, D., Seffah, A., Forbrig, P.: Patterns in model-based engineering. In: CADUI, pp. 195–208 (2004)

227. Petrasch, R.: Model based user interface design: Model driven architecture und hci patterns. GI Softwaretechnik-Trends. Mitteilungen der Gesellschaft für Informatik 27(3), 5–10 (2007), http://pi.informatik.uni-siegen.de/stt/27_3/03_Technische_Beitraege/MDA_HCI_Patterns_Petrasch_Short.pdf (checked: June 27, 2008)

228. Limbourg, Q., Vanderdonckt, J., Souchon, N.: The task-dialog and task-presentation mapping problem: Some preliminary results. In: Paternó, F. (ed.) DSV-IS 2000. LNCS, vol. 1946, pp. 227–246. Springer, Heidelberg (2001)

229. Gulliksen, J., Göransson, B., Boivie, I., Persson, J., Blomkvist, S., Cajander, Å.: Key principles for user-centred systems design. In: Seffah, A., Gulliksen, J., Desmarais, M.C. (eds.) Human-Centered Software Engineering: Integrating Usability in the Software Development Lifecycle, pp. 17–36. Springer, Dordrecht (2005)

230. Trætteberg, H.: Model-based User Interface Design. PhD thesis, Department of Computer and Information Sciences, Norwegian University of Science and Technology (2002)

231. Ratzka, A.: Design patterns in the context of multi-modal interaction. In: Proceedings of the 6th Nordic Conference on Pattern Languages of Programs, VikingPLoP 2007 (2008)

232. Ratzka, A.: Patterns for robust and accessible multimodal interaction. In: Proceedings of the 13th European Conference on Pattern Languages of Programs, EuroPLoP 2008 (2008)

Using Pattern-Based Architecture Reviews to Detect Quality Attribute Issues – An Exploratory Study

Neil B. Harrison[1,2] and Paris Avgeriou[1]

[1] Department of Mathematics and Computing Science, University of Groningen,
Groningen, The Netherlands
[2] Department Computer Science and Engineering, Utah Valley University,
Orem, Utah, USA
`neil.harrison@uvu.edu, paris@cs.rug.nl`

Abstract. Architecture reviews are effective for identifying potential problems in architectures, particularly concerning the quality attributes of the system, but are generally expensive. We propose that architecture reviews based on the architecture patterns and their interactions with quality attributes can be done with small effort. We performed an exploratory study to investigate how much time and effort is required to perform such a review, and how many related issues it uncovers. We performed nine architecture reviews on small systems, and recorded the time and effort spent, and the number of issues identified. On average, a pattern-based review took less than two person-days of effort and less than a day of calendar time. The median number of issues identified was three, one of which was major. We recommend that where extensive architecture reviews are too expensive, a pattern-based review can be done with small effort and time.

Keywords: Software Architecture Patterns, Architecture Reviews, Quality Attributes.

1 Introduction

Some of the most important requirements concern the system's quality attributes. These requirements are characteristics that the system has, as opposed to what the system does, such as usability, maintainability, performance, and reliability. Sommerville notes that functional requirements are services the system should provide, while non-functional requirements (quality attributes) are constraints on the functions offered by the system [1]. Bachmann et al and Bass et al [2, 3] use quality attribute scenarios to describe quality-attribute-specific requirements; such a scenario includes a stimulus acting on an artefact (a system or part of a system) within an environment, and a response and its measure. The set of quality attributes is rich and varied, and various classification schemes are used (see for example [3] and [4]).

A particular challenge of quality attributes is that because they tend to be system-wide characteristics, system-wide approaches are needed to satisfy them; these approaches are defined at the system architecture level and not the component level.

J. Noble et al. (Eds.): TPLOP III, LNCS 7840, pp. 168–194, 2013.
© Springer-Verlag Berlin Heidelberg 2013

Clements et al state the following [1]: "Modifiability, performance, security, availability, reliability – all of these are precast once the architecture is laid down. No amount of tuning or clever implementation tricks will wring any of these qualities out of a poorly architected system." However, they cannot be fully tested until the software is undergoing system test. This creates a large gap between when approaches to satisfy quality attributes are designed and when they are completely validated.

Because quality attributes are largely constrained by the systems' software architecture (see also [5]), the architecture is often reviewed to determine how well the system will meet its quality attribute requirements. Numerous architecture review methods have been developed, and general guidelines have been established [6, 7]. Several of the most prominent architecture review methods are classified and compared in [8], and further classifications are made in [9]. (Note that in this paper a review is an independent examination of the architecture for the purpose of finding potential architectural issues; this is sometimes called an evaluation [10].)

Architecture reviews have been shown to be effective tools in uncovering architectural issues [10, 11], many of which are related to quality attributes. Maranzano et al report that the most common design issues found are in performance engineering, error handling and recovery, reliability and availability, operations administration and maintenance, and system evolvability [11]. Bass et al report common risk themes in projects using the Architecture Tradeoff Analysis Method (ATAM) include availability, performance, security, modifiability, and security [12]. Architecture reviews are, of course, most useful when done early in the development cycle, before too much code has been written [6]. ATAM reviews are well-known, and are similar to other architecture reviews (such as those discussed by Maranzano et al.) For this reason, we have compared pattern-based architecture reviews, described below, to ATAM reviews.

Unfortunately, software architecture reviews have several important limitations. The most significant is that they require significant effort and time to complete. Abowd et al report that the average cost of an architecture review in AT&T was 70 staff days [6]. The SEI Software Architecture Analysis Method (SAAM) requires an average of 14 staff days [6]. Clements et al report that the approximate cost of an ATAM-based architecture evaluation ranges from 32 to 70 person-days (split roughly evenly between the evaluation team and the stakeholders) [10].

Closely related to effort is time. Maranzano et al report that the review preparation time lasts between two and six weeks [11], and the review itself lasts from one to five days. Clements et al state that ATAM-based evaluations should result in about three actual project days being consumed by the process [10].

In spite of the proven benefits of architecture reviews, these limitations make projects less willing to use them. This is particularly true of small projects, where time is severely limited. Many small projects also follow the Agile development philosophy [13], in which documentation such as architecture documentation is eschewed.

In response to this problem, we have developed a lightweight method for reviewing architectures called Pattern-Based Architecture Reviews (PBAR). It is a shift from a comprehensive architecture review to one that focuses on issues related to the satisfaction of the system's important quality attributes. It uses the patterns found in the architecture to identify quality attribute issues.

1.1   Problem Statement

The overall problem can be stated as follows: is PBAR a viable architecture review method for small projects? By viable, we mean that the costs are low enough that small projects might consider using it, and that its benefits outweigh the costs of the review.

As a point of clarification, we are not comparing the effectiveness of PBAR to other architecture review methods; indeed it is obvious that a lightweight review method such as PBAR cannot go into the depth that comprehensive reviews can. Yet even a lightweight review is better than no review at all. To illustrate how its low cost might appeal to small projects, we compare the costs of PBAR with those of ATAM.

It is important to learn this because if PBAR is a viable review method for small software projects, it can help their developers find architectural issues related to quality attributes while the software is still in early development, and such issues are relatively easy to fix.

We note that there are different ways that "small projects" may be defined. For the purposes of this study, we looked at projects with few developers; nearly all were under 10. The rationale is that projects with so few people are unlikely to have any extra time for documenting or reviewing architectures. We do not mean to exclude other measures of size, such as number of requirements, function points, or components, but we haven't examined them in this particular study.

1.2   Research Objectives and Approach

Our research objectives are to empirically analyse the use of PBAR in small projects for the purpose of learning the following:

1. How much effort does a PBAR review take compared to an ATAM-based evaluation?
2. How much calendar time does a PBAR review require compared to an ATAM-based evaluation?
3. How many major and minor architectural issues can a PBAR review uncover?

This paper presents an empirical validation of PBAR with respect to these three questions. For the first question, we examined the effort in terms of person-days required to perform the review. For the second question, we looked at the duration of the review meetings. For the third question, we examined the number and type of issues found. We note that these research objectives are a part of the overall problem as stated above, and do not aim to quantify the effectiveness of PBAR as a whole. They are intended to give evidence that can be used to help reason about the effectiveness of such reviews.

This empirical study was exploratory in nature (see [14]). The type of exploratory study was an observational study done in the field: we collected data on actual reviews done on live projects. We began 9 reviews and completed and analysed data from 7 reviews. Details of the type of empirical study, as well as the setup and execution of the study, are provided in this paper.

The rest of this paper is as follows: Section 2 gives background about key concepts, namely architecture patterns and quality attribute tactics, and describes the PBAR process. It also describes related work. Section 3 presents the empirical study method used and explains how the study was planned and reviews set up. It then describes the execution of the reviews and the data collection. Section 4 gives a summary of the results, and section 5 gives our interpretation of the results. The final section gives conclusions and describes future work.

2   Research Background

In order to understand the background behind using patterns in architecture reviews, one must understand the role of architecture patterns and tactics, and their relationship with quality attributes. These terms and their relationships are described below. A short description of the PBAR process follows thereafter.

2.1   Architecture Patterns

Software patterns are generalized solutions to recurring design problems in software development. They provide a proven approach and guidance on using the pattern solution. The solutions are generic, and are customized to the situation in which a pattern is used. Patterns include information on the consequences of applying the solution; this is important information. The most well-known software patterns are object-oriented design patterns [15]. Architecture patterns give approaches to the design of the entire software system. Architecture patterns dictate a particular high-level modular decomposition of the system [16, 17, 18]. While there are many types of patterns, in this paper we are concerned only with software architecture patterns.

For example, the Layers pattern divides the system into distinct layers so that each layer provides a set of services to the layer above and uses the services of the layer below. Within each layer, all constituent components work at the same level of abstraction and can interact through connectors. Between two adjacent layers a clearly defined interface is provided. In the pure or strict form of the pattern, layers should not be by-passed: higher-level layers access lower-level layers only through the layer beneath [19].

One of the key benefits and unique characteristics of architecture patterns is that they capture the general architectural structure of the system and couple it with the consequences of using that architectural structure. These consequences are the impact of using the pattern on the quality attributes of the system. The impact makes it easier or harder to satisfy a certain quality attribute. In nearly every case, architecture patterns impact multiple quality attributes.

The Layers pattern supports fulfilling many security requirements, because authentication services can be encapsulated into a layer surrounding the main application. On the other hand, the Layers pattern requires that requests pass through multiple layers in order to be fulfilled; this hurts performance. If performance is an important quality requirement, Layers may not be the best choice.

Because the patterns are based on long experience, their impact on quality attributes is usually documented as part of the pattern description (see [18].) This documentation is a valuable resource for the architect. This information is beginning to be organized and summarized for handy use [20].

2.2   Quality Attributes and Tactics

Certain specific measures are often implemented to improve quality attributes. Bass et al call these measures tactics [3]. For example, a duplication scheme to improve the reliability (nonstop operation) of the system is a tactic. The implementation of a tactic may require significant changes to structure and behavior of the architecture patterns in the system. Because of this, future maintenance of the system may be considerably more difficult and error-prone. Tactics may be "design time," or overall approaches to design and implementation, such as "hide information" to improve modifiability, or may be "runtime tactics", which are features directed at a particular aspect of a quality attribute, such as "authenticate users" to improve security. In this paper, we concern ourselves with the runtime tactics, and when we refer to "tactics", we mean runtime tactics.

We find that architects often consider which tactics to use at the time they design the architecture [21, 22]. However, unless the relationship between the architecture patterns and the tactics being used is well understood, architects risk making architectural decisions (either concerning which patterns to use or which tactics to use) that could be difficult to implement correctly and maintain. The relationship between the tactics selected and the patterns used is therefore an important consideration in an architecture review.

2.3   The Pattern-Based Architecture Review (PBAR) Process

The goal of Pattern-Based Architecture Reviews is to provide a ligheweight architecture review process that can be used where traditional architecture review methods would not because of their high cost. The premise is that time and effort can be reduced through focusing review on the most important quality attributes, keeping the number of reviewers to a minimum, limiting the advance preparation, and limiting the meetings to the review meeting itself.

The structure of Pattern-Based Architecture Reviews (PBAR) is based on architecture review processes, namely the AT&T review process [11], which one of the authors used while an employee there, as well as ATAM [3]. PBAR is simpler than these processes chiefly in that the up-front work is reduced, and that the focus is narrowed to the quality attributes and patterns used. While architecture patterns may be identified during ATAM and other reviews, PBAR's pattern focus also comes from

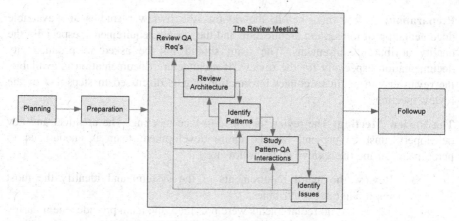

Fig. 1. The PBAR Architecture Review Process

reviews of organizations, where patterns were used to identify organizational issues [23]. The key differences between PBAR and comprehensive architecture reviews are summarized in this table:

Table 1. Key Focus Differences in Review Methods

Comprehensive Architecture Review	Pattern-Based Architecture Review
Focus on all requirements	Focus on key quality attribute requirements
Discovery through analysis and other study methods for satisfaction of requirements	Discovery through pattern identification and association with quality attributes
Extensive preparation by reviewers and stakeholders	No preparation for stakeholders
Documentation often prepared just for the review	Only existing documentation used
Architects and key stakeholders attend review	Entire team encouraged to attend review

We emphasize that this process came from our experience in conducting architecture reviews and our desire to make them simple and practical for small projects. Thus the process is heuristic rather than formal. Its audience is practitioners who need simple solutions, hence the description of the process is also simplified and oriented towards this audience. It is aimed at producing pragmatic results rather than rigorous verification and validation of an architecture. The flow of the reviews is as follows:

Resources and Planning: At least one reviewer is needed. On the project side, all developers are encouraged to take part in the review; other stakeholders are desired.

Preparation: A few days before the review, the reviewer studies any available documentation of the system architecture and the system requirements, especially the quality attribute requirements. The team should not be asked to produce any documentation especially for the review. If architecture documentation is available, the reviewer can begin to collect information that is discussed in steps 1-4 of the review meeting.

The Review Meeting: The review is a face-to-face meeting. The architect and key developers must be present, but the entire development team is encouraged to participate. During the review, do the following:

1. Review the major requirements of the system, and identify the most important quality attributes.
   a. If no requirements were provided, the team provides them during the review. The reviewer usually asks what the major capabilities of the system are.
   b. With the team, identify the most important quality attributes. Ideally, stakeholders provide input to determine the most important quality attributes.
   c. Elicit more detail about the quality attributes by discussing scenarios of the functional requirements. For example, when walking through a purchase scenario in an e-commerce system one might ask, "What should happen if the link to the customer drops just before a purchase is finalized?"

2. Review the architecture of the system. If no architecture diagram was provided, ask (or help) the team to draw one. In general, a components and connectors view is the most useful diagram for PBAR.
   a. It is useful to draw the architecture on a white board, even if it was provided beforehand.

3. Identify the architecture patterns used in the architecture. Because published patterns have rich documentation about their consequences; in particular their impact on quality attributes (see [20]), one should look for established architecture patterns. A comprehensive list of architecture patterns can be found in [19].One can identify the patterns by doing the following:
   a. Look for common pattern names (see [19]) in architecture documentation, module names, or annotations on modules. For example, a module named "Shared Database Layer" would indicate the presence of the Layers pattern as well as a member of the Repository family (Shared Repository, Active Repository, or Blackboard; for descriptions, see [18, 19].) Of course, the use of a pattern name does not necessarily mean that the pattern is actually present; the reviewer should question the architects about it and delve into the structure to verify whether the pattern is present; see below.

    b.   Match structural decomposition (components and connectors) to the structures of the patterns. For example, data flow through sequential modules indicates the use of Pipes and Filters [18]. This method is a common way of identifying patterns, particularly where architects are unfamiliar with patterns. Note that it has been shown that architecture patterns can be found through architecture diagrams [24].

4. Study the architecture and quality attributes together to determine the effects of each pattern on the system's quality attributes.

    a.   Identify the tactics used and map them to potential patterns that may implement them. Several important tactics have been identified in [3], and extensive reliability tactics are given in [25].For example, the security tactics of Limit Exposure and Limit Access [3] suggest the use of the Layers [18] architecture pattern. Note that tactics may not be spelled out in any architecture documentation; an effective way to identify them is to ask the architects how they address each of the quality attributes. This will reveal the use of tactics, and may also reveal important omissions. Examine how the tactics might be implemented in the patterns, and how easy such implementations are. For example, see [26] for information on reliability tactics and patterns.

    b.   Review the scenarios previously used, and discuss what tactics will be used to implement the quality attribute measures discussed, and where in the architecture they belong. This highlights both missing tactics and tactics that may not be fit well in the patterns used.

    c.   It is useful to annotate the architecture diagram on the white board with notes showing where the various tactics are (to be) implemented.

5. Identify issues; including the following:

    a.   Quality attributes not addressed or not adequately satisfied. If feasible, discuss possible solutions (e.g., certain tactics that might be used.)

    b.   Patterns that are not used that might be useful

    c.   Potential conflicts between patterns used and quality attributes. They may be specific to this architecture, but may also include general characteristics the patterns, such as the fact that a layered architecture is often incompatible with a high performance requirement.

Follow-up: After the review, the reviewer may perform further analysis of the data. In any case, create a short summary report for the project. It is useful to meet with the entire team for a feedback session.

2.4   Related Work

Related work consists of surveys and descriptions of architecture review methods, and empirical studies related to architectural review. We begin with surveys and descriptions of review methods.

Numerous architecture review methods have been developed. Virtually all the well-known methods are based on using scenarios to evaluate the architecture; these include Scenario-Based Architecture Analysis Method (SAAM) [27] and some variants, Architecture Tradeoff Analysis Method (ATAM) [28], Active Reviews for Intermediate Design (ARID) [31], Architecture-Level Modifiability Analysis (ALMA) [32], Architecture-Level Prediction of Software Maintenance (ALPSM) [33], and Scenario-Based Architecture Reengineering (SBAR) [34]. Dobrica and Niemelä have surveyed these architecture analysis methods, and compared eight elements of them [8]. Ali-Babar et al included additional elements [9] in a subsequent study. The following table shows five elements selected from these two studies where PBAR has significant differences from many other methods, and shows how they are done in PBAR. These differences reflect tradeoffs made in order to accommodate the low cost needs and characteristics of small projects, such as minimal architectural documentation.

Table 2. SA Review Method Classification Applied to PBAR

Method Element	PBAR's Focus; Key Differences From Other Methods
Method's goals [9]	Evaluate the ability of system architecture to achieve quality attributes (QA). Focus only on QAs and not functional requirements (Similar to SBAR [34], but SBAR is for analysis of existing systems.) PBAR trades off comprehensive coverage such as ATAM [28], for lower cost, focusing on a high payoff area.
Quality attributes [8]	Multiple quality attributes, similar to SBAR [34] and ATAM [28]. This trades off depth in a single QA for breadth across many. Some methods focus on a single QA (e.g., ALMA [32] focuses on maintainability.)
Architectural description [9]	Uses whatever the project has; if none is available, use verbal descriptions and whiteboard sketches. All other methods require some architectural description; PBAR attempts to work with inferior or nonexistent documentation, because if extensive documentation is required, projects may not afford the review at all.
Reusability of existing knowledge [8]	PBAR uses existing (external) architecture pattern and tactic knowledge [3, 26]. Other methods tend to focus on internal experience repositories [28, 32]. PBAR may also use internal experience repositories, but can also work for small projects which have no such repositories.
Resources Required [9]	Very few resources required; see later section. All projects that specified resource requirements were much higher; see [28] for example.

We note that we are not comparing PBAR to any existing method, but rather propose that PBAR provides a way for projects to get some of the quality attribute-related benefits of reviews in cases where the costs of such reviews are prohibitive. PBAR can also be an inexpensive way to identify issues, prior to following up with a more rigorous review method.

Bachmann et al [2] propose a method for designing software architectures to achieve quality attributes that is based on a reasoning framework. The reasoning framework helps architects create an architecture that meets the needs of quality attribute scenarios, which may include the selection of patterns and tactics. PBAR is similar in that it focuses on quality attributes, as well as uses patterns and tactics. However, PBAR is a review approach rather than an architectural design method, and uses pattern and tactic documentation rather than a reasoning framework.

Zhu et al describe an approach to examine patterns to find tactics that may be applied, for the purpose of selecting and calibrating a quality attribute reasoning framework [29]. The reasoning framework is then used, as noted above, in architecture reviews. Our approach is somewhat the other way around: quality attribute scenarios are derived from user stories, and compared against the architecture patterns in use.

An empirical analysis of architecture reviews was performed by Bass et al, who extensively analysed data from 18 final reports of architecture reviews [30]. They categorize the most common risk themes identified. They also note that about twice as many risk themes are risks of "omission" rather than risks of "commission." We did not classify the issues we found into their risk theme categories, nor did we identify risks of omission vs. commission; although we saw issues of both types. We note that all their reviews were of large projects, while ours were almost exclusively small projects. We do not know if this has an effect on the number and type issues identified.

3 Case Study Design

In order to fully understand the implications of any empirical study, one must understand how the study was designed. This includes the type of study, as well as the selection of subjects and how the study was carried out. These topics are explored in more detail in this section.

3.1 Study Type

This study is exploratory in nature (see [14]), meaning that we set out to learn about the nature of the effort and calendar time required by PBAR, and number of issues it identifies (treatment), rather than to formulate a hypothesis to test the treatment against. We were also not attempting to compare PBAR to established architecture review methods. It is also exploratory because there have been no other empirical observations of pattern-based architectural reviews such as PBAR, and thus the underlying theory has not been established yet. This study should provide a basis for future formal studies testing hypotheses about the effectiveness of these reviews.

The empirical method we used was an observational study, which is an in situ study of industrial practice [14]. Alavi and Carlson call it a field study, and state that it entails no manipulation of independent variables and is carried out in the natural settings of the phenomenon of interest [35]. In our studies, independent variables included project size, domain (in particular, which quality attributes were important), and background of participants.

We report the details of the study and its results in the next sections, following the model given by Wohlin et al [37], which Jedlitschka and Ciolkowski note is for generic empirical research [38]. (As their proposal describes guidelines for reporting controlled experiments, it was not a good fit for this study.) The introduction and problem statement are given in section 1. The following section, case and subject selection, describes the projects selected. The next section, Experiment Operation describes how the reviews were done. Section 4 presents the data, and sections 5 and 6 discuss its interpretation, including threats to validity and limitations of application. We finish with conclusions and future work.

3.2   Case and Subject Selection

We selected nine projects for the experiment. The projects were selected for their availability and ability to participate in the study.

We classified the projects based on the number of developers involved. Large projects had more than 30 developers, medium had 10 to 30 developers, and small were less than 10. The projects were as follows:

All the projects studied except one were medium or small, with 30 or fewer people on the project. Most of the projects had fewer than 10 people working on them. The reason we use number of people on the project as a size metric is twofold. First, most of the reviews were done before the code was complete, so the size in terms of implementation (e.g. lines of code) was not known. Second, a functionality metric such as function points, feature points, or even user stories could not be used because few if any of the projects used them. We did not observe any notable differences in the results of the review due to the sizes of the projects.

The methodology the projects used (e.g., Agile, waterfall) was not specified.

Architecture reviews are generally done in the early phases of projects [6]. We performed most reviews during the development phase, although two were done in later phases. The reviews that were performed in later phases ended up serving as validity checks for issues identified (see interpretation of results.) The only difference we observed between early and late phases was that the projects in late phases did not make changes based on the issues found. One would expect this; indeed, architecture reviews are to be done as early as is practical.

There were no constraints put on the application domains. Of course, the size of the project plays a significant role in the type of application; for example one would not expect life-critical systems to be done in the teams such as we studied. Our domains were concentrated more in web-based applications, but the driver was size, rather than application domain.

Five of the projects were student capstone projects, the rest were industry projects. Note that the capstone projects were all projects done for real external customers; none was a canned project for the students. In addition, nearly all the students who participated had part-time or full-time jobs in industry, and had several years of professional experience. Each team had at least one team member with over 3 years professional experience. The reviews were scheduled at the convenience of the project.

The following table identifies each project studied.

Table 3. PBAR Projects Studied

System	Size	Project Phase	Project Description
A	Large	Implementation	Streaming data manipulation and analysis
B	Med.	Architecture	Computer-controlled process control (similar to an automated assembly line)
C	Small	Post release	Embedded GPS platform application
D	Small	Early Implementation	Web-based time tracking system
E	Small	Early Implementation	Distributed data entry and subscription management system
F	Small	Early Implementation	E-commerce inventory management system
G	Small	Early Implementation	Android™[1] phone application
H	Small	Early Implementation	Web-based game platform
I	Small	Architecture	Web-based business process support system

We note that other classifications of projects, such as number and complexity of requirements, etc., may also be useful for understanding the applicability of PBAR, and recommend such studies be done.

---

[1] Android is a trademark of Google Inc. Use of this trademark is subject to Google Permissions.

3.3   Experiment Operation

We performed each review according to the process described in Section 2.3. The independent variable in the study was the review approach, namely PBAR, as compared to ATAM. We collected data for the following dependant variables:

- Number and importance of issues uncovered, as well as which quality attributes were affected.
- Time required for the review
- Effort required for the review

We also measured the following extraneous variables, in order to calibrate the results as necessary:

- Project size, as measured by number of people on the project.
- Phase in development
- Quality attributes important to the project
- Number of patterns identified

In order to avoid "false positives;" identifying issues that weren't really there, we did the following to verify the validity of the issues we found:

- Asked the participants whether each issue was indeed a real problem.
- Followed up at a later time to see whether the team acted on the issues. Lack of action does not mean that an issue is not real, but action does indicate that an issue is real.
- Ascertained whether the issues had already been considered, and possibly corrective action taken.

For each project, we filled out a summary report template that contained a description of the project and the data collected, and returned it to the project. A sample is found in the appendix.

Two of the reviews were not completed. In project I, the review was not completed at all. In project A, the review itself was completed but feedback from the architects was not obtained. Both these reviews involved deviations from the process and thus provide possible insights into the process, as we will discuss later.

4   Data Analysis

Our research objectives stated in section 1.1 were to determine how much effort is required for a PBAR review, how much calendar time is required, and how many issues are typically found. As this is an exploratory study, we did not test a hypothesis, but rather gathered information so that hypotheses about the effectiveness of PBAR can be made.

4.1   Case and Subject Selection

The effort required depends on the number of reviewers and the number of stakeholders involved in the review. This is important not only for determining the effort required, but also when comparing the efforts of different types of reviews.

In all our studies, a single reviewer was involved, so the reviewer effort can easily be calculated. The number of stakeholders participating varied, so we calculated the effort per person. Because there is no preparation required for stakeholders (unlike other review types), the total stakeholder effort was in the review meeting and the follow-up session. So we were able to average the meeting time to come up with the per stakeholder effort. Table 4 shows the breakdown of effort for the reviewers, compared to various versions of the ATAM method as reported in [10]. We note that Clements et al [10] do not precisely define the difference between ATAM-Medium and ATAM-Small; it appears that ATAM-Small is a scaling down of the medium review.

Table 4. Reviewer Effort in person-days, by Phase

	PBAR *(review team size: 1)*	ATAM-**Medium** *(review team size: 1)*	ATAM-**Medium** (using **Checklists**) *(review team size: 1)*	ATAM-**Small** *(review team size: 1)*
Preparation	1/2	1	1	1
Review Meeting(s)	1/4	20	12	6
Follow-up	3/4	15	12	8
Total Effort	< 2	36	25	15

Using a second reviewer would be desirable, and we surmise that adding a second reviewer would not double the effort of a single reviewer. The reason is that much of the follow-up effort is devoted to writing a summary of recommendations; the effort for this task would not double with the doubling of the reviewers.

Table 5 summarizes the effort of the stakeholders. The descriptions of ATAM split the stakeholders into project decision makers and other stakeholders. Project decision

Table 5. Stakeholder Effort in person-days, by Phase

	PBAR *(5 stakeholders)*	ATAM-**Medium** *(3 stakeholders)*	ATAM-**Medium** (with **Checklists**) *(3 stakeholders)*	ATAM-**Small** *(2 stakeholders)*
Preparation	0	3	1	3
Review Meeting(s)	1.25	12	9	6
Follow-up	< 1	3	3	2
Total	2	18	13	11

makers include architect, project manager, and in the case of the medium reviews, the customer. In these tables, the ATAM entries show only the effort of the project decision makers.

In PBAR, as many as all developers may attend, so the total effort will vary. We found that the effort required for each person averaged 2-2.5 hours for the review meeting and half an hour or less for the follow-up meeting, for a total of 3 hours per person. The table shows a team of 5; larger organizations will have a proportionally larger effort.

4.2   Calendar Time Required

In the following table, we see that PBAR requires somewhat less calendar time than ATAM-Small reviews. Clements et all do not summarize calendar time, but the time given below is based on times given for various parts of the review.

Table 6. Calendar Time for Review Types, in days

	PBAR	ATAM-Small
Calendar Time	< 1	3

Clements et al state that for ATAM reviews, the calendar time added to a project is minimal. Preparation and follow-up are done behind the scenes, and thus have no schedule impact. The review meetings usually consume about three days [10]. In PBAR reviews, preparation and follow-up were also done behind the scenes. The difference then is that PBAR review meetings consumed less than one day, while ATAM meetings generally last two or more days. Note that because the entire development team is encouraged to attend PBAR meetings, the schedule impact is equivalent to meeting length: a PBAR that consumes half a day causes half a day impact to the schedule. ATAM reviews appear not to require the entire time, so the calendar time is estimated; Bass et al do not give an exact figure.

4.3   Number of Issues Identified

The following table summarizes the issues found in the reviews (as noted above, reviews A and I were omitted because they were not completed):

The following table summarizes the issues found in the reviews (as noted above, reviews A and I were omitted because they were not completed):

The number of patterns identified is consistent with patterns found in other systems (see [24]). Since patterns provide ready-made documentation (at the very least the structure and behaviour of the pattern, and its generic advantages and liabilities), they are useful during the review. However, the number of patterns is not expected to be correlated with the number of issues identified; indeed, a simple inspection of the data indicates it is not.

Table 7. Issues Found in Reviews

System	Development Phase	Patterns Identified	Total Issues Identified	Major Issues	Major Issues Implemented
B	Architecture	6	4	1	0
C	Released, Legacy	7	2	0	0
D	Early Impl.	4	7	1	1
E	Early Impl.	3	3	2	1
F	Early Impl.	3	3	1	1
G	Early Impl	2	3	1	1
H	Early Impl	3	5	0	0
Median		3	3	1	1

Issues were defined as potential problems with satisfying a quality attribute. Major issues were those issues that had the potential to compromise the satisfaction of a quality attribute, as agreed by the team. Examples of major and minor issues are:

- Major issue: In the time tracking system (project D), if a user logs in, and the link between the user's client (which tracks their work session) and the server goes down, and later comes up, an inaccurate time record may be generated. (Quality attribute: Reliability.)
- Minor issue: In the e-commerce support system (project F), the system allowed file transfers, but the verification of the file transfer was left to the user to do manually. Automated transfer verification would be nicer, but users were billed for per message, so automated verification would cost them. Perhaps a future change would be to allow the verification to be free. (Quality Attribute: Usability.)
- An important consideration in any review is whether important issues are missed by the review. We do not know of any information about how many issues are missed by any architecture review method; PBAR or published methods such as ATAM. However, one might consider comparing the issues found by each method on a review of the same architecture, to determine whether one method finds issues missed by the other. We have not done this

yet. Such a comparison will be most effective if the nature of the issues found and missed is explored; it may show, for example, that PBAR is well-suited or ill-suited for identifying issues related to certain quality attributes.

5   Interpretation of Results

In analyzing the results, we consider three things, the effort required to perform the reviews, the time it takes, and the number and type of issues uncovered by the reviews.

5.1   Effort Required

It is striking to see the large difference in effort between PBAR and review methods such as ATAM. We describe the probable reasons that the effort for PBAR is so low, based on observations of these experiences. This validates the intent of PBAR given above.

1. Much of the time difference is in the review meetings. PBAR has a narrow focus. Rather than trying to discover every potential issue, PBAR focuses on the characteristics of the most important quality attributes of a project. This means that the review does not have to exercise a complete set of scenarios, but rather focus only on a rather limited set of scenarios associated with the most important quality attributes.
2. Another reason for the differences in review meeting effort is that PBAR has a simple, single meeting format. ATAM has a two-phase evaluation activity, which accounts for one fourth to one half of the meeting effort. Some of the effort in the first phase might be considered preparation for the review; PBAR has few preparation activities for the stakeholders.
3. Because the review has a narrow focus, fewer issues will be found. Thus, the follow-up work will be less.
4. In our study PBAR employed only one reviewer; this reduces the overall effort.
5. The projects we reviewed with PBAR were small, so the architectures will surely be simpler than large projects. It should take considerably less time to go through a small architecture than a large one.

Is the cost low enough that small projects are likely to use PBAR? Clearly, small projects are more likely to use a low-cost review method than a high cost one. Not only is the effort small, but the calendar time required for the review meeting is short; under a day. This is important, as many small projects have short release cycles (3-4 weeks [39]), and may have daily units of work [40]. We recommend that this validation be done.

5.2   Time Required

PBAR requires somewhat less calendar time than reviews such as ATAM, although the difference is not as striking as the difference in effort. The main reason for the difference is that the review meeting, being focused rather than comprehensive, is considerably shorter. This begins to suggest that PBAR may present an opportunity for a project to make tradeoffs: a project where development schedule is critical may choose the focus of a PBAR-style review, where a project that needs comprehensive examination will wish a review similar to ATAM. We speculate that there may be approaches to reviews between PBAR and ATAM that may be more comprehensive than PBAR yet lighter weight than ATAM.

5.3   Number and Type of Issues Identified

We see that all the reviews found relevant issues, some of which were major. This indicates that PBAR is successful at finding issues. This begs the question of whether PBAR finds all the issues, or even a significant portion of important issues. Naturally, we cannot know if PBAR – or any architecture review method – detects all the issues. It is logical to assume that PBAR does not find all the issues that a comprehensive review does, but we have no data that quantifies the difference. In order to quantify the difference, one would need to compare PBAR with another method in a formal experiment. This may be an area of future research.

We note that the projects studied had a wide range of important quality attributes. We also note that issues were found among nearly all the quality attributes that were identified. This shows some diversity among the projects, and indicates that PBAR is likely to be useful across several different domains.

Bass et al [3] list several benefits that architecture reviews have beyond identification of errors. It is useful to see whether PBAR provides the same benefits. Based on our observations of the reviews, but not based on any rigorous study, we suggest that PBAR may have the benefits that Bass et al present:

Bass et al [3] list several benefits that architecture reviews have beyond identification of errors. It is useful to see whether PBAR provides the same benefits. Based on our observations of the reviews, but not based on any rigorous study, we suggest that PBAR may have the benefits that Bass et al present:

1. Puts Stakeholders in the Same Room: Because PBAR employs a review meeting, it does this. In six of the nine reviews, all developers were present, but non-developer stakeholders were not present. Thus PBAR has some of this benefit.
2. Forces an Articulation of Specific Quality Goals: During each of the reviews, the teams were asked to identify the most important quality attributes, and their acceptable levels. Goals not associated with quality attributes were not explored.
3. Results in the Prioritization of Conflicting Goals: Teams were asked to identify the most important quality attribute goals, although it was informal.
4. Forces a Clear Explication of the Architecture: Each team was required to explain their architecture; some teams without architecture documentation produced architecture diagrams during the review. In fact, people from two different projects mentioned this benefit in their feedback. One of these was a team of only four people and there was different architectural understanding even within such a small team.

5. Improves the Quality of Architectural Documentation: Where no architectural documentation existed, teams produced architecture diagrams during the review. Improvements to existing architecture documentation were not assessed.

6. Uncovers Opportunities for Cross-Project Reuse: We observed no evidence of this benefit.

7. Results in Improved Architecture Practices: Bass et al explain that organizations that use architectural reviews as part of their development process have improved architectures over time. We observed some evidence of this benefit in that teams increased their knowledge and use of architecture patterns. At the beginning of the reviews, none of the participants had extensive knowledge of architecture patterns, and some were completely unfamiliar with them. In the review, as patterns came up, they were discussed, along with their advantages and disadvantages.

Our experiences with the two reviews that were not completed gave us some insights into the process. In project A we were unable to meet with the team. Because the project had extensive architecture documentation, we performed the review offline, in the spirit of Johnson et al [41]. While we found several issues including two we considered major, the project did not give us feedback about the nature of the issues. This indicates the value of a face-to-face meeting, although one could certainly consider a distributed meeting. In project I, we attempted to use a different reviewer, but the reviewer did not have architectural expertise, and the review fell flat. It seems obvious that the reviewer should be highly experienced with architecture; we found it to be true.

We also considered types of issues identified, where types are based on applicability to different quality attributes. The data in table 8 show that reliability issues were prominent, and may indicate that PBAR reviews are well suited to find such issues. However, we note that the data are not conclusive.

Table 8. Quality Attributes in the Systems

Quality Attribute	Number of Systems where Important	Total Issues Found	Number of major issues
Performance	5	3	0
Reliability, (inc. Fault Tolerance)	7	12	1
Usability	3	3	1
Security	5	4	1
Maintainability, Extensibility	5	5	2
Portability	3	0	0
Configurability	1	0	0

6   Limitations of the Study

The validity of the study is limited by several factors. We note the following limitations:

1. Kitchenham et al [14] note that evaluating one's own work, as we have done here, can lead to positive bias. In this case, there could be bias to overstate the effectiveness of the reviews; e.g., find more issues than were really there. In order to avoid this bias, we draw no conclusions about the effectiveness of the reviews, and instead have focused on effort and issues. We validated the issues identified by asking participants during the review whether the issues were legitimate or not.

2. Some of the participants were students of the reviewer, and may have felt pressure to conform. This would not affect the number of issues identified, but might have affected whether they fixed the issues. To counter this, the students were instructed that the review was for research purposes, and the results of the review, and their response to it, in no way affected their grade (i.e., there was no requirement at all to fix any of the issues that came up.)

3. The number and quality of issues found by a review depends not only on the review process, but on the quality of the architecture (including the experience of the architects involved as well as the quality and quantity of architectural documentation) and the maturity of the architecture. Therefore, we do not make claims about how many issues one might find in a typical PBAR. We also note the phase of the project (see table 7), although we did not have enough projects, particularly in phases other than early implementation, to make any distinctions based on project phase.

4. The study does not identify important architectural issues that PBAR may miss. Therefore, we do not recommend that PBAR substitute for more extensive architecture review methods, but rather as a tool where expensive architecture methods are not practical.

In addition, Falessi et al [42] describe lessons learned from applying empirical software engineering to software architecture, and note several challenges that may threaten the validity of such studies. We note the following challenges are particularly relevant to this study:

1. Describing the Desired Return on Investment: In our case, this relates to cost versus the benefit of PBAR reviews as compared to ATAM-style reviews. While the costs of each can be quantified, the benefits are difficult to characterize. A major reason for this is that PBAR reviews have a narrow focus, which makes the benefit difficult to compare against ATAM. But a more basic issue is that benefit itself is difficult to measure; number of issues identified, for example, is at best a gross indicator of benefit. Therefore, we do not draw any conclusions about the benefit of the reviews.

2. Describing Social Factors: In particular, the development team size can influence the architecture process, and the subsequent architecture.

Of course, the results of an architecture review are dependent on the quality of the architecture reviewed. Nearly all of the projects studied had uniform (small) team sizes, so there was consistency across projects. We note that the larger projects we studied had similar results, but we do not claim similar results for larger teams.

3. Evaluating the Software Architecture Without Analyzing the Resulting System: The fact that we did not evaluate the resulting systems weakens the validation of the issues identified: we did not verify that the issues were indeed important to have identified. One mitigation action we undertook was to determine whether the issues were resolved – a resolution of an issue indicates that the development team felt it was important enough to rectify. This adds some credibility to the issues.

4. Subjects: Falessi et al note that software architecture decision making requires a high level of experience. Inexperienced architects can be expected to make architectural errors, including errors of omission: not considering important issues such as quality attribute issues. Reviews of architectures produced by inexperienced architects would therefore logically be expected to find a greater number of issues. Many of these projects' developers were students, although most students did have professional experience as well. In addition, every project studied did include at least one highly experienced person. Nonetheless, the number of issues identified could be somewhat high. We expect that this would have no impact on the time and effort required.

5. Training: The particular issue with this study is that the effectiveness of a pattern-based review requires that the reviewer have significant knowledge of architecture patterns and their interactions with quality attributes. Our reviews all used the same reviewer, which ensured consistency across reviews, but exposes a significant weakness in that the technique may not have the same results with a reviewer who has a different background. We recognize this limitation in generalizing the results, and recommend this be addressed in future work.

6. Complexity: Falessi et al note that software architecture is really useful only for large software systems, but empirical studies frequently use small of simple systems. This is true of this study. We note that complex systems may indeed have more issues than we saw in the small reviews, but the time and effort require may well increase. However, our focus was on small projects as the main target group for PBAR.

7   Conclusions and Future Work

The problem driving this work is to find out whether a pattern-based architecture review method is an effective tool for small projects. In this study, we learned that in reviews of small projects, architecture patterns can be identified and used to identify potential problems related to satisfying the projects' important quality attributes. We learned that these issues may be significant enough that the projects fixed them. We stress that we did not determine that all the important issues were identified. Such reviews require little effort, about two person-days each for reviewers and stakeholders. The calendar time required for such reviews is less than a day.

Our findings suggest that these reviews can be beneficial for small projects early in the development cycle that are unable or unwilling to undergo a comprehensive architecture review. A review requires a very small amount of effort as well as calendar time, and can be expected to uncover about three issues, one of which is major. The reviews may be well suited for systems where reliability is important. We would not recommend them for projects late in the development cycle. We also do not recommend them for projects that have many highly critical quality attributes; comprehensive analysis of the architecture is likely required in such situations. The study does not draw any conclusions about the suitability of PBAR for large projects, although many such projects will have many critical quality attributes. We propose, though, that the interaction of patterns with quality attributes may be a fruitful area of study as part of a large comprehensive architecture review.

We plan to perform other studies with different reviewers to strengthen the results and to give greater insights into the requirements of the qualifications of the reviewers. We recommend studying PBAR as part of a traditional architecture review in large projects. In other words, use the identification of the architecture patterns and their impact on quality attributes as one of the investigative tools within, for example ATAM. PBAR might complement such existing approaches.

References

1. Sommerville, I.: Software Engineering, 8th edn. Addison Wesley Longman (2007)
2. Bachmann, F., Bass, L., Klein, M., Shelton, C.: Designing Software Architectures to Achieve Quality Attribute Requirements. IEE Proceedings 152(4), 153–165 (2005)
3. Bass, L., Clements, P., Kazman, R.: Software Architecture in Practice, 2nd edn. Addison-Wesley (2003)
4. International Standards Organization, Information Technology – Software Product Quality – Part 1: Quality Model, ISO/IEC FDIS 9126-1 (2000)
5. Bengtsson, P.: Towards Maintainability Metrics on Software Architecture: An Adaptation of Object-Oriented Metrics. In: First Nordic Workshop on Software Architecture, Ronneby (1998)
6. Abowd, G., Bass, L., Clements, P., Kazman, R., Northrop, L., Zaremski, A.: Recommended Best Industrial Practice for Software Architecture Evaluation. Technical Report CMU/SEI-96-TR-025, CMU Software Engineering Institute (1997)
7. Obbink, H., Kruchten, P., Kozaczynski, P., Hilliard, R., Ran, A., Postema, H., Lutz, D., Kazman, R., Tracz, W., Kahane, E.: Report on Software Architecture Review and Assessment, SARA (2002),
http://philippe.kruchten.com/architecture/SARAv1.pdf
8. Dobrica, L., Niemelä, E.: A Survey on Software Architecture Analysis Methods. IEEE Trans. Softw. Eng. 28(7), 638–653 (2002)

9. Ali-Babar, M., Zhu, L., Jeffery, R.: A Framework for Classifying and Comparing Software Architecture Evaluation Methods. In: 15th Australian Software Engineering Conference, Melbourne, pp. 309–318 (2004)
10. Clements, P., Kazman, R., Klein, M.: Evaluating Software Architectures: Methods and Case Studies. Addison-Wesley (2002)
11. Maranzano, J., Rozsypal, S., Zimmerman, G., Warnken, G., Wirth, P., Weiss, D.: Architecture Reviews: Practice and Experience. IEEE Software 22(2), 34–43 (2002)
12. Bass, L., Nord, R., Wood, W., Zubrow, D.: Risk Themes Discovered Through Architecture Evaluations. SEI Report CMU/SEI-2006-TR-012 (2006)
13. Beck, K., et al.: Manifesto for Software Development, http://agilemanifesto.org (accessed October 2008)
14. Kitchenham, B.A., Pfleeger, S.L., Pickard, L.M., Jones, P.W., Hoaglin, D.C., Emam, K.E., Rosenberg, J.: Preliminary guidelines for empirical research in software engineering. IEEE Trans. Softw. 28(8), 721–734 (2002)
15. Gamma, E., et al.: Design Patterns: Elements of Reusable Object-Oriented Software. Addison-Wesley (1995)
16. Harrison, N., Avgeriou, P., Zdun, U.: Architecture Patterns as Mechanisms for Capturing Architectural Decisions. IEEE Software 24(4), 38–45 (2007)
17. Shaw, M.: Toward Higher-Level Abstractions for Software Systems. In: Proc. Tercer Simposio Internacional del Conocimiento y su Ingerieria, pp. 55–61 (October 1988); reprinted in Data and Knowledge Engineering, vol. 5, pp. 19–28 (1990)
18. Buschmann, F., et al.: Pattern-Oriented Software Architecture: A System of Patterns. Wiley (1996)
19. Avgeriou, P., Zdun, U.: Architectural Patterns Revisited – a Pattern Language. In: 10th European Conference on Pattern Languages of Programs (EuroPLoP 2005), Irsee, Germany (2005)
20. Harrison, N., Avgeriou, P.: Leveraging Architecture Patterns to Satisfy Quality Attributes. In: Oquendo, F. (ed.) ECSA 2007. LNCS, vol. 4758, pp. 263–270. Springer, Heidelberg (2007)
21. Harrison, N., Avgeriou, P.: Pattern-Driven Architectural Partitioning - Balancing Functional and Non-functional Requirements. In: First International Workshop on Software Architecture Research and Practice (SARP 2007). IEEE Computer Society Press (2007)
22. Harrison, N., Avgeriou, P., Zdun, U.: Focus Group Report: Capturing Architectural Knowledge with Architectural Patterns. In: 11th European Conference on Pattern Languages of Programs (EuroPLoP 2006), Irsee, Germany (2006)
23. Coplien, J., Harrison, N.: Organizational Patterns of Agile Software Development. Prentice-Hall (2004)
24. Harrison, N., Avgeriou, P.: Analysis of Architecture Pattern Usage in Legacy System Architecture Documentation. In: 7th Working IEEE/IFIP Conference on Software Architecture, Vancouver, pp. 147–156 (2008)
25. Utas, G.: Robust Communications Software: Extreme Availability, Reliability and Scalability for Carrier-Grade Systems. Wiley (2005)
26. Harrison, N., Avgeriou, P.: Incorporating Fault Tolerance Techniques in Software Architecture Patterns. In: International Workshop on Software Engineering for Resilient Systems (SERENE 2008). ACM Press, Newcastle upon Tyne (2008)
27. Kazman, R., Bass, L., Abword, G., Webb, M.: SAAM: A Method for Analyzing the Properties of Software Architectures. In: 16th International Conference on Software Engineering (1994)

28. Kazman, R., Klein, M., Barbacci, M., Longstaff, T., Lipson, H., Carriere, J.: The Architecture Tradeoff Analysis Method. In: Proceedings of IEEE, ICECCS (1998)
29. Zhu, L., Babar, M.A., Jeffrey, R.: Mining Patterns to Support Software Architecture Evaluation. In: Fourth Working IEEE/IFIP Conference on Software Architecture (WICSA). IEEE Computer Society, Washington, DC (2004)
30. Bass, L., Nord, R., Wood, W., Zubrow, D., Ozkaya, I.: Analysis of architecture evaluation data. J. Syst. Softw. 81(9), 1443–1455 (2008)
31. Clements, P.: Active Reviews for Intermediate Designs, SEI Carnegie Mellon University CUM/SEI-2000-TN-009 (2000)
32. Bengtsson, P.-O., Lassing, N., Bosch, J., Van Vliet, H.: Architecture-Level Modifiability Analysis. Journal of Systems and Software 69 (2004)
33. Bengtsson, P.O., Bosch, J.: Architectural Level Prediction of Software Maintenance. In: 3rd European Conf. on Software Engineering Maintenance and Reengineering (1999)
34. Bengtsson, P.O., Bosch, J.: Scenario-based Architecture Reengineering. In: 5th International Conference on Software Reuse (1998)
35. Alavi, M., Carlson, P.: A Review of MIS Research and Disciplinary Development. Journal of Management Information Systems 3(4), 45–62 (1992)
36. Holz, H., Applin, A., Haberman, B., Joyce, D., Purchase, H., Reed, C.: Research methods in computing: what are they, and how should we teach them? SIGCSE Bull. 38(4), 96–114 (2006)
37. Wohlin, C., Runeson, P., Höst, M., Ohlsson, M.C., Regnell, B., Wesslén, A.: Experimentation in Software Engineering: an Introduction. Kluwer Academic Publishers (2000)
38. Jedlitschka, A., Pfal, D.: Reporting Guidelines for Controlled Experiments in Software Engineering. In: Intl. Symp. on Empirical Software Engineering (2005)
39. Cockburn, A.: Agile Software Development: The Cooperative Game, 2nd edn. Addison-Wesley (2007)
40. Schwaber, K.: Agile Project Management with Scrum. Microsoft Press (2004)
41. Johnson, P.M., Tjahjono, D.: Does Every Inspection Really Need a Meeting? Empirical Softw. Eng. 3(1), 9–35 (1998)
42. Falessi, D., Ali Babar, M., Cantone, G., Kruchten, P.: Applying empirical software engineering to software architecture: challenges and lessons learned. Empirical Swre. Eng. (2010) (to appear)

Appendix A: Sample PBAR Report

The following is a report from an actual PBAR session:

System Description and Requirements

A local company provides discount magazine subscriptions to its customers, and has found a rather lucrative niche market for their business. Inmates in prison have a lot of time on their hands, and appreciate magazines. So this business mainly targets prisoners.

The main part of the business consists of receiving orders, and then placing the orders with the magazine companies. The service they provide is one-stop shopping for magazine subscriptions at a very good price. (I assume they get good volume prices from the magazines themselves.)

At this time, all their orders are received on paper through the mail. This system allows employees to enter the customer information and the order information from the paper orders into a database, where it can be used later.

There are several key requirements:

1. Customers may have multiple addresses, and the addresses change often. It is important to keep former addresses around (at least one former address), because customers sometimes move, and their magazines don't catch up to them. So they complain to this company.
2. In the future, customers will be able to be entered directly from the customer website.
3. In the future, orders might be taken via the web.
4. One order may contain orders for several different magazines.
5. Orders arrive with payments, which can be cash, check, or credit card. Payments may be of two or more types (e.g. two different checks).
6. Customer complaints are common, and the company spends considerable time and money resolving them. Besides the forwarding address problem noted above, a common complaint is that an order is placed, and the subscription never starts. So tracking order information and status is desirable. (Note that the original vision of the system included support for handling customer problems, but that has been deferred to a later release.)
7. Data entry errors are a fact of life. In the future, the system should support a double-entry system, where two different employees enter the same information, and it is compared for accuracy.
8. Data entry employees may work remotely.

Key Quality Attribute Requirements

1. Reliability (accuracy and fault tolerance): The consequences of inaccurate data are serious: Customers get angry because they don't get the magazines they paid for. And it costs time and trouble to hunt down the error, even to the point of finding the original paper order and verifying it. This is a key quality attribute.
2. Capacity: The amount of data being handled is quite large for a system of this size. There are currently around 90 thousand customers, and roughly one million orders. There are around 1000 different magazine titles. However, because each magazine can come from multiple suppliers, the real number of magazines is three to four times that number. The system must handle not only this load, but larger amounts of data as the business expands. This is a key quality attribute.
3. Extensibility: There are numerous important capabilities that will be needed in the future, so the system must be easily extended. This is a key quality attribute.

4.   Security (authentication and authorization): It is important to keep the system safe from unauthorized use. In particular, data entry employees must be authenticated, and may have different privileges. This quality attribute is important.
5.   Performance: The system has no hard or soft real time needs, but operations on this large database should be quick.

System Architecture

This system is a student team project, and as such is rather small, and has work left to be done. The architecture relies heavily on existing software packages. These packages, and the way they are designed, play a major role in shaping the architecture. Prominent patterns include the following:

1.   Repository: The database is central to this application.
2.   MVC: MVC is really central to the human interface of the application. The framework they used for implementing the UI is based on MVC, and even identifies its components as such. However, see the note in Layers, below
3.   Layers: The system is also highly layered. The Views, Controllers, and Model form (almost) the top three layers, which is really not a true use of the MVC pattern. Underneath that, there is another layer associated with the Model layer, and then the database. There is another layer that is sometimes present on top of (or in) some of the Views. It is called "widgets." Its purpose is to go nearly directly to the database for certain actions (e.g., large queries) to improve performance. It bypasses intermediate layers.
4.   Broker: There is some possibility for a Broker to manage efficient and reliable access to the database. However, at this time, it is simply potential.

Patterns and Quality Attributes

In general, the patterns are compatible with the important quality attributes of the system. Of note:

1.   (Performance) The most notable liability of the Layers pattern is its performance. Indeed, this architecture uses the common "wormhole" variation of Layers to circumvent some layers in order to improve performance. However, this variant has some issues:
     a.   It's a bit harder to understand.
     b.   It's a bit more problematic for extensibility, in that as new capabilities are added, one must always consider whether or not to use the 'wormhole" in the new features. This will almost certainly be an issue in this application. That said, the "wormhole" appears to be worth the tradeoff.
     c.   In this case, it required a bit of data to be replicated.
2.   (Security) The Layers pattern is so compatible with authentication and authorization that they are normally a slam-dunk in a Layered architecture.

Unfortunately, it isn't quite so easy here. The "wormhole" causes security checks to be done in two different places. So it isn't quite as clean as we might like. It doesn't appear to be a big problem, and is likely not worth doing differently.

3. (Extensibility) The MVC architecture will make it easy to add future web capabilities, such as adding customers or orders. This is a key strength of this architecture.

4. (Capacity) The use of a commercial database package takes care of any capacity worries. In addition, one of the commercial layers can easily become a Broker, thus adding further support for capacity, if needed. No worries here.

5. (Reliability) The commercial database package also takes care of most reliability concerns. It provides the ability to group actions into transactions which can be committed as a unit. We discussed the possibility of race conditions that might allow a record to be lost and appear to the employee as if it had been entered. Upon further reflection, I suspect that the easiest way to deal with this (if it even it possible) is simply to implement the double-entry system that will be put in place for catching erroneous data entry. That should take care of it. We also discussed running audits on the data to ensure that customer and order records are not missing anything. Given the importance of correct data, it still might be a good idea.

Summary Notes

There was no architecture documentation on the project, yet the review still worked. The architect was very knowledgeable.

Overall assessment: Successful: Few issues were raised, but that was because the system appears to be well-designed.

Statistical assessment:

1. Time: 1 hour, 15 minutes
2. Size: small
3. Team size: 4 people (students)
4. Domain experience: 1 person – high, 3 people – moderate by this time
5. Project phase: mid implementation, first release.
6. Patterns found: 3 (Broker doesn't count, because it is potential, not present)
7. Issues found: 3
    a. Reliability; in particular issues about potential loss of data in rare conditions. (Discussed during first part)
    b. Extensibility, with respect to the Layers "wormhole" (discussed during the second part – strong pattern discussion) (Major Issue)
    c. Security, with respect to the Layers "wormhole" (discussed during the second part)
    d. Pattern awareness: The team knew all the patterns we discussed.

Author Index

Avgeriou, Paris   168

de Souza, Jerffeson   55

Fernandes, Clovis   55

Guerra, Eduardo   55

Harrison, Neil B.   168

Köppe, Christian   24

Ratzka, Andreas   111

Rüping, Andreas   1